"Today savvy marketers realize that traditional mass marketing is essentially dead. This fascinating book reviews targeted marketing opportunities for identifying 'receptive consumers' in the growing over-40 segment. The end-result is intriguing and valuable insights for marketers serious about using segmentation methodology to target baby boomers and their elders more effectively."

John H. Bissell
Partner, Gundersen Partners, LLC
former columnist *Brandweek*

"I loved reading this book: it's a real gold mine of data, figures and proof that the mature market must urgently be considered THE top-priority target for every marketing and communications manager. It also provides a tool box for adopting the efficient segmentations described in order to reach consumers with the highest potential in a wide range of product categories. If you are an open-minded marketing executive, then, no doubt, this book is a must!"

Jean-Paul Tréguer
CEO Senioragency International
Author of *50+ Marketing* and other books

"This book is essential reading for every person trying to sell to consumers 40 or older. The psychographic segmentation strategies described present a sharp tool for optimal marketing. This book offers numerous insights on how to improve the return on the marketing investment—and the descriptions and analyses are uniformly engaging."

William J. Muggli, Ph.D.
former Director of Corporate Market Research
Wells Fargo Company

"This book offers a mix of micro and macro viewpoints, examining specific segments and their buying habits and motivations, while also providing a thorough and informed overview of how to communicate with those over 40. Best of all, the authors' many insights are based on exhaustive research, not theory or supposition, giving marketers a wealth of valuable and actionable real-world information."

Joseph Rydholm
Editor
Quirk's Marketing Research Review

"*Marketing to the Mindset of Boomers and Their Elders*, based on years of research by Strategic Directions Group, provides a refreshingly unique approach to the motivations of those 40 and older. Its application spans across multiple product and service categories. It's important reading for any marketing professional targeting the mature market."

Janice Shimokubo
former Executive Director of Marketing
Qwest Communications International, Inc.

"Morgan and Levy have not only challenged conventional assumptions about marketing to the 'mature' market, they've proven how shallow and ineffective most of those assumptions are. Their work deeply explores the motivations of this key demographic group and provides an actionable approach to reaching it. Any marketer hoping to reach baby boomers and their elders needs to read this book and take it seriously."

Michael Blumfield
Director of Marketing
Community Reinvestment Fund

"Marketing to the mature market—this vast, elusive, and ever-expanding opportunity for sales and services—in this new century requires new information and insights. Those who seek to reach the mature market will welcome the unique segmentation strategies developed so extensively by Morgan and Levy. I can't say it more emphatically—READ THIS BOOK!"

Connie Goldman
Author of *The Gifts of Caregiving—Stories of Hardship, Hope, and Healing* and *Secrets of Becoming a Late Bloomer*

"*Marketing to the Mindset of Boomers and Their Elders* is at once two books, the definitive desk-reference handbook of who this historically vast bulk of the American populace is, and a detailed roadmap of where they, and thus the U.S. economy, are going in the next two decades."

Matthew Grimm
Columnist for *American Demographics*
former editor *Brandweek*

"I know of no greater single cultural force in America over the next thirty years than the aging of baby boomers, including both the continued strain on boomers caring for their own aging parents and the eventual care of boomers themselves by their children. *Marketing to the Mindset of Boomers and Their Elders* is required reading for anyone trying to navigate this morass of social and economic tension."

David Kiley
Detroit Bureau Chief
USA Today

MARKETING *to the* MINDSET *of* BOOMERS *and* THEIR ELDERS

Carol M. Morgan *and*
Doran J. Levy, Ph.D.

Saint Paul, Minnesota

The Brewer House
1029 Lombard Avenue
Saint Paul, MN 55105-3256
651-228-7250 (Voice)
651-228-7260 (Fax)
email: cmorgan@attitudebase.com

Cover design by 45 Degrees/Minneapolis

Typesetting by Minnesota Technical Typography, Inc.

50+® is a registered trademark of Strategic Directions Group, Inc.

Simulator® and Marketer® are registered trademarks of Doran J. Levy, Ph.D.

Library of Congress Catalog Number: 2002091275

ISBN: 0-9705605-1-6

Marketing to the Mindset of Boomers and their Elders is available at special discounts for bulk purchases by corporations, institutions, and other organizations. For more information, please contact Attitudebase at 651-228-7250 or email: cmorgan@attitudebase.com.

This book is dedicated to
Donald J. Brenner, Ph.D. and Daniel P. Deneau, Ph.D.,
two professors who provided us with
enormous inspiration and direction.

Second book on ongoing studies

Marketing to the Mindset of Boomers and Their Elders is the authors' second book based on insights from their ongoing multiple-client studies on boomers and their elders. Beginning in 1989, these studies have been conducted seven times with over 20,000 people in this market. This book includes nine separate segmentation strategies based on attitudes. Data on demographics, behaviors, and Internet and media usage were also gathered.

The authors' first book, *Segmenting the Mature Market* (Probus), was published in 1993. It describes three of the segmentation strategies and set the stage for their ongoing work.

TABLE
of CONTENTS

LIST OF FIGURES

Acknowledgments

We are extremely grateful for the suggestions and insights that Doris DeLuca brought to this book. Her editing skills helped bring many of our views into a clearer perspective. Doris' commitment and interest in the project also spurred us onto complete it.

Edward M. Morgan admirably assisted us in the data processing that serves as the book's foundation. His highly developed analytic skills and critical insights helped guide us as we delved through our data.

Thanks also to William Muggli and Janice Shimokubo for their highly useful comments delivered from their own unique perspectives.

Finally, we wish to thank the 25 major U.S. corporations who, by participating in our multiple-client studies, helped support our research into a vibrant and growing market.

Chapter 1

ATTITUDES: WHAT DRIVES THE MARKET

Need to understand motivations

Ten years ago, Peter Francese, founding publisher of *American Demographics*, commented that "The attempts by marketing executives to reach those over 50 have been miserably unsuccessful. No market's motivations and needs are so poorly understood. A new way of segmenting those over 50 based on their underlying motivating factors is desperately needed."

We do not find that much has changed since Francese made his comment. As the influx of baby boomers feeds the monumental growth of the highly diverse mature market, the need to be able to target profitable segments within it has grown. Seeing this obvious need, other marketers have continued to segment the mature market, a subject we take up in Chapter 3. We believe, however, that their attempts have been less than effective.

In our view, segmentation strategies of the mature market —or any market—should be based on motivations and attitudes—what are commonly called psychographics. This approach defines segments *receptive* to a product or service and delineates which messages that segment considers *relevant*. In these days of painfully tight marketing budgets, the need for this approach is evident. Marketers can no longer afford to market to non-receptive prospects. Customers and prospects defined through a psychographic segmentation can be further qualified by such data as demographics, behaviors, and media and Internet usage. Using this approach, marketers will be able to make their decisions based on complete and integrated profiles of their best target(s).

What we've done

Our explanation of the mature market, unlike all others, is based on *why* those in the mature market behave as they do. Recognizing the need to segment the mature market by its motivations and attitudes, we conducted our first study on the market in 1989. Since then we have conducted a total of seven studies, surveying 20,000 persons and creating nine separate psychographic or motivational segmentation strategies on this market.

As far as we can determine, no other researchers have ever created multiple segmentation strategies on any one market. Our achievement is singular. This book presents a unique perspective on the motivations of those 40 and older that is not available elsewhere. The proprietary methodologies we have used to create these nine segmentation strategies are the same as those we apply in our custom studies.

Based on motivational research

Motivational research, the type of research on which this book is based, is derived from clinical psychology. Many researchers intuit respondents' thoughts and motivations, making unsupported assumptions based on behavioral and demographic measures. In contrast, we have measured the respondents' motivations and concerns regarding a product or issue directly.

Decades ago, motivational researchers believed that purchase decisions were based primarily on unconscious, deeply rooted emotional reasons. One of these earlier motivational researchers, Pierre Martineau, states that the consumer "wants more from life than bargains. And his behavior stems more often from emotional and non-rational causes than from logic."

While Martineau's position may be considered extreme, it is obvious that many of the goods and services people buy are related to self-enhancement. One's choice of beer, perfume, or an automobile may be made on the basis of hopes, fantasies, and dreams, rather than particular functional product characteristics. On the other hand, many product decisions are made entirely on the basis of logic.

Understanding various appeals

In developing successful strategies for the mature market, both rational and emotional appeals must be understood and exploited. Growing old is a physical as well as an emotional condition. Some women, for example, buy face cream because the product softens their skin or reduces roughness. These are entirely rational decisions based on the product's ability to perform some function.

Other women, however, buy face cream because they want to look younger. The buyer purchases a skin cream, such as Lancôme's Absolue, for example, based on the promise that the aging process will be delayed. Understanding what motivates different types of women will lead to more effective appeals, whether they are purely functional, emotional, or a combination of the two.

Our nine segmentations of the mature market are based on our assessment of the concerns, motivations, and views of U.S. consumers 40 and older living their lives as they continue to mature. We have incorporated both rational and emotional motivations for buying specific types of products into our nine segmentations.

Our research process

Our view of the mature market is based on large and extensive original studies. We define the mature market as comprised of persons 40 and older. However, our first attitudinal or psychographic segmentation study in 1989 was based on persons 50 and older. In 1994, we decided to include the leading edge of the baby boomers within our research, and in our subsequent studies we lowered our age requirement to persons 40 and older. While we have had no upper age limit in our studies, our oldest respondents are in their late 80s and are all living independently. Our samples were selected randomly and proportional to each state's population. The results were then weighted to reflect the U.S. population in terms of age, gender, income, and U.S. Census Region.

We have gathered a massive amount of information from more than 20,000 people 40 and older across the contiguous U.S. This data includes purchase information, media and Internet usage, activities, brand information, and demographics. We have also gathered behaviors that range from food consumption at home and in restaurants to travel destinations, financial investments to car purchase, mail order profiles to health behaviors, and societal concerns to participation in organizations such as AARP.

This extensive database of information enables us to link many relationships to form a cohesive picture of the diverse aspects of the mature market. Other researchers may have snap shots of parts of the mature market. We are unique in capturing the depth of this market through our nine segmentation strategies and also its breadth through the immense number of demographics and behaviors we have collected.

Unlike global segmentations that are too general to be of much use, the nine separate segmentation strategies we've developed are sufficiently specific to apply to scores of products and services. By examining persons 40 and older in nine different ways, we have simplified this complex market, but have provided enough detail to give marketers clear direction.

Procedure adapted from psychology

To determine the motivational segments that comprise the mature market, we used a procedure from mathematical psychology or psychometrics. The process involves devising a set of attitude statements that reflects various aspects of the issues to be studied. Nine separate groups of statements were used, each concentrating on various aspects of the purchase of a specific product or a particular issue.

After reviewing hundreds of articles and numerous books on the mature market, interviewing mature consumers, and talking with professionals involved in providing goods and services to the mature market, we created the attitude statements used. For example, in constructing the Lifestyle segments, called the Self segments in our first book, we used 60 statements. Two of these are:

"I am interested in products that will make my skin look younger."

"I wish I could move to a safer neighborhood."

These statements reflect the mature market's concerns and views about themselves as growing older and were used to determine the Lifestyle segments.

Eight more sets of attitudinal statements, each containing from 50 to 100 statements, were sorted by respondents to develop our total of nine separate segmentation strategies. The statements were sorted by respondents to indicate their degree of agreement or disagreement with the statement. A computer analysis determined groups of people with similar rankings. The needs of each of our motivational segments can be understood by examining its rankings of these attitudes.

Why are motivations important?

While behaviors and demographics each contribute to the purchase decision, they do not explain it entirely. Their importance also varies considerably depending on the specific product or service. The purchase of a high chair for a grandchild is driven by demographics, but the purchase of one made of wood versus one constructed of steel may be based on attitudes or psychographics.

For some discretionary purchases, motivations and attitudes are overriding. For example, our data shows that only 3% of those 40 and older with sufficient discretionary income to purchase a fur coat actually did so within the past three years. In this case, their income, a demographic, shows they are financially able to make such a purchase and yet they have not done so.

What are the differences in motivations between those who have purchased a fur coat compared to those who have not? Do non-buyers feel that owning a fur coat is not part of their lifestyle, a crime against animals, or are they dissatisfied with the coats currently on the market? Unless attitudes and motivations are explored, a marketer will never know the answers to these questions. Furthermore, unless a marketer understands the market's motivations by segment, he or she will never be able to target his or her most receptive segment(s).

Frequent product failures

While an understanding of demographics and behaviors is critical to designing successful products, it is also necessary to understand the attitudinal segment to whom the product would most strongly appeal. Thousands of products are currently designed and marketed to a mythical "average" consumer.

With half of all products disappearing within five years after launch, it's not surprising that a Booz Allen & Hamilton study found that "46% of all new product development costs go to failures." Perhaps these product failures were targeted at a huge mass market that never materialized in terms of sales. Designed for no one in particular, many new products end up satisfying no one. There is, however, an immense payoff in targeting new products to qualified receptive psychographic segments. Yoram Wind, a professor of marketing at the Wharton School, notes that if companies improved "their effectiveness at launching new products, they could double their bottom line. It's one of the few areas left with the greatest potential for improvement."

Another very different type of problem can occur when a marketer focuses on an "average" consumer and also fails to segment a market by its attitudes. What the marketer may see as overriding problems affecting an entire market place may be almost totally concentrated in one or two attitudinal or psychographic segments. For example, in doing a customer satisfaction study a client of ours found that a worrisome percentage of its customers gave it a very poor rating on service.

When we looked at this problem from the perspective of an attitudinal segmentation strategy, we found that virtually all of those who gave it a poor ranking were in one attitudinal segment. The sources of this segment's dissatisfaction with our client sprang from the segment's own life situation, not a problem our client could remedy. A psychographic segmentation helped our client realize that the remaining segments were very satisfied with its service and there was nothing that could be done for the dissatisfied segment. In this way, our client could make a sound marketing decision and thereby save millions of dollars in attempting to fix a problem that it could never solve.

Markets in flux

We live in a world marked by such rapid change that in an instant tomorrow becomes today. Marketers dependent on behaviors have data on what has occurred in the past. With only historical data, they have no way of measuring the market's receptivity to new products, products never before created. While Toyota collects data on the behaviors of Camry owners, a car it has produced for years, it has far less behavioral data on the Prius, a mass-produced hybrid vehicle only recently introduced.

When measured accurately, an attitudinal or motivational segmentation strategy has a singular ability to identify future trends. Such a segmentation will identify segments frustrated with current products and services with needs which current products do not satisfy. These attitudinal segments with unmet needs represent areas of opportunity which a marketer should at least be aware of and consider.

For example, all new car buyers are not frustrated with car dealerships. Among those 40 and older, only one of our Car Purchase segments, the Uninvolved, has strongly negative feelings toward the new car purchase process. The Uninvolved are 19% of those 40 and older. When the Uninvolved are further defined by behaviors, demographics, and geodemographics, a dealership can decide whether or not it would be sufficiently profitable to change how it sells cars in order to reduce the Uninvolved's frustrations.

Incorporating attitudes into databases

In tracking behaviors and recording demographics in an immense database, marketers are still stymied by not knowing *why* a particular customer has purchased a product. Answers to the *why* question would help database marketers target even more successfully. The more robust the initial psychographic segmentation, the more reliable and useful will be any database classification. Thanks to new methods and powerful computers, database prospects can now be categorized by attitudinal or motivational segment. By correlating attitudinal segments with behavioral and demographic data, psychographics can be mapped onto a customer database.

Including attitudinal segments in a database helps marketers focus on collecting only necessary data. In many cases we've seen immense databases filled with irrelevant data. Collected and maintained at great expense, this irrelevant data is useless for planning good campaigns. The issue is not the collection of terabytes of data, but the collection and use of the right data.

A new way to select media

In purchasing media, advertisers are most typically presented with demographics and behaviors. In an attempt to get the most for their advertising dollar, advertisers are struggling with the difficulty of understanding the attitudinal differences between readers of various magazines as they relate *to their specific products*. If a pharmaceutical company knew the psychographic profiles of *Prevention* and *Health* readers he or she could decide on which magazine best suited its product. Part III of this book describes how our nine segmentation strategies on the mature market can be used in the promotional portion of the marketing mix.

Our data show that there are substantial differences between our attitudinal or psychographic segments in terms of the magazines they read and the other types of media they rely upon. Seeing that advertisers could enjoy immense savings in the selection of magazines, we created our Simulator media selection program, incorporating our nine mature market segmentation strategies.

The Simulator program arrives at the most cost-effective magazine selections for reaching potential buyers within a product category based on the psychographic segment most receptive to that category. The psychographic segment is further defined by demographics and behaviors. In the case of a statin, a pharmaceutical drug for high cholesterol, our Simulator program may select magazines that are subscribed to or regularly purchased by Faithful Patients, one of our Health segments, who have had their cholesterol tested and who also have insurance coverage.

Searching for lifetime value

Focused on assessing the market place based on lifetime value (LTV), marketers may dismiss the mature market as headed to its grave. The reality is that at 60 a person in the U.S. may enjoy 20 or 30 more years of life. For some psychographic segments, we have found that those years will be enjoyed in relatively good health and with sufficient income. Indeed, as discussed in the next chapter, the mature market actually enjoys a high degree of discretionary income.

Our research and that of others supports a conclusion that the mature market as a whole cannot be dismissed as entrenched in its brand loyalties. In Chapter 11, we discuss the findings of a study on brand loyalty to various food products which supports this viewpoint. Our own research shows that some attitudinal or psychographic segments in the mature market are more brand loyal than others and their loyalties are to specific classes of products, not to all products across the board.

For the reasons outlined above, we believe it is worthwhile to view the mature market as presenting marketers with LTV. Furthermore we conclude that in measuring LTV, attitudes or motivations are just as important as behaviors—regardless of the market being studied—in signaling those customers who are really brand loyal. A study by Allan L. Baldinger and Joel Rubinson of the NPD Group, Inc. suggests a "definition of loyalty that includes both attitudinal and behavioral components." In addition, their study validated that "highly loyal buyers have a probability of staying with a brand over the coming year that is related to their attitudes about the brand."

Why us?

As a small firm with a specialized expertise, Strategic Directions Group has focused on the development and application of psychographic or attitudinal segmentation strategies. We've accumulated a total of 35 years of experience in this area. Our proprietary methodologies are applied with equal success to business-to-business issues as well as to those on consumers.

We believe that our years of experience and our work in a wide variety of industries, from utilities to packaged goods and from pharmaceuticals to financial services, contributes to the success of each custom project. Over the past 12 years we've applied the same expertise and commitment to our studies of the mature market, creating the unique body of data outlined in this book.

REFERENCES

Francese, Peter. Personal interview. 1991.

Martineau, Pierre. *Motivation in Advertising*. New York: McGraw-Hill, 1957.

Power, Christopher, Kerwin, Kathleen, Grover, Ronald, Alexander, Keith, Hof, Robert D. "Too many new products fail. Here's why — and how to do better." *Business Week* 16 August 1993.

Baldinger Allan L. and Rubinson, Joel. "Brand loyalty: The link between attitude and behavior." *Journal of Advertising Research* November-December 1996.

Chapter 2

GETTING A BEAD ON BOOMERS AND THEIR ELDERS

How real is the market

Massive and contradictory generalizations about the mature market abound. Some perceive those in the mature market as having high net worth and discretionary incomes, with expenditures that reach the stratosphere. At the same time, others view this market as either impoverished or made up of frugal tightwads who refuse to spend.

Those in the mature market are pictured as getting healthier and more vigorous every day and yet in desperate need of a drug benefit to cover all the pills they must take for their declining health.

They are rejected as a market because they will die soon, and hyped as a market that will live longer and healthier lives than any other previous generation. The mature market is pictured as open to new adventures and dismissed as too brand loyal to pursue.

As is characteristic of generalizations and stereotypes, there are shreds of truth in all these views of the mature market. Each position is actually one demographic cut or one attitudinal segment posing as a representation of the entire market. Applying mass market strategies to any market fosters the creation of such misconceptions, particularly in the case of the highly diverse mature market. Seeking to reduce any market's complexities to a few descriptors, mass marketing gives us only generalizations instead of a multi-dimensional, segmented perspective.

Rejecting a homogeneous perspective on the mature market, this book is a testament against such stereotypes. In their place we've identified *receptive* segments based on motivations and attitudes toward a specific product or service, and we've linked them to demographics, behaviors, and media usage. These detailed profiles allow for the abandonment of misleading generalizations and the efficient and effective pursuit of best prospects.

Defining the market

While a mass market strategy defines a market with a couple of demographics — "moms with kids under 10" — our work, regardless of the market or product studied, supports a synthesis of many types of information and insights. As we point out in the next chapter, the mature market is extremely varied and will only reward marketers who are willing to deal with its complexities and pursue a targeted strategy.

We've defined the market by nine separate psychographic or motivational segmentation strategies and plan to create additional segmentation strategies in the future. These motivational segments exist to a greater or lesser degree in all ages of the mature population. There are Stylish Fun, one of our Car Purchase segments, among those 65 and older, although in smaller numbers than among those 40 to 64. Conversely, the Proactives, one of our Health segments, occur in greater numbers among those 65 and older, as compared to those 40 to 64. A significant life event, such as a massive heart attack, may motivate someone to change their bad habits and take on Proactive attitudes.

Phenomenal net worth

U.S. Census data from 1995, analyzed and released in February 2001, shows that households headed by someone 40 and older enjoy 91% of our population's net worth. In addition, those 40 and older have amassed $9.7 trillion in assets, including home value. These assets almost equal the $10.2 trillion 2001 U.S. Gross National Product. Chapters on our Financial segments and the mass affluent market discuss the products and services demanded for the management of such wealth by each psychographic segment.

High discretionary incomes

While the net worth of mature households is staggeringly high, much of that wealth is in illiquid assets. Only a home equity loan, reverse mortgage, or an outright sale will liberate the money trapped in the equity of a home, for example. Rather than dwell on the mature market's net worth, then, we explore the high discretionary income enjoyed by those 40 and older here and in our chapter on marketing to empty nesters. Essentially, discretionary income is what is left after taxes and necessities, such as food, utilities, and clothing, have been paid for. In the U.S. 74.2% of all households had discretionary income in 2000.

The concentration of discretionary income in the mature market is apparent regardless of one's demographic perspective. Among households with discretionary income, 65% of that discretionary income is enjoyed by households headed by someone 40 and older. But discretionary income is not uniform across the mature market. Expenses such as mortgage payments and college tuition actually lower the percentage of those 45 to 64 households with discretionary income.

At the same time, households 55 to 64 enjoy the highest amounts of discretionary income per household member: $12,774. Although their discretionary income was not the highest, in 2000, when baby boomers were in the 35 to 54 age group, the Consumer Expenditure survey (CEX) shows they possessed 52% of the country's discretionary income, then totaling more than $1 trillion dollars.

Marketers who dismiss the mature market to pursue younger consumers should consider the attractive levels of discretionary income enjoyed by those in even the upper reaches of this market. A few myths about the so-called impoverished mature market should be dispelled by the fact that virtually identical percentages of 25 to 34 households (82.5%) and 65 to 74 households (82.7%) have discretionary income. But persons 65 to 74 actually have a higher level of discretionary income per household member ($9,612) as compared to those 25 to 34 ($8,859).

We see, then, that contrary to the stereotype of cash-strapped mature consumers, on average those 65 to 74 have money to spend on nonessential products and services. Other misconceptions about the mature market are taken up in Part II of this book. For example, the supposed entrenched brand loyalty of those in the mature market is dealt with in Chapter 11.

Tackling stereotypes

If marketers examine those 40 and older in aggregate it becomes easier to dismiss them as flat and unexciting. Boomers and their elders have been around for years, and marketers mistakenly assume that they know all about them. The fact is, their knowledge of this market is only fragmentary. Until now, marketers have lacked an integrated perspective and have not always been successful in targeting the mature market.

The mature market is the dominant market in the U.S. economy, responsible for the majority of expenditures in virtually every category. As 64% of all U.S. households in 2000, mature households enjoyed 64% of pre-tax income and were responsible for 65% of the expenditures as tracked by the CEX. It is difficult to understand why a marketer could dismiss the mature market as unexceptional and focus solely on Generations X and Y.

In addressing stereotypes about the mature market, it is useful to begin by segmenting it by age. The mature market's potential and its diversity starts to become apparent when we break out households headed by someone 40 to 64 from those 65 and older. Doing so also begins to reveal the complexities of this market and the need for finely honed target marketing.

Boomers spend big

While households headed by someone aged 40 to 64 represent 44% of all households, in 2000 they enjoyed 52% of all pretax household income. In 2000, according to the CEX, those 40 to 64 were also responsible for 49% of all the expenditures tracked. Most marketers recognize that the sales of financial, beauty, travel, and health care products and services are highly dependent on those 40 to 64 who are massive over consumers of them.

Although not often recognized, those 40 to 64 generate a major portion of sales for several other industries. Compared to all other demographically defined groups, those 44% of U.S. households headed by someone 40 to 64 are dramatic over consumers in categories from health to entertainment, food to furniture, and gifts to cash contributions, all tracked by the CEX.

A few specifics lend support

Responsible for 50% of all expenditures on furniture, those 40 to 64 are prime targets for Ethan Allen and other furniture manufacturers. Those in this demographic group represent 49% of all expenditures for shelter. They are reshaping the products offered by the housing industry, from one-level houses to inner-city rental units.

Considering entertainment, which includes expenditures on such items as movie theater tickets, pets and their care, and television equipment, those 40 to 64 made 52% of these expenditures, although they represent just 44% of all U.S.

households. In 2000 movie attendance reached $7.7 billion, an all-time high according to the Motion Picture Association of America. While the average American aged 12 and older watched at least five movies per year in a theater, those 40 and older were the most frequent moviegoers, viewing 12 or more per year and making up 40% of U.S. moviegoers by age, the largest demographic group.

Art museums, the ballet, opera, and other fine arts venues all find their audiences graying. Older baby boomers, those born between 1946 and 1955, especially dominate fine arts audiences. A new analysis commissioned by The National Endowment of the Arts (NEA) of the 1997 Survey of Public Participation in the Arts compared this data to trends in 1982 and 1992. This analysis found that older boomers, 22% of the U.S. population at that time, were 27% of ballet patrons and 25% of art museum visitors. In 1997 the median age of those who attend the opera was 45, while visitors to art museums had a median age of 43 in 1997. At classical music festivals such as Tanglewood, half of the concert goers are 55 and older.

The conundrum faced by these arts organizations—and by virtually every other industry—is how to satisfy current customers in the mature market while increasing participation and purchases by younger consumers. This problem can be solved by marketing to a motivational mindset, not a demographic. A psychographic segmentation completed on an entire market will show that motivations are not restricted to one demographic category, but actually permeate various demographics.

Mail order catalog sales

In its October 2000 Consumer Buying Trend Report, Abacus, a division of Doubleclick Inc., noted that of households 25 and older which had bought from a catalog, households aged 66 to 75 had the highest number of transactions (4.0) for the one-year period. Households aged 56 to 65 were a close second with 3.9 transactions. The most dollars per transaction ($112) were spent by 46 to 55 year-old households; they also spent the most in catalog purchases, an average of $415 per household. Abacus also found that those 40 and older accounted for 73% of all catalog sales.

Packing their bags

Among international travelers, those 40 to 64 — as well as those 65 and older — are clearly over consumers. Examining international travel in 2000, D.K. Shifflet & Associates Ltd., a market research and consulting firm specializing in travel, found that those 40 to 64, 29% of the population, represented 48% of the dollars spent. In addition, those in this demographic group took 45% of all trips. Considering the length of these international trips, those 40 to 64 accounted for 45% of international vacation days in 2000. But while the 40 to 64 demographic is exceptionally appealing in aggregate, we have to dig further using our Travel segments in order to understand what motivates them to travel and their expectations of it.

Specific niches within the travel industry are also heavily dependent on baby boomers and their elders. Contrary to the myth that mature consumers hoard their money, those 50 and older actually account for 80% of all luxury travel according to the Business Forum on Aging, a division of the American Society on Aging (ASA). *Hotel & Motel Management* magazine reports that half of timeshare sales (50%) in 1998 were to baby boomers. But the market of timeshare owners and prospects is further defined by the Global Explorers, one of our Travel segments. While they are 25% of the 40 and older population, Global Explorers represent 38% of timeshare owners and 38% of those interested in buying a timeshare.

In viewing domestic travel, the Travel Industry Association of America (TIAA) reports that in 2000 baby boomers took the most domestic trips, accounting for 45% of all domestic trips, including both recreational and business travel. Baby boomers also spent the most on their trips, averaging $479 per trip. In contrast, those 18 to 34 spent an average of only $431 per trip.

Elder potential exists

At the present time, households headed by those 65 and older constitute 20% of all households. The CEX shows that in terms of income, they represent 12% of household income before taxes and 14% of all expenditures. At the same time, we've already pointed out the high discretionary income of those 65 to 74, who are free of mortgage and college-tuition payments and child-rearing expenses.

While it is true that the median pre-tax income of households headed by someone 65 and older was $23,048 in 2000, such households are frequently composed of a person living alone (31%). In 2000 among *individuals* 65 and older, 17% enjoyed an average income of $37,500 or more. In 2000 among individuals 25 to 34, as well as those 65 and older, 2% had an average income of $100,000 and above. A few years ago great hype surrounded dot com affluent consumers barely out of high school. At the same time, far less attention was paid to similarly affluent consumers 65 and older.

Marketing to the 65 and older affluent demands razor sharp targeted marketing that encompasses an identification of psychographic segments specific to a product or service, as well as further delineation by demographics, behavior, and media usage. When considering the 5% of those 65 and older having an average *individual* pre-tax income of $75,000 and above as a market, a cruise marketer, for example, must still identify the even smaller percentage of those within that 5% for whom an around-the-world cruise is appealing.

Expenditures on health

The market for health-related products and services is far larger than that for high-end cruises. At the same time, the health-related market is a highly competitive one. Our chapters on direct-to-consumer advertising and specific pharmaceuticals show that the successful marketing of health-related products and services still requires a high level of insight and targeting.

Households headed by someone 65 and older, 20% of all households, are responsible for 32% of all expenditures on health care, including health insurance, drugs, medical services, and medical supplies according to the CEX. Those in these households are of great importance to such companies as Medtronic, Pfizer, and Blue Cross & Blue Shield.

Donations top list

In addition, those 65 and older make 31% of all cash donations. It's no wonder that non-profit organizations from alumni organizations to the Public Broadcasting Service (PBS) are targeting those 65 and older for contributions. That a high level of donations and the bulk of health-care expenditures are made by those 65 and older may come as no surprise. At the same time, there are many opportunities in marketing to this demographic which have been overlooked.

Fashions for those 65+

For example, according to the NPD Group, a market research firm, women 65 and older spent $14.7 billion on apparel in 1999, almost as much as that spent by 25- to 34-year-olds. While spending by the older women increased from the previous year by 12%, that of the younger group increased only 0.1 percent. But who in the fashion industry is currently pursuing this market?

Seeking new horizons

While they represent just 13% of all persons in the U.S. population, those 65 and older are exceptional targets for the travel industry. In examining 2000 figures supplied by D.K. Shifflet & Associates regarding international travel, we see that those 65 and older accounted for 18% of all trips to foreign countries, 19% of trip days, and 17% of the total spending on these trips.

Those in the mature market, including those 55 and older, accounted for 31% of all domestic trips. They spent an average of $447 on such trips, which was less than baby boomers, but more than those 18 to 34. TIAA reports that mature Americans 55 and older "average the longest stays away from home" even as they maintain the highest share of day trips.

But knowing that the expenditures of those 65 and older on travel are disproportionate to their size in the market isn't enough. We have to abandon a mass-market perspective and take up a targeted approach. Certain Travel segments we've identified within the mature market are exceptional customers and prospects for manufacturers of recreational vehicles, packaged tour operators, and cruise lines.

U.S. population ages

While the aging of the U.S. population is inevitable, it is difficult for us to totally comprehend the problems and opportunities these changes will bring. Visit Florida to see what the population of the U.S. as a whole will look like in 2025. At the present time, virtually one out of every five (18%) Florida residents is 65 or older. By 2025 the U.S. population as a whole will mirror what Florida is today, with 18.5% being 65 and older. The oldest baby boomers, now in their mid-40s and 50s, will then be approaching their 70s and 80s. By 2025, the dramatic aging of our population will also be seen in the fact that 48% of our population will be 40 and older.

A more short-term perspective shows that from now through 2010 the population of those 34 and younger will decrease by 4%, while those 35 and older will increase by the same percentage.

World populations age

In this era of globalization, marketers will also have to adjust to the aging of the entire world's population. The rate at which the U.S. population is aging has been mitigated by factors such as an influx of immigrants and a higher birthrate as compared to countries such as Italy, Germany, and Japan.

These countries are already facing an aging population with 16% to 17.5% of their populations 65 and older. The most rapidly growing demographic group in Japan, for example, is its Silver Generation, those 65 and older. Now 17% of its population, those in this age group will be one in four (25%) of Japan's population in 2015.

Opportunities and challenges

The generalizations and stereotypes that abound about baby boomers and their elders provide only fragmentary views of the market, and misleading ones at that. Demographics, insufficient for targeting any market, are especially weak when tackling this extremely diverse market. In addition, many behaviors do not yet exist. Since the majority of baby boomers, for example, have not yet retired, we don't know how they will react to it or to other changes in their lives. Until now we have actually known very little about those 65 and older as consumers. In 1935, after all, only 5% of the population was 65 and older, a percentage that now stands at 13%.

Supplanting misconceptions about the mature market, our nine separate psychographic segmentation strategies, when layered with demographics, behaviors, media usage and other measures, structure the mature market in a manner useful for both strategic and tactical marketing decisions. These psychographic segmentations help us to define the current needs and motivations of baby boomers and their elders and also provide insights into what will motivate them as they age.

REFERENCES

Bureau of Labor Statistics. *Consumer Expenditure Survey* 2000. Table 3, "Age of reference person: Average annual expenditures and characteristics."

U.S. Census Bureau. *Household Net Worth and Asset Ownership.* 1995, issued February 2001. Table I.

American Incomes: Demographics of Who Has Money. Ithaca, New York: New Strategist Publications, 2001.

"Movie ticket sales up, but attendance down." *Research Alert* 6 April, 2001.

Wellner, Alison Stein. "Make love, not art?" *American Demographics* April 2001.

Lach, Jennifer. "Summer overtures." *American Demographics* June 1999.

Abacus News release. "Abacus trend report details catalog buying habits," November 14, 2000.

Abacus, a division of Doubleclick, Inc., custom tables.

D.K. Shifflet & Associates Ltd., custom tables.

Business Forum on Aging, a division of the American Society on Aging (ASA). *Tips and Facts: A Handbook to Reaching the 50+ Market.*

Malley, Mike. "Baby boomers fuel growth of timeshare opportunities." *Hotel & Motel Management* 16 November, 1998.

Travel Industry Association of America (TIAA). *Domestic Travel Market Report* 2001.

U.S. Census Bureau. *Statistical Abstract of the U.S.* 1999. Table 61, "Living Arrangements of Persons 15 Years Old and Over, by Selected Characteristics: 1998."

"Vogue tentatively breaks fashion's taboo on age." *StarTribune* 28 July, 2001.

D.K. Shifflet & Associates Ltd., custom tables.

Travel Industry Association of America (TIAA). *The Mature Traveler* 2000.

U.S. Census Bureau. *Statistical Abstract of the U.S.* 1999. Table 33, "Resident Population, by Age and State: 1998."

U.S. Census Bureau. *Statistical Abstract of the U.S.* 1999. Table 24, "Projections of Resident Population, by Age, Sex, and Race: 2000 to 2025."

Belson, Ken. "These oldies look golden to Japan Inc.: Companies finally start targeting the aging population." *Business Week* 7 August, 2000.

Freedman, Marc. *Prime Time: How Baby Boomers Will Revolutionize Retirement and Transform America.* New York: Public Affairs, 1999.

Chapter 3

SEGMENTING THE MATURE MARKET

Two points of agreement

Many marketers agree on two points regarding the mature market. Point number one is simply that the mature market is critical to many businesses. In industries such as pharmaceuticals, travel, financial, and real estate, marketers readily acknowledge their dependence on the mature market for sales and profitability. In other industries, such as apparel and packaged goods, the mature market provokes far less interest, if any at all.

The mature market's significance was first recognized in the professional literature over 40 years ago. In 1958, Robert D. Dodge predicted in the *Journal of Retailing* that the mature market would become an important one. "The numbers in this age group," stated Dodge, "will continue to increase, and problems will lessen if marketers understand the nature and characteristics of the market." Over the next several years, the journal articles that followed generally stressed the size and importance of the mature population as a whole.

The second point on which marketers generally agree is that the mature market is not a homogeneous one. Over the past 30 years, the need to identify and target specific prime prospects in the mature market has spurred the development of segmentation strategies. These developments were also influenced by gerontologists who believed that those in the mature market were not a homogeneous group, but differed in how they adapted to such events as retirement and aging.

While psychologists such as Erik Erikson have postulated that children pass through determined psychosocial stages on their way to adulthood, it is also recognized that each person in the mature market has accumulated singular life experiences. These experiences differentiate each individual. Having had fewer life experiences, five-year-olds share more similarities with their cohort than their parents and grandparents do with theirs. As sociologist Leonard Pearlin has remarked, "There is not one process of aging, but many; there is not one life course, but many courses; there is no one sequence of stages, but many."

The many "process[es] of aging" have created an incredible diversity within the mature market. Many marketers concede that this diversity makes it ineffective to attempt to reach the mature market with a mass-market strategy. Writing for the *Baltimore Sun*, Adrianne B. Miller noted that "Companies looking for foolproof strategies to market products and services to older Americans have learned the hard way that there's no one marketing formula, no one medium, no one message."

The need to segment the market

The mature market's importance and its diversity have created the need to segment it based on one assumption or another. Over the past 30 years a number of approaches have been tried, each with its own limitations. In 1989 we reviewed virtually all publicly available segmentation approaches then in existence. Concluding that none provided a comprehensive way of effectively targeting and reaching best prospects within the mature market, we embarked on our own segmentation research.

In the 12 years since we began our work on the mature market we have found that the segmentation strategies developed by others still do not demonstrate a correction of the major drawbacks we identified. Some largely ineffectual approaches, such as segmenting the mature market based on demographics, have never entirely fallen out of favor. In other cases, a particular approach, deemed useless 30 years ago, has once again been resurrected. This is the case with studies using general psychological traits such as "loving" or "remote" to define segments and their tendency to buy a product or service.

Our criticism of many existing segmentation strategies springs from our 35 years of experience focused on developing proprietary segmentation strategies for clients on a wide variety of topics, as well as our work in segmenting the mature market. We have found that the most reliable and actionable segmentation strategies fulfill the following five criteria.

Actionable segmentation strategies fulfill the following five criteria:

1. Are closely tied to a specific product, issue, or service.

2. Are based on multiple and redundant measures.

3. Overlay multiple psychographic segmentations.

4. Present a multi-dimensional approach.

5. Are measured empirically.

---

1. The segmentation strategy itself must be closely tied to a specific product, issue, or service.

The more specifically a segmentation study is focused on a product, service, or issue, the more actionable will be the segmentation strategy that results. Studies based on cohort analysis, general personality traits, lifestage, values, general psychographics, and lifestyle are inherently weak because they do not tie mature consumer segments to anything specific. The usefulness of such studies for sales and marketing tasks, such as product development, messaging, pricing, or database marketing, is extremely limited.

These studies are appealing because they are available as off-the-shelf products and also provide a simple, easily understood view of the market place. Because they are so general, marketers can be seduced into thinking that they can be applied to many products or services within their portfolios. But the very attributes many marketers find attractive about such general strategies also lessen their usefulness.

An example of a very general segmentation strategy based on values is one created by the Seniors Research Group (SRG), a division of Market Strategies Inc., working with J. Walter Thompson's Mature Market Group. This segmentation strategy is described in a newsletter published by the American Society on Aging, as well as in marketing communication materials from J. Walter Thompson.

This value-based strategy violates the first of our key tenets of useful segmentation strategies: a strategy must be built on the examination of an issue, specific product, or product class. Instead of targeted segments, the value-based SRG strategy results in segments such as the Hearth and Homemakers who value "family, belonging, and conformity" and the "In-Charge Intellectuals" who believe "scholarship, power, and variety" are most important.

This segmentation is described as a magic bullet and marketers who use it "will find themselves awash in opportunity." In using the SRG segmentation, marketers, we are told, will be able to "identify the market most likely to purchase their product or service." It is obvious, however, that without a great intuitive leap it would be difficult for these segments to reveal anything about their expectations of a luxury cruise or a drug for high cholesterol or a carton of soy milk. A segmentation strategy such as this one does not yield specific attitudinal perspectives on any market.

Commercially available VALS 2

A similar situation is encountered with SRI International's Values and Lifestyles (VALS). First introduced in 1978, VALS is a commercially available psychographic segmentation system. In 1989 VALS was replaced by VALS 2. Although VALS 2 does not focus on segmenting the mature market, some of its segments are made up heavily of those who are in the mature market. According to SRI, two-thirds of the VALS2 Strugglers and Believers segments are mature consumers. While VALS 2 explores what motivates consumers to buy, rather than isolates what they are buying, it has one severe limitation. The self-orientation dimension that is part of the VALS 2 system and around which the segments are organized poses three different motivations for buying.

The system is built on the faulty premise that there is a general and static foundation to purchasing behavior that can be applied to all products and services. The "principle oriented" Believers would be driven by the same underlying motivations in purchasing a car or ice cream or luggage. In contrast to VALS 2, the approach we advocate in this book links one population or market to a particular class of products or services. VALS 2 and other value-based segmentation strategies are so general that their ability to identify best prospects, either by segment or by individual consumer, is extremely limited. Because of this they don't fulfill our first principle of an effective segmentation strategy.

Values manifested as attitudes

Those who create segmentation strategies based on "values" such as VALS2 and the SRG study differentiate them from studies focusing on attitudes and psychographics. While we seek to avoid possibly endless semantic arguments, we believe it is important to clarify what is being measured in a segmentation based on values. We approach this question by suggesting that three levels exist within each person's core, whatever those levels may be called.

The first and deepest of these levels makes up our fundamental belief system which remains internal, is largely unchanging, and is possibly unconscious. While the second level also resides internally, we can be conscious of its contents. The contents of the second level can be manifested in verbal statements or behaviors, but these manifestation of our values or beliefs — or whatever we label them — again remain internal. It is only when these values or beliefs are made external or public that we reach the third level.

Our position is that values cannot be measured directly. They are internal. A value can only be measured when it expresses itself externally as a statement of an attitude or a behavior. Marketers touting segmentation strategies based on values suggest that they represent a deeper element in the consumer's personality than attitudes. We would argue that these researchers are actually measuring statements of attitudes or psychographics and only inferring the subject's deeper value system through these attitude statements.

Psychographic versus lifestyle

Semantics are also involved in the confusion that exists between the words *psychographics* and *lifestyle*. Some writers and researchers use the two words as if they are interchangeable. For example, writing in *Discount Store News*, Mike Duff describes a study by Roper Starch which developed "five psychographic profiles to delineate basic lifestyle differences." For us, a *psychographic* segmentation covers the hopes, needs, fears, beliefs, opinions, and attitudes which shape the actions and choices a person makes. *Lifestyles* are a tangible, external expression of a person's psychographics.

Moving from concrete evidence of a person's lifestyle, such as frequent trips to Europe or living in a mobile home, to that person's psychographics requires an unsupported intuitive leap. Because lifestyle information is far easier to gather and less expensive to create than psychographics, marketers take such leaps all the time. Marketing plans that result from this type of thinking are based on shaky foundations. It would be far more effective to create a proprietary psychographic segmentation strategy and attach lifestyle choices.

Gerontographics: another general attempt

George P. Moschis, a professor of marketing at Georgia State University, attempts to understand the mature market through a model he calls Gerontographics. In devising his segmentation, Moschis used 136 measures that focused on older adults' needs, attitudes, lifestyles, and behaviors. His four segments reflect variations in attitudes about health, psychological and social connection with society, consumption, and numerous other categories. While focused on the mature market, Moschis' segments are again too general to be useful in planning the marketing of a specific product or service.

Moschis himself comments that as he completed the research on which Gerontographics is based, he found that "older consumers in each of the four segments ... respond differently to various marketing stimuli across different types of products/services (industry groups) ... suggesting the need for industry-specific gerontographic segmentation and marketing-response models for greater effectiveness."

Cohort analysis also too general

Another general segmentation is created when an entire population is divided by the demographic of age. Marketers using cohort analysis seek to explain an entire generation's motivations by their commonly shared experiences. We have noted the belief of gerontologists and sociologists that as we age we collect unique experiences, creating highly diverse, rather than similar, populations. In our view, a commonly shared experience might be the popular music heard by virtually everyone in a generation and with which they can identify. But in virtually all other respects, distinctly individual experiences cannot be submerged into generalities in order to explain the motivations of millions of baby boomers — or of any other generation.

A major example of the cohort approach is seen in the book *Rocking the Ages* by J. Walker Smith and Ann Clurman of Yankelovich Partners, Inc. Rather than accept the position of gerontologists and sociologists, Smith and Clurman believe that "the experiences of a generation determine what they like and dislike, how they spend their money, and how they aspire to live their lives—in short, what their values are." The authors tell us that "Only by knowing how the consuming motivations of your customers are tied to the underlying values of the generation to which they belong will you be able to tailor your products, services, and communications to their needs, interests, and desires."

It is difficult to see how a marketer attempting to define his or her best target market could rely on cohort analysis for this task. Using cohort analysis, Smith and Clurman describe the baby boomers in mind-boggling generalities. Among other things, those in this cohort are "self-absorbed" and prize "individuality." What types of cars, for example, should we attempt to sell to "self-absorbed" baby boomers—vans or SUVs or sports cars? Our own everyday observations show baby boomers driving many different types of vehicles. Our Car Purchase segments, described in detail in Chapter 20, reveal four attitudinal or psychographic segments that exist in the mature market, each with very different motivations and expectations regarding the cars they drive.

No competitive advantage

The generalizations presented by cohort analysis are not, as Smith and Clurman would have us believe, "a *key* [their italics] source of competitive advantage." We consider them to be quite the opposite. Since the generalizations offered by cohort analysis require little work or investment, they are easily accessible to everyone and, therefore, provide no competitive advantage. In these days of ferocious competition and reduced marketing resources, the ill-founded generalizations of cohort analysis will not enable marketers to target their best prospects. Instead of a set of the finely honed swords required for today's marketing battles, cohort analysis delivers only a roughly hewn club.

Geography as destiny

Another type of segmentation that defines a market from one perspective is that of geodemographics. Systems such as Claritas' PRIZM are based on the assumption that "You are where you live." Using U.S. Census data and incorporating behaviors, the PRIZM system has created "62 clusters across 15 social groups." Because none of these neighborhood clusters is limited to those 40 and older, the PRIZM system is too general for those interested in targeting boomers and their elders.

Claritas believes that "It's a worldwide phenomenon that people with similar cultural backgrounds, needs, and perspectives naturally gravitate toward one another." If one believes that "birds of a feather flock together," then the PRIZM system is a "simple way," as the company itself describes it, to "identify, understand, and target consumers." The simplicity of such systems is appealing, but a quick analysis of one's own neighborhood would reveal its fallacies.

While we link our psychographically defined segments to their geographical location, we object to basing an entire segmentation approach on one perspective, where consumers live, and drawing conclusions from it. The "flocking together" assumption on which geodemographic segmentations is based is too simplistic. Rejecting geography as destiny, we would begin by segmenting a market by its attitudes and motivations toward a specific product or service. Knowing the segment(s) attitudinally receptive to a particular product or service, we would then layer on behaviors, demographics, and geographic data gathered *from the same study* in order to thoroughly define the target.

2. A segmentation strategy should be based on multiple and redundant measures.

Today virtually all psychographic segmentation studies, although not ours, are created using statistical techniques that mislead marketers and reduce the value of such studies. In the process of creating a psychographic segmentation, these scientific techniques define some of the attitudinal measures as redundant. The statistical software used pulls out a group of scales as related in some way.

As a next step, these methods require that marketers reduce the number of attitudinal measures or scales the program has selected. In this second step, marketers use intuition, not scientific methods, to figure out the relationship or shared meaning among the group of scales, selecting a scale as representative of the group.

For example, differing scales, measuring the dimension of frugality, such as an interest in saving, a dedication to investing, and a search for value, may all have been included in the original set of scales to which respondents reacted. These commonly used techniques and the marketer's resulting need to find a representative scale could lead him or her to intuit that any one of these scales actually represent the dimension of *frugality*.

This approach can result in incorrect interpretations and a vast reduction in the insights that a psychographic segmentation can deliver. From our perspective, these conventionally created segmentations provide little depth. The nuances, shadings, and details of a target segment's motivations, all of which provide marketers with valuable guidance, are missing.

3. A segmentation strategy should overlay multiple psychographic segmentations.

In order to understand and reach their best target(s), we believe companies need multiple psychographic segmentation strategies focusing on various aspects of a product or service. This approach recognizes the great difficulty in understanding human motivations and their complexity. Evidently some major corporations deny this difficulty as they apply one segmentation to all the products within their portfolio.

While we have already criticized other aspects of segmentation approaches based on values, we also find that another inherent weakness these studies have is presenting only one perspective. Conversely, the practice of some major corporations to commission multiple psychographic segmentation studies on the same topic or issue in order to compare them is not what we are suggesting either. But multiple psychographic segmentation studies on *different aspects* of a specific product can be overlaid to obtain a far richer and far deeper understanding of segments within a market.

For example, our Health Information segments address a specific topic, the search for and use of health-related information. But such a segmentation shouldn't supplant a study specifically focused on how diabetics view the management of their disease. Overlaying the Health Information segmentation strategy with a proprietary one on a specific disease, such as diabetes, would result in important insights not obtained from viewing the market from a single perspective. But one isn't a replacement for the other.

4. Successful segmentation strategies present a multi-dimensional approach.

Rather than a one-dimensional approach to the mature market, or any market, our years of experience demonstrate the need for a multi-dimensional perspective. No single perspective can identify a marketer's best prospects. While the percentages vary depending on the product or service, demographics can perhaps explain 20% to 60% of why someone buys a product or service. For example, a certain percentage of women in the mature market who are incontinent use absorbent undergarments. A physical need that occurs more frequently among mature women explains a significant part of their purchase of these products. Behaviors add a similar range of percentages. We can infer that women who purchase absorbent undergarments are either incontinent themselves or are buying them for someone who has this condition.

Getting to the why

But even knowing the demographics and behaviors of a target market, a gap in our understanding of this market still exists. *Why* have these buyers of absorbent undergarments opted for this solution to their problem of incontinence rather than others, such as having surgery, implants, medication, biofeedback, or doing Kegel exercises?

Without an attitudinal or psychographic segmentation, we don't know the *why*, the motivation, behind their purchase decision. This knowledge gap weakens our ability to predict future behaviors, particularly for new products and services for which behaviors don't yet exist. Lacking a psychographic or motivational segmentation, we are also at a disadvantage in predicting behaviors among a population—such as the baby boomers—undergoing a new experience—such as growing old—for the first time.

Extreme simplification

The effort to create an easy-to-use segmentation, as well as a lack of understanding regarding the complexities of human motivation, has led marketers to create segmentation strategies based on only a couple of dimensions. And such simplistic segmentation strategies are cropping up with ever-increasing frequency. Perhaps the lure of tagging everyone in a database with what someone is trying to pass off as a psychographic segmentation has encouraged the creation of these skeletal strategies.

One such segmentation strategy was created by Daimler-Chrysler to carve up the Mercedes Benz C-Class customer. Two dimensions, youth/mature and simple/luxury, create four segments or possible combinations. In this case, the mature buyer, one of the dimensions, can either be motivated by a classic product line seeking "neither frills nor extras in their Mercedes" or an elegant product line and "desirous of more luxury." How the mature buyer, whether classic or elegant, feels about safety features, payment options, warranties, or a host of other issues is not explored. Instead of a full, rich, and detailed profile, a marketer using this segmentation has only two product-related dimensions to work with: very little indeed.

Integrate around psychographic segments

As demonstrated by Figure 1, we advocate that an attitudinal or psychographic segmentation be placed at the core of all marketing efforts, informing and integrating all of them. As this figure illustrates, we would view sales data and geodemographic coding from the perspective of our target psychographic segment(s). We believe marketers will make the most of their budgets and be most successful in targeting prospects who are already receptive to their products or services. The cost of convincing someone who has no interest in your product or service that he or she must buy it is immense and probably futile.

It is unfortunate that most of the segmentation strategies on the mature market do not offer a multidimensional perspective. As we've already seen, these one-dimensional segmentation strategies can be based on demographics, behaviors, lifestyle, or lifestage. For example, in marketing to heavy and light users of a product or service, behaviors are used to segment the market.

Lifestage insufficient label

Using lifestage to segment the mature market has resulted in examples such as defining certain baby boomers as empty nesters, saying nothing about the motivations of psychographic segments within this group. Labeling those of a certain age whose children have left home as empty nesters and then intuiting that they as a class will make various types of purchases and adopt a new lifestyle cannot be supported. Our

ORGANIZING AROUND MOTIVATIONS

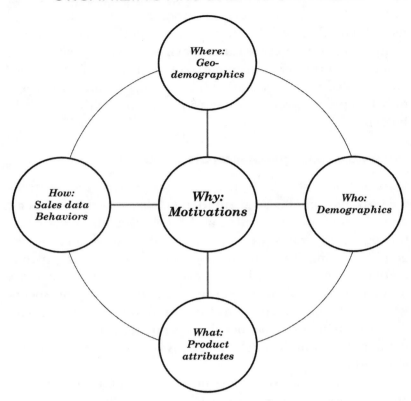

Figure 1: *Psychographic or attitudinal segments explain* why *prospects would buy or current purchasers do buy. Such segments form the hub around which other aspects of sales and marketing can be integrated.*

chapter in this book on marketing to the empty nester shows that *some* child-free baby boomers will indulge themselves, while others decidedly will not.

Dangers of demographic segments

Demographic segmentation is another example of the one-dimensional approach. Making its first appearance 35 years ago, demographic segmentations of the mature market have been the most prolific of all approaches, particularly those based on age. The authors of age-based segmentation studies face the problem of defining the age at which a consumer enters the mature market. Does the mature market begin at 40 or 50 or at 62? A second problem for marketers and researchers occurs in considering actual, chronological age versus felt or perceived age or physical age.

Demographics provide no insights on motivations and attitudes. If a consumer is 72 but feels 52, how can products be designed or effective advertisements created using an age-based segmentation? If someone is 72 but has superb health and the stamina of someone 42, how can he or she be classified with someone of the same age who has multiple chronic diseases?

One example of a study using demographics to divide up the mature market is an immense one, commissioned by The Markle Foundation in 1988. The study examined the "values, attitudes, behavior and overall outlook on life" of America's mature population. The study interviewed 3,000 Americans in person and then segmented respondents according to their age.

One "critical finding" of the Markle study was that " . . . those over 60 tend to be a relatively content and secure group . . . . " The weakness of categorizing the mature market based on one gross variable, such as age, is seen in this statement. Considering that at that time women over 65 comprised 58 percent of those in this age group, but were 74 percent of the elderly poor, this generalization is misleading. For example, the lives of many elderly women could very well have lacked "contentment" and "security." Placing all "those over 60" into one general category distorts reality. Some in the mature market are very content and secure in their lives, but others are far less so.

Combining two demographics: age and income

The mature market has also been segmented based on other demographics, such as financial status. Considerations based on household income, disposable income, and assets form the basis of this segmentation approach.

In her now-classic article in the January–February 1980 issue of *The Harvard Business Review*, Rena Bartos outlines a segmentation approach based on both age and finances. We include it here because it exemplifies the intuitive leaps made by some marketers, relying either on secondary research or focus groups or both, to segment markets. More art than science, the reliability of such non-quantifiable approaches in determining attitudinal segments should be questioned.

Bartos states that " . . . age by itself is not differentiating enough to reveal the marketing opportunities that exist within it [the mature market]." Her belief is that "The socioeconomic conditions that shape people's lives are far more differentiating than age alone." After outlining six segments, Bartos states that marketers of "general products" need not concern themselves with three of the segments: the poor, the sick, and a segment she has labeled as "other." The remaining three segments, based on age and financial position, are the Active Affluents, the Active Retireds, and the Homemakers.

Although Bartos' segmentation provides an interesting perspective, we believe it has certain limitations. As Bartos herself acknowledges, her segments are not based on an objective, comprehensive, or quantifiable study. Bartos fashioned her segments by reviewing U.S. Census data and other available studies. Having completed her analysis, she then made an intuitive leap to create the segments that she believed *should exist*. Our objection to this work is that it violates both Tenet number 5, addressed on the next page, regarding empirically measured segments and Tenet number 4, including multiple dimensions.

Limited applications

Bartos' segmentation is not applicable to the marketing of many products and services. For example, the interests of one product group, health care, is not addressed by Bartos' segmentation strategy. She puts to one side that group of the mature market that is most ill to focus on those she views as being largely in good health. The marketing of pharmaceutical drugs to mature consumers with chronic diseases would fall outside Bartos' segmentation.

In focusing on only the affluent, Bartos assumes that a single demographic can determine the market. As we will demonstrate in the chapters that follow, having substantial financial resources does not necessarily mean that one feels motivated to spend money on travel, a new car, or plastic surgery. Conversely, less affluent consumers may be highly motivated to make such purchases, and frequently do so.

5. Successful segmentation strategies are measured empirically.

In the initial phases of developing a segmentation strategy a market researcher must decide if the segmentation will be developed *a priori* or before the fact or from the data provided by the respondents themselves. For example, a researcher who decides to carve up the mature market by those 40 to 64 and those 65 and older before any research has been done, has created an *a priori* segmentation scheme. In contrast, an *a posteriori* segmentation develops from the data itself and the way in which respondents have reacted to specific questions or materials. We strongly advocate the later approach, which allows the market to speak for itself.

Earlier in this chapter we mentioned the work of Professor Moschis and his Gerontographics segmentation strategy. We objected to this segmentation's lack of specificity: it is too general to be useful. We also are troubled by another facet of Moschis' work. He determined the number and names of his segments before he analyzed his data. He states that "the number of subgroupings (segments) and their corresponding names are derived or specified on an *a priori* basis, based on our knowledge about human behavior in late life." As a first step, Moschis determined his segments. Then he collected the data used to categorize people into his pre-existing segments.

The inherent weakness in this approach is that it is based on the assumption that everything about the aging process and the psychological makeup of mature persons is already known. It also assumes that what is now known is perfectly accurate in describing the behavior of older adults. A third weakness in this approach is that it rests on Moschis' ability to be an authoritative and unbiased interpreter of that pre-existing body of gerontological knowledge.

DOES OUR WORK FULFILL THE CRITERIA?

1. The segmentation strategy itself must be closely tied to a specific product, issue, or service.

Of the nine segmentation strategies presented in this book those on Health Information and Health Compliance best represent our idea that a segmentation strategy must be closely linked to a specific product, issue, or service. These two segmentations are tied to two different issues in health care.

Since it would be impossible for us to fund and create every possible segmentation strategy that could conceivably exist, the remaining seven segmentation strategies presented here are of a slightly more general nature than what we would suggest to a client planning a proprietary or custom study. We would counsel a cruise marketer to consider a custom segmentation specifically examining attitudes toward cruises or, even more specifically, one examining how destination affects motivations to cruise. But cruise marketers face competition from all forms of travel, from recreational vehicles to packaged tours. Important insights can be obtained by overlaying our more general Travel segmentation with a custom one specifically on cruising.

2. A segmentation strategy should be based on multiple and redundant measures.

Given the complexity of human motivation, the construction of an attitudinal or psychographic segmentation on simplistic dimensions is ludicrous. In creating our segmentation strategies we believe in casting the widest possible net and examining scores of attitudes.

These attitudes represent different perspectives on a dimension, such as cost or convenience or ease of use, related to a product or service. Furthermore, each area we examine is addressed in various ways. It isn't sufficient to measure, for example, a respondent's reaction to one scale addressing cost. For greater assurance that cost is or is not an important motivator, cost—or any other dimension—should be explored from several different perspectives.

Our wide-ranging approach, as well as a sufficient level of redundancy built into our studies, creates a higher level of certainty that we have developed a credible segmentation.

3. A segmentation strategy should overlay multiple psychographic segmentations.

Our chapter on the Morgan-Levy Health Cube illustrates our belief that in order to understand complex human motivations it is useful to overlay multiple psychographic segmentations. In this example, the Morgan-Levy Health Cube creates Super Segments based on combinations of segments within our Health, Health Information, and Health Compliance segmentation strategies. The result is a far deeper understanding of consumer motivations, as well as a far more targeted and realistic viewpoint of the market place.

4. Successful segmentation strategies present a multidimensional approach.

The most useful segmentation strategies of any market combine multiple perspectives of that market. We strongly advocate to our clients that the psychographic or attitudinal segmentation strategies we create serve as the hub of all marketing efforts. In these competitive times, marketing to non-receptive consumers is far too expensive and impossible to justify. No amount of advertising of Boca Burgers will entice a Traditional Couponer, one of our Food segments, to buy that product. Why bother?

In terms of existing customers or clients, customer relationship management (CRM) efforts are more successful if the attitudes of existing customers are known. Different customer segments demand various types and frequency of contact. Even lucrative and loyal customers do not all demand the same level and type of service. For example, a loyalty program may be of great importance to one psychographic segment and of no importance to another. One segment may be religious in having their card punched or scanned at every purchase, while another refuses to even carry the card, considering it a bother. Tailoring customer service to a customer's psychographic segment increases the effectiveness of CRM efforts.

5. Successful segmentation strategies are measured empirically.

All of our segmentation strategies are created empirically. We do not approach a research project from an *a priori* perspective—assuming that we know which segments we will find before we have even begun a project. Nor do we divide a market into any type of segmentation before the fact. For example, we did not conclude that those 40 to 64 were necessarily similar or different from those 65 and older.

We believe that the point in doing research is to allow the market, whatever it is, to speak for itself. We don't assume that we know what exists before we examine it as objectively and as thoroughly as possible.

As we worked on each of the nine separate segmentation strategies on the mature market discussed in this book, we began by determining the general issues that were important and relevant to the mature market in reference to that product category or behavior. The initial process entailed a review of secondary research, as well as interviews with mature consumers. We also relied on the knowledge we've accumulated in our 35 years of experience in conducting segmentation studies for a wide variety of clients. All of these efforts generated the hundreds of relevant attitude statements used to create our nine segmentation strategies.

Improvement needed

The diversity of the mature market and the increasing competition faced by marketers demands that they improve their ability to target their best prospects and retain their most lucrative customers. Because of these trends, segmentations have to be both comprehensive in how they segment the market and also specific to a product or service.

While the importance of the mature market and the need to segment it has been established, the segmentation approaches that have been used to date to categorize this diverse population have been only partially successful. The result has been some confusion over the actual nature of the mature market. One study states that those in this market are extremely brand loyal, while another suggests that they are willing to switch brands. Study "A" concludes that those in the mature market are frightened of high-tech products, whereas study "B" finds them willing to try new, innovative technologies.

It isn't surprising that the results of these studies appear contradictory and confusing. The methodologies used in these studies to segment the mature market have frequently produced partial views, rather than comprehensive scenarios. At times the basis for a segmentation has been too general, as in the case of an age-based approach, or too narrow, as in the case of segmentations based on only a couple of dimensions.

While today's technology enables us to embed attitudes or psychographics into databases or use them for media selection, many marketers remain mired in simplistic views of the mature market. Profitable marketing to the mature entails capturing this population's complexities. Rather than segment the mature market based on only one variable, such as age or lifestage, what's needed is a comprehensive approach that takes into account an entire range of variables. Behaviors, demographics, media and Internet usage, informal sources of information, and lifestage issues must be layered on a psychographic segmentation strategy in order to develop realistic and effective targets. The nine segmentation strategies described in this book combine all of these elements to allow marketers to both understand and reach their best targets within the mature market.

REFERENCES

Dodge, Robert D. "Selling the Older Consumer." *Journal of Retailing* Summer 1958.

"Erik Erikson's Eight Stages of Psychosocial Development." 10 February, 2002 www.snycorva.cortland.edu.

Gelb, Betsy. "Discovering the 65+ Consumer." *Business Horizons* May–June 1982.

Miller, Adrianne B. "Companies finding older consumers hard to categorize." *Minneapolis Star and Tribune* 5 November, 1990.

Livewire, 7. JWT Specialized Communications, Mature Market Group.

Leinweber, Frank. "Evaluating the Older Adult Market: New Research Highlights Key Values." *The Business & Aging Networker* Summer 2001.

Maturity Market Perspectives, December 1989.

Duff, Mike. "The customer connection: seniors." *Discount Store News* 26 October, 1998.

Moschis, George P. "Gerontographics: A Scientific Approach to Analyzing and Targeting the Mature Market." *Journal of Services Marketing* Summer 1992.

Smith, J. Walker and Clurman, Ann. *Rocking the Ages*. New York: HarperBusiness, 1997.

"DaimlerChrysler: Losing out to Lexus." JMR Lifestyle Research Institute, Ltd. 2001. February 10, 2002 www.jmrlsi.co.jp.

The Markle Foundation. *The Pioneers on the Frontier of Life: Aging in America* 1988.

Morrisett, Lloyd N., president, The Markle Foundation. Letter to authors. 11 June, 1988.

Bartos, Rena, "Over 49: The Invisible Consumer Market," *The Harvard Business Review* January–February 1980.

Moschis, George P.

Chapter 4

THE LIFESTYLE SEGMENTS

UPBEAT ENJOYERS

Upbeat Enjoyers are enthusiastic, active, and involved. They believe they are successful and are optimistic about their futures. Because of these attitudes, they tend to view the world—and themselves—through rose-colored glasses. For Upbeat Enjoyers, age has increased their attractiveness. Those in this segment would like to spend their retirement expanding their intellectual horizons. They will work when they find it convenient or interesting to do so. Upbeat Enjoyers show little concern about their future financial security.

An optimistic lot

The key to understanding Upbeat Enjoyers is realizing their profound and pervasive optimism. They are optimistic about their futures and feel that their best years are now and yet to come. Upbeat Enjoyers aren't looking backward to some golden past, but forward to an even better future. The optimism that Upbeat Enjoyers radiate apparently makes them attractive and appealing to others, because those in this segment are the least likely to report feeling lonely.

Upbeat Enjoyers have a positive attitude toward life and every change they encounter is seen within this perspective. In fact, Upbeat Enjoyers strongly believe that their quality of life is directly linked to being open to change. Those in this segment consider themselves to be successful people and attribute some of that success to good luck.

Looking great

Their attitudes about how they look really separates Upbeat Enjoyers from the other Lifestyle segments. When Upbeat Enjoyers look in the mirror they don't see crows feet, wrinkled brows, or sagging jowls. For them the mirror reflects a face that has actually become more attractive with age. Upbeat Enjoyers are convinced that they have become sexier with every passing year.

These attitudes about looking young are also connected to exceptionally strong convictions that they feel young. With the vitality of youth surging through their bodies, Upbeat Enjoyers aren't interested in stores having chairs where they can rest while shopping. They don't find that physical or mental limitations make it difficult for them to get around stores.

Upbeat Enjoyers believe that we live in a society that demands that we be young and beautiful. However, you won't find Upbeat Enjoyers visiting a plastic surgeon or slavishly using Clairol's Nice'n'Easy every three weeks on their gray roots. Those in this segment like the look of gray hair. Upbeat Enjoyers do get a boost by wearing clothes that are in the latest styles. But convinced that they look great and feel young, Upbeat Enjoyers are free to turn to other interests.

Energy translates to action

Upbeat Enjoyers, more than the other Lifestyle segments, want to enjoy life and remain active—both mentally and physically. Those in this segment clearly feel capable of continued intellectual pursuits—they're the only segment that does not believe their memories have declined with age. Only

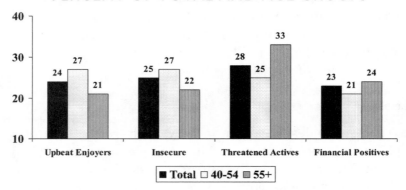

LIFESTYLE SEGMENTS: PERCENT OF TOTAL AND AGE GROUPS

■ Total □ 40-54 ▨ 55+

Figure 2: *At a statistically significant level, a higher percentage of Threatened Actives exists among those 55 and older as compared to those 40 to 54. At the same time, lower percentages of Upbeat Enjoyers and Insecure exist in the older population as compared to the younger.*

Upbeat Enjoyers are interested in going to lectures. They find taking courses through the mail or on television appealing. Upbeat Enjoyers also tell us they enjoy day trips to educational attractions, such as museums.

Upbeat Enjoyers are flexible in their travel options and have a relaxed, spontaneous view regarding an ideal vacation. They feel extremely comfortable making their own travel arrangements without depending on a travel agent. Sitting on a beach or going on a cruise are two vacations Upbeat Enjoyers would clearly enjoy. Although Upbeat Enjoyers also favor taking long trips by car or in a recreational vehicle (RV), they don't feel totally dependent on their cars. Consequently, they don't object to laws requiring that older people be retested for a driver's license.

Retirement a continuation

When they picture their lives as mature adults, what we consider a conventional retirement doesn't figure into the Upbeat Enjoyers' plans. They don't believe they will ever retire, but plan to keep working in some capacity. Continuing to work on a flexible schedule—when they find it interesting or necessary—fits the Upbeat Enjoyers' plans. Besides working for pay, those in this segment are the only ones interested in doing more volunteer work.

While continuing to work is an integral part of the Upbeat Enjoyers' mature years, they show little concern about investments, savings, and future financial security. Other interests have far greater importance to Upbeat Enjoyers as compared to these types of financial issues. Vacationing on a beach or buying trendy clothing are at the top of their list; how these items will be paid for is a lesser priority.

Upbeat Enjoyers can see themselves living in a condominium, the only Lifestyle segment that finds this option appealing. They certainly won't need their children's help in deciding where to live. Moving to a condominium isn't linked to any desire on the part of Upbeat Enjoyers for a safer neighborhood. They aren't concerned about being crime victims and are strongly against the idea of older people learning how to use guns.

Between working and volunteering, Upbeat Enjoyers have less time to shop. They are the only Lifestyle segment that is enthusiastic about shopping through a catalog. Upbeat Enjoyers are the Lifestyle segment least focused on mature consumer discounts.

INSECURE

The Insecure are deeply troubled by their lack of financial resources. They view their lives as bleak and offering little chance of improvement. Looking back on a difficult past, they see themselves facing uncertain, lonely futures. Retirement for the Insecure may include working because of financial need, but few other plans and goals. Those in this segment are also concerned with the possibility of being a crime victim. Least pleased about the effects of age on their appearance and their memories, the Insecure are open to products that will make them younger physically and mentally.

Scrimping through life

Not having enough money to live on is the one issue which sets the Insecure apart from the other three Lifestyle segments. Only their financial lives are laced with serious uncertainty, and being financially secure is the Insecure's greatest concern. Worried about their finances, the Insecure plan on working through their retirement — especially if they can be flexible as to when and where they work. What spare cash the Insecure have is invested conservatively.

The Insecure's tenuous financial position may be reflected in additional concerns. They are worried about becoming a crime victim, although they don't believe older people need to learn how to use a gun. With few financial resources, the Insecure are the only Lifestyle segment that plans on spending them solely on their own needs. Their children will have to take care of themselves. The Insecure, however, don't plan to show up at their children's doorsteps seeking assistance. But if they were seriously ill, only the Insecure would turn to someone to help them make final plans.

Because of their lack of financial resources, the Insecure do not plan a particularly active retirement. They enjoy going on escorted tours and day trips to such attractions as museums. When traveling, Insecure are the Lifestyle segment most interested in receiving special discounts for mature people from hotels and airlines. Those in this segment prefer to shop in well-established stores and look for value. They don't expect special courtesy from salespeople due to their age.

Aging a negative

In their view, life has not been kind. Lonely and isolated, the Insecure are the only Lifestyle segment that sees themselves as unlucky in life and unsuccessful. Far more than the other Lifestyle segments, the Insecure feel that the best years of their lives are over. In their mature years the Insecure don't find themselves with a stock of golden memories. At the same time, they see a cruel and grim future closing in on them. It's no wonder that this segment is the most pessimistic about its future.

Living in a society they believe is obsessed with youth and beauty, the Insecure feel that they have to look as young as possible. Achieving this goal is a challenge because the Insecure believe that they have grown less attractive with age. With every passing decade their sexual appeal has diminished. When they look in the mirror they see bags and wrinkles; in their view, this evidence of aging is too obvious to deny.

To look as young as possible the Insecure must invest in treatment products that will make their skin look younger. They are the only segment interested in hair dyes that will easily return their gray hair to its natural color. Besides their diminished physical attractiveness, Insecure find that aging has also brought them a decrease in stamina. For example, they would like stores to provide shoppers with more chairs so they can rest.

Not only has their appearance declined, the Insecure believe that their memories aren't as good as they used to be. Perhaps for this reason, Insecure are against laws requiring older people be retested when renewing driver's licenses.

While the Insecure believe age-related changes have not been positive, they view receptivity to change as important to one's quality of life. At the same time, the Insecure do not rush to embrace all aspects of change. They would be happiest if they could live out their lives in their own homes. And the Insecure also don't like the way American values are changing.

THREATENED ACTIVES

Threatened Actives want to preserve their independence by working in retirement, remaining in their own homes, and, especially, continuing to drive their cars. Nothing should impinge on these necessities. Those in this segment do not view retirement as a time for growth and the cultivation of new interests. Threatened Actives have a general-

ly positive outlook on life and accept themselves as they are. While concerned about their safety, Threatened Actives feel somewhat financially secure. They would like to pass on some of their assets to their children.

The three needs

The need Threatened Actives have to preserve their independence and the continuity of their lives focuses on three basic needs. This segment's most important need is that of staying in their own homes. They reject retirement communities such as Sun City as the perfect places to retire. Neither do they find condominiums appealing. They would, however, like to move to a house in a safer neighborhood.

Far more than the other Lifestyle segments, Threatened Actives also want to continue working—but on their own schedules. They tell us they don't believe in retirement. Perhaps they want to work because they don't view retirement as a time to grow intellectually. Threatened Actives don't want to go to lectures, and they reject the idea of taking courses through the mail or on television. They have absolutely no interest in sitting on a beach watching the waves lap in. Continuing to work will give their lives meaning and fill up the hours.

Lastly, the Threatened Actives' independence is clearly preserved through the ability to drive their car, which is at the center of their lives. Threatened Actives are, after all, the most interested of all the Lifestyle segments in taking long trips by car or in an RV. They need their car and very strongly oppose efforts to have older people retested when it comes time to renew their driver's licenses.

Not only do these needs suggest a resistance to change and an emphasis on continuity, the Threatened Actives themselves tell us that openness to change is not important to the quality of their lives. This segment isn't comfortable with changes in American values, changes that may increase crime. And Threatened Actives are terrified of becoming crime victims. Threatened Actives very strongly believe that older persons should learn how to use a gun.

Content with their lives

Although adamant about preserving their three basic needs, Threatened Actives are content with themselves and their lives. As they look back over the years, Threatened Actives feel they have been successful and that the future will bring more good times.

Threatened Actives accept their appearance and wouldn't spend a lot of energy improving it. Wearing stylish clothes doesn't make them feel good, and they don't think it is important to look as young as possible. Threatened Actives have no interest in hair dyes that will return gray hair to its natural color. They are very much opposed to such things as having their sagging eye lids attended to by a plastic surgeon; they have no interest in skin treatments to make themselves look younger.

Some financial pressures

Although Threatened Actives feel somewhat secure about their financial futures, it's still a concern of theirs. Their independent way of operating is seen in the fact that Threatened Actives are the only segment opposed to going to financial planners for advice. They are also the only segment that plans to spend some of their savings on their children, rather than solely on themselves.

Threatened Actives want to buy things that will last a long time. Stores offering discounts for mature shoppers will attract Threatened Actives, who also expect special treatment because of their age.

FINANCIAL POSITIVES

Financial Positives are realists and long-term planners. And they have definitely planned not to work in retirement. Very financially secure, Financial Positives are also relent-

less seekers of value. Those in this segment are savvy buyers, whether they are purchasing a couch or a cruise. Although Financial Positives have a positive view of their lives, they are not satisfied with their current appearance or their memories. Of all the Lifestyle segments, plastic surgery would be of greatest interest to Financial Positives.

Planned for financial security

Motivated by a concern to be financially secure, Financial Positives believe very strongly that they have attained their goal. They have done so through planning and have made conservative financial investments. Unlike the other Lifestyle segments, Financial Positives have relied on the advice of financial planners. Even when they can no longer care for themselves, Financial Positives don't foresee relying on their children.

Having achieved a high degree of financial security, Financial Positives want to relax, not work, in retirement. They have planned so that they will not have to work.

Besides saving and investing, Financial Positives are savvy shoppers who are careful with every dollar. They are wholeheartedly committed to shopping for value and purchase items they believe will last a long time. Such items are found at the well-known stores Financial Positives prefer.

Enjoying success

Financial Positives consider themselves to be very successful people who have been very lucky in their lives. They are optimistic about their futures and are not at all lonely.

While Financial Positives are the only ones interested in living in a retirement community, they are even more interested in living in their own homes for the rest of their lives. They find their current neighborhoods to be low in crime, and they aren't interested in moving for greater safety.

For Financial Positives retirement will include going on escorted tours. They have a slight interest in hotels and airlines offering discounts to mature customers.

Emphasis on youth

Although open to change, Financial Positives would agree that aging has created changes with few benefits. Their memories, they believe, aren't as good as they used to be, and Financial Positives, who place a great emphasis on looking as young as possible, find their appearance in their mature years to be less than acceptable. In this they go along with society's emphasis on youth and beauty.

Financial Positives certainly don't feel sexier than ever, nor do they feel younger than they are. Their realistic perspective prompts Financial Positives to favor rejuvenating cosmetics and plastic surgery as ways to recapture a youthful appearance.

Chapter **5**

BEYOND THE EMPTY NEST

Some distracting events

They've finished paying for their children's braces and college tuition, soccer equipment and trips to the Gap. Now empty nesters are ready for exotic vacations, expensive jewelry and designer clothing for themselves — or so marketers believe. Marketers focused on these generalizations often forget that other life stage events may actually be draining the resources of empty nesters, rather than channeling them to luxury products and new indulgences.

Even if their children have flown the nest, baby boomers and their elders have parents who may themselves need support, whether emotional or financial, or both. In addition, having spent more than 20 years funneling their resources into their children's lives, empty nesters may find themselves playing catch up in saving for their own retirement.

A variety of life-stage events, then, add complexities to our perspective on mature persons who are without a child under 18 in the home. But life events themselves are not sufficient for optimal target marketing. Any market, but particularly the mature market, is heterogeneous, exhibiting a wide range of attitudes and motivations toward specific products and services, as well as diverse demographics, behaviors, and media usage. It appears that many marketers don't realize that without an organized perspective, specifically a psychographic segmentation, it's impossible to pursue one's most profitable targets. As one article on empty nesters notes, "few marketers have figured out how to best target the new empty-nest boomer. Perhaps that's because trying to neatly define the boomer's empty-nest psyche is proving as vexing as trying to discern the messages hidden in the Beatles White Album.... Marketing products to this tie-dye mix of consumers may prove challenging."

A simplistic view

In their pursuit of empty nesters, some marketers rely on the easy use of one simple demographic perspective: their children have all left home. These marketers have bypassed the efficiencies and effectiveness that a psychographic segmentation strategy can bring to every facet of marketing, from product development to messaging. Defining their target in the most simplistic fashion, marketers note that a major change in household composition takes place in the homes of many married couples as they move into their 40s and 50s.

Married couples 25 to 39 make up 51% of all U.S. married couples with a child of their own in the household, a percentage which drops to 42% among those 40 to 54 in this population. A massive exodus occurs, and those 55 and older account for only 3% of married couples with a child of their own under 18 in the home. This departure combines with other factors, such as two-income households and prime-earning years, to give empty nesters in the total U.S. population the highest level of discretionary income of any group defined by household composition and marital status.

Impact of discretionary income

But even if an empty nester enjoys a higher level of discretionary income, that fact in and of itself does not suggest how it will be spent — or even if it will be spent. Becoming an empty nester is both an event in time and the state or condition of being child free. While the event of becoming an empty nester happens annually within millions of families, its impact on discretionary purchases depends on each family's economic situation. High-income families have always enjoyed elevated levels of discretionary income, even with a child or children at home. When high-income families transition to empty nester status, it's not as significant an economic event as compared to what middle- or low-income families experience when they become child free. Lower-income families have struggled for years to provide their children with just the basics.

Given that the economic impact of becoming an empty nester varies by income, the essential condition of being an empty nester — that is, not having a child under 18 at home — should lead marketers of discretionary purchases to target all currently child-free affluent mature couples or singles, whether they have ever had a child or not.

A high level of discretionary income is also not limited to empty nesters and focusing solely on them leaves out two other attractive demographic groups: couples, whether married or not, who have never had children and persons who have never married and have also remained childless.

The current interest in marketing to gays, for example, is related to this group's higher incomes and the fact that the vast majority of them have never and will never support a child. Fixating on empty nesters suggests a 1970s view when 75% of all adults were married, a percentage that dropped to only 56% in 1998. As reported by the University of Chicago's annual General Social Survey, of all U.S. households — regardless of age—only one in four (26%) are married couples with children, a significant drop from the early 1970s (45%).

Demographics weak predictor

At best the empty nester label may be somewhat helpful to a mass marketer intent on acquiring new customers or retaining existing ones. Target marketers trying to find the most receptive customer and deliver a relevant message will find the empty nester designation of very limited use. How can identifying empty nesters help a travel marketer find the small percentage of mature consumers convinced that a three-week luxury cruise to Tahiti is their perfect vacation? A marketer for BMW needs to know far more than the empty nester designation to target affluent mature consumers.

What should one say to those 40 and older to trigger their phone call to a plastic surgery clinic? Considering all the sagging eyelids and relaxing jaw lines among mature consumers, why is it that scarcely one in ten women in the 55 to 64 age group, the "age for cosmetic surgery," has had such surgery?

If demographics alone determined who gets nipped and tucked, access to several credit cards, healthy incomes, and companies specializing in loans for cosmetic surgery would induce many more mature consumers to have such surgery. Rather it's motivations that distinguish those with an interest in cosmetic surgery and other age-defying acts from those who accept themselves as they are. Whether plastic surgery or sun screens, hair dyeing or wrinkle creams, the Financial Positives, one of our Lifestyle segments, are by far the most receptive to all these strategies.

Focusing on prime target

The challenges of marketing to empty nesters, or any market, are best met by focusing on specific psychographic or motivational segments overlaid with demographics, behaviors, and media and Internet usage. In this chapter we'll show which of our Lifestyle segments, limited to those of comparable age and income, are the best targets for certain products and services, whether children under 18 are present in the home or not. Our Lifestyle segments are described in Chapter 4.

Age, income define sample

In our analysis, we considered persons 40 to 59, whether they are child-free or have a child of their own under 18 living at home. The median ages of the child free, as well as those with a child under 18 living at home within this age group, are virtually the same, 46 and 45 years of age. The age group we selected encompasses baby boomers who had children in their late 30s and early 40s. By age 59 even those persons who had children comparatively late in life would largely have finished providing them with financial support. Those 55 and older, for example, make up only 3% of all married couples with a child of their own under 18 in the home.

We also limited our sample to couples with an annual pretax household income of $50,000 and above and singles with an income of $30,000 and more. Within this sample we found that child-free households actually have a lower median household income ($69,525) as compared to households with children ($80,000). A higher likelihood of marriage (77%) occurs in households with children as compared to those without children (51%). The higher incomes of households with children are a result, we assume, of multiple income earners.

Comparing discretionary income

While not in the upper reaches of affluence, the income levels we selected generate at least average discretionary income. The U.S. Census Bureau defines discretionary income as "money available for luxuries after all necessary expenditures," such as taxes, food, and shelter. Approximately one quarter of all household income in the U.S. is discretionary. In 1999, 82.4% of all households had discretionary income, and the average amount per household member was $6,867. To put the levels of discretionary income discussed in the following paragraphs into perspective, we note that the 40 and older population enjoys 65% of all discretionary income in the U.S. and those 40 and older have discretionary income per household member that ranges between $6,000 and $7,900.

Based on their median household income of $69,525, we estimate that child-free married couples in our selected sample enjoy a discretionary income of $6,699 for each household member. Those who are married with one child under 18 at home have a higher median income of $80,600, but a lower discretionary income of $5,166 per household member. Discretionary income sinks to only $3,213 per individual among married couples with a median household income of $80,600 and three children under 18 at home.

It is true that in our sample those who are married and child free have about $1,500 more annual discretionary income, as compared to those with one child under 18 in the home: a difference of about $125 per month. This modest amount of increased discretionary income isn't a sufficient reason for limiting a marketing effort to just empty nesters. Doing so would leave out the single and child free who also have a median income of $69,525 and enjoy $12,505 in discretionary income just for themselves.

Impact of Lifestyle segments

Rather than focus only on empty nesters, then, there is great benefit in casting a wider net and including those 40 to 59 with the income levels we've described, whether or not they have ever had children. Having better defined the demographic target, even greater benefits develop from adding the perspective of a psychographic segmentation, in this case our Lifestyle segments. No demographic target, however focused, will provide the insights needed when products are to be designed, media selected, customer relationship management (CRM) programs set up, and messages crafted. In these areas, the questions of what motivates a target—the *why* questions —are only answered by motivations and attitudes. A psychographic segmentation is the clearest way to lay out a market's motivational landscape and address marketing tasks at an optimal level.

In this chapter we examine discretionary purchases by our Lifestyle segments within the selected sample. We focused our examination on travel, luxury cars, original art, designer clothing, fur coats, and fine jewelry. How do patterns of consumption differ by the Lifestyle psychographic segments? While it's true that Upbeat Enjoyers and Financial Positives segments have the highest median household incomes, our emphasis on them in this chapter is due to their patterns of consumption. For example, Threatened Actives in our sample with a child under 18 at home have a median household income of $81,394, slightly above the median for this population, and yet they are under consumers of the luxury products we examined.

Segments reveal preferences

In some instances, an activity or product appeals most strongly to one of our Lifestyle segments, whether they have children in the home or not. In other instances, something may be used or purchased more frequently by persons without children in the home than those with — but even more frequently by one Lifestyle segment within that category. In other instances, different Lifestyle segments within each group, whether child free or with a child, lead in consumption of a product or service. These situations suggests that motivations and attitudes, not merely demographics, heavily influence these choices.

For example, looking at those who have gone on an escorted tour in the past five years we see that among those without children in the home, Financial Positives are the prime consumers. In contrast, among those with children it's the Upbeat Enjoyers. An escorted tour appeals to child-free Financial Positives because of their high level of interest in fixed-price travel. Conversely, the highly social Upbeat Enjoyers find the intense, contained experience of an escorted tour an experience they can enjoy with their children. We should keep in mind that an escorted tour for the Upbeat Enjoyers may mean white water rafting down the Colorado River or crossing the Plains in a covered wagon.

Where do you usually stay?

Whether in our defined sample or in the 40 and older population as a whole, out of 14 alternatives the top three places to stay while on vacation are at a hotel or motel, with relatives, or with friends. But of those in our selected sample staying with friends is something that Upbeat Enjoyers do at higher levels, whether they have children (41%) or not (41%), in contrast to the sample as a whole (35%). In this instance, more of the gregarious Upbeat Enjoyers are comfortable staying with friends, whether or not they themselves have a child under 18 at home.

Not only do Upbeat Enjoyers stay with friends, more of them with children plan to stay at a timeshare on their next vacation (14%) as compared to those in our defined sample (9%). Another home-like accommodation, the bed and breakfast, also appeals to Upbeat Enjoyers. More of them plan to stay at a bed and breakfast, whether they have a child under 18 at home or not (17% and 22%) as compared to our sample (14%). Besides offering social and familial experiences, many bed and breakfasts would also appeal to the Upbeat Enjoyers' interest in history and unique objects.

Staying at a cabin, whether owned or rented, is something more of those in the sample with children plan to do on their next vacation (22%). But among those with children, we see that more Financial Positives (25%), but fewer Upbeat Enjoyers (19%), find staying at a cabin appealing. As we've noted, Financial Positives are motivated to seek a set-price vacation and many of those in this segment also favor driving to vacation destinations.

Next vacation's activities

We've asked our respondents which of 22 activities they planned to include on their next vacation. It is evident that some of the activities enjoyed on vacation clearly show a demarcation between those with children and those without. But even within these two groups, we find that an activity appeals even more to one of our Lifestyle psychographic segments than to others. While only 24% of those without a child 18 or younger in the home plan to visit a theme park on their next vacation, 42% of those with a child in the home plan to do so. But among those with at least one child at home, a whopping 51% of the Threatened Actives say that visiting a theme park is definitely part of their vacation plans.

Conversely, 28% of those without a child at home say they will gamble on their next vacation compared to just 23% of those with a child. But gambling on their next vacation is something that far more child-free Insecure (39%) are planning to do as compared to the other Lifestyle segments. The 10% decline in skiing from 1987 to 1997 has been at least partially attributed to the aging baby boom's decrepitude, a perspective that we believe is too simplistic. A child or children at home certainly impacts on plans to downhill ski on one's next vacation. Although only 5% of the child free say they will do so, 12% of those with at least one child under 18 at home plan to ski on their next vacation. But among those with at least one child, the Upbeat Enjoyers are the Lifestyle segment Mount Sunapee and Aspen should target: 19% of them plan on this activity.

It is true that not having a child at home increases the likelihood of attending cultural events and concerts (28% versus 24%) when those in our sample take their next vacation, but far more dramatic differences are seen in one of our Lifestyle segments. It is overwhelmingly the Upbeat Enjoyers, with their interest in continuing education, the arts, and history, who plan to participate in these activities, whether they have children in the home or not (33% and 37%).

Two segments prefer cruising

Child-free Financial Positives are the most frequent cruisers. As we've noted, this segment likes a vacation arrangement where all charges are known up front. Over the past five years, 8% of child-free Financial Positives have gone on three or more cruises, compared to 2% of the qualified sample as a whole. Over the next five years, two Lifestyle segments present the cruise industry with excellent possibilities. Financial Positives remain the very best target among the child free, with 62% planning to go on one or more cruises and 6% planning to go on three or more cruises in the next five years.

We also see that certain cruise lines have succeeded in widening their appeal from the value-seeking Financial Positives, to another of our Lifestyle segments. Virtually every cruise line from Disney to Carnival, Holland America to Royal Caribbean is positioning itself as selling fun for the family. Offering kids and teenagers free passage and classes, dance parties and sports, cruise lines are focused on enticing kids and their parents on board. And it's working. Now 61% of Upbeat Enjoyers with at least one child under 18 at home are planning on going on at least one cruise over the next five years: 5% say that they will go on three or more. This appeal fits perfectly with the Upbeat Enjoyers' focus on enjoying themselves today and on social contact.

Vacation length varies

In examining vacations of different lengths taken over the last 12 months, we found several relationships. For example, of those with a child at home and those child free, the same percentage (76%) has taken one or more short trips of from one to four days over the past 12 months. Considering trips of this length, the most frequent travelers are child-free Upbeat Enjoyers and Financial Positives. While 10% of the child free in our qualified sample have taken six or more of these short trips over the past 12 months, 13% of the child free in both of these Lifestyle segments have done so. In contrast, only 4% of Upbeat Enjoyers and 3% of Financial Positives with at least one child at home have taken six or more short trips.

Using a travel agent

Our studies show that one in five (20%) of the 40 and older population books all of its travel through a travel agent. The percentage rises considerably to more than one in three when we consider Upbeat Enjoyers (36%) in our qualified sample with no children at home. More than half (54%) of those in this segment who are child-free make more than half (51%) of their travel arrangements through a travel agent, the highest of all the Lifestyle segments regardless of child-related status. The Upbeat Enjoyers' desire for hassle-free experiences and lack of concern about their cost make it natural for them to put themselves in the hands of a travel agent. Travel agents would do well to identify Upbeat Enjoyers in their databases and lavish attention on them in CRM programs.

Destinations differ by segment

Examined only by demographics, the percentage of the qualified sample who have visited Alaska over the past five years doubles among the child-free (2% versus 4%). And among the child free, one of our psychographic segments is the very best target for Alaska tourism: the Upbeat Enjoyers. Eight percent of them have made a trip to Alaska, double the number of all the child-free who have visited this state. In our qualified sample who are child-free, 17% have visited Hawaii over the past five years. But the percentage of child-free Financial Positives who have done so is 29% higher and the highest of all the segments (22%).

Of trips to the 27 countries we track, we note that France has been visited by 6% of those 40 and older in the past five years, whether in the total population or our qualified sample. Fewer of those who are qualified with a child or children under 18 at home have visited France (4%) as compared to the child-free (9%). But 56% more child-free Upbeat Enjoyers as compared to all the child free have vacationed in France in the past five years (14%).

The idea that France complements the Upbeat Enjoyers' own *joie de vivre* and appeals to their interest in museums and history, enjoyment of fine wines and food is borne out by their assessment of the country. Besides telling us of their past and future visits, our respondents also rated six countries on seven measures such as safety, friendly people, good value and offering enjoyable activities.

France rated highly

When rating France, child-free Upbeat Enjoyers reserved their highest ratings for its activities. While 30% of those in our sample who are child free thought that offering activities they enjoyed was a phrase that described France "very well," 36% of Upbeat Enjoyers gave France this highest rating. No other of our Lifestyle segments, whether with or without a child, gave France such a high rating on this point. On other measures, more child-free Upbeat Enjoyers than the child-free group as a whole consider France to have a clean environment and interesting sights and to be a good value. But this segment's scores on the friendliness of the French and the ease of traveling in that country were similar to the scores of the child-free sample overall.

Our data shows that in appealing to the U.S. mature traveler, French tourism should target not just empty nesters, but Upbeat Enjoyers. And while this segment rates certain aspects of their travel experience in France very highly, there is room for improvement. Specifically, what can be done to improve the Upbeat Enjoyers' ratings of France that are just average? What information and experiences do Upbeat Enjoyers need in order to rate the ease of traveling in France as exceptionally good? Increasing travel to France among the U.S. mature market clearly means that tourism marketers in France must know and anticipate the needs of Upbeat Enjoyers.

Moving up to a luxury car

Examining five brands with 5% or more market share in our selected sample, we find that 55% of those with at least one child under 18 at home drive a Chevrolet, Ford, Dodge, Honda, or Toyota as their newest car. This percentage drops to 50% when only the child-free are considered. Which car brands take up this 5% difference? In examining 12 luxury brands, including Cadillac, Lincoln, Porsche, Mercedes-Benz, Saab, Audi, and BMW, we see that just 10% of those in our sample with at least one child owns a luxury brand as their newest car. In contrast, among the child-free, 15% do so. There is, then, a 50% increase in luxury brand ownership between the child free and those with a child at home.

True insights into the child free who buy a luxury car are found when the car brands owned by our Lifestyle segments are examined. For example, the same percentage (2%) of our sample with or without kids owns a Mercedes-Benz. Any increase in ownership of this brand comes from the Upbeat Enjoyers, which increase from 3% to 4% ownership among the child free. No Upbeat Enjoyers in our sample with a child at home owns a Jaguar or Porsche. While only miniscule numbers of child-free Upbeat Enjoyers own a Jaguar (1%) or Porsche (1%), they are the only Lifestyle segment to do so.

Conversely, whether or not Financial Positives have a child at home or not, only 2% of them own a Mercedes-Benz. This segment's ownership of a Cadillac, however, increases from zero to 6% among the child free. In our sample the Upbeat Enjoyers' ownership of a BMW remains flat at 1%, whether a child is in the home or not, but among Financial Positives it increases from 1% to 3% among those without a child under 18 at home.

Car marketers have to create marketing strategies that are based on the fact that specific brands appeal to specific attitudinal segments. The purchase of a luxury brand may or may not be triggered by the departure of the last child from the home. What is certain is that the consumer's preference for a specific brand is directed by his or her motivations. Manufacturers of luxury vehicles must thoroughly understand the car-related attitudes and motivations of the U.S. mature market. We further explore these motivations in this book's chapters on our Car Purchase and Car Maintenance segments and on Chapter 22 on the purchase of luxury cars.

Purchase of luxury goods

In analyzing the purchase of six classes of luxury goods, including designer clothing and fine gold jewelry, we see that for certain items consumption is not influenced by whether or not a child under 18 remains in the home. As with other items we have examined, distinguishing insights lie within the Lifestyle segments themselves.

For example, in our sample 15% of both the child-free and those with a child have purchased original art in the last three years. Whether the Upbeat Enjoyers (17% and 19%) or Financial Positives (19% and 18%) have a child at home or not, their purchase of original art remains the highest of all the Lifestyle segments. Laying a proprietary segmentation specifically on motivations to purchase art over our Lifestyle segments would be even more revealing.

In selecting the best target for a particular product, the presence or absence of a child or children in the home becomes irrelevant compared to other far more critical considerations. Should the Oval Room and fur salon at Marshall Field's target the Financial Positives or Upbeat Enjoyers? Within our selected sample, the percentages of child free and those with a child who have purchased a fur coat in the past three years are virtually the same (4% and 3%). One of our Lifestyle segments, however, stands out as a prime target: more child-free Financial Positives have purchased a fur coat (7%). But before singling out this segment as the most valuable fur coat buyer, we must note that the majority of child-free Financial Positives will spend only $1,000 to $3,000 on such a coat. While only average in their level of fur coat purchases, the majority of child-free Upbeat Enjoyers would spend $3,000 or more.

Upbeat Enjoyers spend more

Whether among the child free or those with a child, more Financial Positives have purchased designer clothing in the past three years (45% and 51%). The vast majority of them, however, will spend in the $100 to $500 range for such pieces, with only 15% spending at $500 and above. Although slightly fewer Upbeat Enjoyers with or without a child at home have purchased designer clothing in the past three years, more of them will spend $500 or more (22% and 27%).

Before targeting a prospective buyer of any luxury product, whether designer clothes or a fur coat, a psychographic segmentation should be integrated with relevant behaviors, demographics, and media usage.

Financial Positives buy jewelry

The purchase of fine gold jewelry set with precious stones by those in our selected sample presents a complicated picture. More of those with children (48%) in our sample have purchased such jewelry over the past three years as compared to the child free (41%). Among the child free, Financial Positives stand out as exceptional consumers (47%). Over half (51%) of both the Upbeat Enjoyers and Financial Positives with one or more children 18 and under have purchased such jewelry. No doubt many of the jewelry purchases of those with children went to the children themselves, perhaps for graduation, a bar mitzvah, or a wedding, or simply to mark a special birthday.

Those with children and those child free within our selected sample spend rather modestly on 18-karat or 24-karat gold jewelry with precious stones. Considering a jewelry purchase of $1,000 or more, we find that 29% of those child free and 33% of those with a child would spend at this level. Among the Lifestyle segments, more Upbeat Enjoyers with at least one child at home would spend this much on a piece of jewelry (39%). And while we've noted that large numbers of child-free Financial Positives have made a fine jewelry purchase in the past three years, only 30% would spend $1,000 or more. Within this particular sample, we see no evidence that the child free spend more than those with a child on purchases of fine jewelry. In terms of other luxury goods, our studies demonstrate that the presence or absence of a child does not influence the amount of money spent on them.

Reaching these targets

To better understand the media which would be most efficient in targeting the Upbeat Enjoyers in our selected sample, we used our Simulator program. Simulator targets media buys using a psychographic segment, in this case the Upbeat Enjoyers, as well as specific demographics and behaviors. Upbeat Enjoyers in our sample are over consumers of magazines. And magazines such as *Condé Nast Traveler*, *Martha Stewart Living*, *The New Yorker*, *New York Times Magazine*, and *Smithsonian* are efficient at reaching them, although not Financial Positives.

When marketers decide to sponsor a program on the Public Broadcasting System (PBS), such as Masterpiece Theatre, the Lifestyle segment they will reach in disproportionate numbers from our selected sample are Upbeat Enjoyers. Eighty percent of Upbeat Enjoyers in our sample watch public television one or more hours a week, as compared to only 68% of Financial Positives.

Based on hours viewed per week, Upbeat Enjoyers are also over consumers of cable television, while they are under consumers of network television. To achieve the greatest efficiencies in marketing and communication, all efforts, from direct marketing to media buys, public relations to telemarketing should be integrated around a targeted psychographic segment, further defined by demographic and behavioral variables.

Detailed profile needed

Rather than limit their focus to empty nesters, marketers of discretionary products must begin with a psychographic or motivational segmentation that determines receptive segments and the messages they consider relevant. We've demonstrated in this chapter that both Upbeat Enjoyers and Financial Positives are prime targets for the marketers of many luxury goods. Using a selected sample, we've also shown that applying behaviors, demographics, and media usage to this psychographic segmentation further focuses marketing initiatives. In addition, marketers of discretionary products must know what designs, brands, payment methods, locations, colors, and level of service are preferred by each Lifestyle segment they wish to target.

REFERENCES

Raymond, Joan. "The joy of empty nesting." *American Demographics* May 2000.

U.S. Census Bureau. "Family Households with Own Children Under Age 18, by Type of Family, 1980 to 1998, and by Age of Householder," 1998.

"One quarter of income is discretionary." *Research Alert* 7 January, 2000.

"Study finds decline in number of married couples with children." *Jet* 13 December, 1999.

Grant, Priscilla. "Face time." *Modern Maturity* March-April 2001.

Balaban, V. and Exter, T. *American Incomes: Demographics of Who Has Money*. Ithaca, New York: New Strategist Publications, 1999.

American Sports Data, Inc. *Sports Participation Trends Report* 1997.

Chapter **6**

THE TRAVEL SEGMENTS

HIGHWAY WANDERERS

Those in this segment are spontaneous travelers who prefer to drive their car or recreational vehicle to their travel destination. Highway Wanderers are motivated to travel because of their love of nature and their interest in visiting friends and family. Once they find a beautiful area, they return to it again and again. Those in this segment prefer to avoid crowds and consider cities dangerous. Highway Wanderers say they find their travel plans restricted because of both insufficient time and money.

Hitting the road

Highway Wanderers are focused on traveling on wheels, whether in their own car or in a recreational vehicle (RV). These choices, well suited to the domestic travel preferred by Highway Wanderers, give them the freedom and economy they seek. Traveling in their own car also fits with the spontaneous travel Highway Wanderers favor. They never make any real vacation plans and don't consider it important to know exactly where they're going to be and when. They want to be free to follow their whims as they drive down the highway.

Given their preference for vacation travel by car, it's not surprising that Highway Wanderers are least interested in flying. For this group, frequent flyer programs hold little appeal. Because of their domestic travel focus, those in this segment have little interest in a travel company, such as American Express.

Reasons for travel

Highway Wanderers think of vacations as a time to visit friends and family. Only Highway Wanderers have this take on vacations, and their position colors virtually every nuance of their vacation experience. For example, because they are probably visiting friends and family on vacation, being pampered is not a top priority for Highway Wanderers. Nor do those in this segment find either bed and breakfasts or time-shares appealing; their friends and family offer much the same type of accommodation. Since their travel is focused on the U.S. and they may very well be visiting friends and family, it isn't surprising they have little fear of getting sick while traveling.

Seek an independent experience

Because traveling by car fits their travel expectations and patterns so perfectly, it's understandable why Highway Wanderers don't find organized escorted tours or chartered transportation appealing. Perhaps when they can no longer drive, Highway Wanderers will take organized escorted tours; even now they don't believe such tours are just for old people.

Cost considerations

Travel by car also fits the Highway Wanderers' need for a low-cost vacation. Of all the Travel segments, only the Highway Wanderers report difficulties in having enough money to spend on vacation travel. They want to enjoy their vacations, but feel pressured by cost considerations. If they do fly on a vacation, Highway Wanderers would be willing to be packed

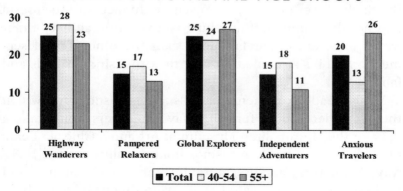

Figure 3: *At a statistically significant level, a higher percentage of Anxious Travelers exists among those 55 and older compared to those 40 to 54. In contrast, lower percentages of Independent Adventurers, Highway Wanderers, and Pampered Relaxers exists in the older population as compared to the younger.*

into a filled coach-class section as long as they knew they were getting the lowest price.

Far from the crowd

While on vacation, Highway Wanderers want to enjoy natural beauty away from hoards of people. They have found that off-season travel is one way of avoiding the masses. To them big cities are unsafe places.

Those in this segment are creatures of habit; they aren't seeking new vacation thrills. Once they find a beautiful natural area, they return there again and again. Highway Wanderers are content to travel in the U.S. and have little interest in experiencing other countries and cultures.

A limited range of activities

Highway Wanderers think of themselves as adventurous travelers, but this belief appears to be related more to their spontaneity than to participating in a wide range of exciting activities. You won't find those in this segment rafting down the Snake River or hiking in Yosemite. In fact, sitting around and not doing much of anything is a vacation activity Highway Wanderers prefer far more than the other Travel segments. And it's also one that may fit with visiting friends and family.

While heading to theme parks such as Disneyland, which they consider a lot of fun, Highway Wanderers would take a pass on the Metropolitan Museum of Art and a Chicago Bears football game. Gambling casinos hold no allure for the Highway Wanderers, and Restaurant Chez Louie will not find Highway Wanderers seated at its white-linen draped tables. Neither is the idea of shopping at the Mall of America a big draw for the Highway Wanderers.

Relying on travel clubs

Given their commitment to traveling in their own car or in an RV, it isn't surprising that Highway Wanderers would get their travel information and reservations from travel clubs such as the American Automobile Association (AAA). They are the only Travel segment that relies on information from friends in planning a vacation. On the other hand, the friends and family of Highway Wanderers don't regard them as a source of travel information.

Other than travel clubs and their friends, Highway Wanderers have few other sources of travel-related information. Travel agents don't function within the Highway Wanderers' vacation orbit. Those in this segment wouldn't use a travel agent to plan their entire vacation, nor do they consider travel agents a good source of information. Highway Wanderers ignore brochures on a destination that have been mailed to them, and they aren't interested in using an online service to make travel reservations.

Strapped for time

Of the five Travel segments, only Highway Wanderers feel they can't get enough time off to go on a vacation. Perhaps because of this they are the most interested in taking several short vacations, rather than one long one. But Highway Wanders still consider even short vacations of less than a week as worthwhile.

PAMPERED RELAXERS

Those in this segment view vacations as times to pamper themselves and luxuriate in first-class service. They want to enjoy the best of everything, perhaps while on a cruise. Cost does not seem to be a limitation to them. Clearly, Pampered Relaxers don't want to do anything mentally or physically taxing while on vacation. Those in this segment want to enjoy their holiday without the encumbrance of friends or family. Shopping and visiting gambling casinos are primary vacation activities for this segment, as are visiting theme parks.

Kid-glove service

Of the five Travel segments, only Pampered Relaxers definitely want to spend their vacation being pampered through exceptional service. Great attention must be focused on their every need. If Pampered Relaxers don't get the service they think they deserve, they get upset.

If all of this pampering costs a great deal of money, that is of little importance to Pampered Relaxers. Those in this segment go on a vacation to have a good time, and they tell us they don't care how much it costs.

Vacations that don't lend themselves to pampering are not at all appealing to Pampered Relaxers. For example, they're the segment least interested in doing their own cooking in a hotel suite's kitchenette. Fine dining, yes; doing the dishes, no.

Spending money on activities

More than anything else, Pampered Relaxers consider sitting on the beach, relaxing, and doing nothing as their favorite vacation activities. Mental and physical exertion are not an important part of a Pampered Relaxers' vacation. Those in this segment don't want vacations that offer plenty of intellectual stimulation or cultural activities. For them, adventure travel experiences such as rock climbing and canoeing hold no appeal.

Besides sitting on the beach lathered in suntan lotion, Pampered Relaxers are extremely enthusiastic about visiting theme parks, such as Busch Gardens or Sea World. Returning home laden with souvenir tee shirts, tea towels, and ash trays appeals to Pampered Relaxers. Shopping at new and different stores, fine-dining experiences, and visiting gambling casinos are other activities that are extremely high on the Pampered Relaxers' list of things to do on their vacations. They prefer to stay in hotels located near points of interest so they can be close to the action.

Cruises provide pampering

Pampered Relaxers' great enthusiasm for cruises stems from their need to be pampered—and most cruises certainly provide that quite well. The cruise package with everything provided for a single price also appeals to this Travel segment. In contrast, a non-pampering situation, the timeshare, is of no interest to Pampered Relaxers. And neither tour buses nor chartered transportation are seen by Pampered Relaxers as a great way to take a vacation trip. While they themselves would avoid organized escorted tours, they don't consider such travel to be only for blue-haired ladies.

Favoring the familiar

Besides their desire to sit on the beach and do very little, Pampered Relaxers are also interested in settling down and staying in one place while on vacation. Since they have no interest in meeting new people or mixing with the locals, it isn't surprising that not knowing the language wouldn't stop a Pampered Relaxer from traveling to a foreign country. Not seeking intellectual stimulation or new experiences, Pampered Relaxers wouldn't find it boring to find a vacation spot they like so that they can go back often.

And because they may be returning to a favorite spot or planning a vacation to one location, it isn't important for Pampered Relaxers to have detailed travel plans. Some vacation planning, however, is viewed as necessary by those in this segment; they aren't spontaneous travelers popping off on a trip with little notice.

The people factor

Pampered Relaxers have a Greta Garbo-like attitude toward their vacations: they want to be alone. In contrast to the Highway Wanderers, Pampered Relaxers do not see vacations as a time to be with friends and family. Nor is vacationing with friends or even people they know something Pampered Relaxers would find appealing, even if it is safer to do so. Meeting new people and exchanging views with persons from other countries or areas aren't things Pampered Relaxers have an urge to do.

No safety concerns

Pampered Relaxers have no concerns about their personal safety in big cities. They don't worry about getting sick while traveling or encountering problems when they eat foods in different countries.

Transportation

While driving their own car or RV on vacation does not appeal to them, Pampered Relaxers do favor picking up a rental car. Nor do those in this segment think that the train is a fun way to travel on vacation. Pampered Relaxers like to fly to their vacation destinations, but being packed into coach class, even if they are getting the lowest price, isn't something they would want to do.

Travel info & arrangements

Pampered Relaxers don't read articles and books in preparation for a trip. This segment views a travel club such as AAA as a knowledgeable source for travel information and reservations. Pampered Relaxers find travel agents helpful because they know about different destinations, but they wouldn't rely on a travel agent to take care of all of their travel needs. Going online to make travel plans isn't something Pampered Relaxers are likely to do.

GLOBAL EXPLORER

For those in this segment vacations have to include intellectual stimulation, authentic experiences, and encounters with new cultures. Global Explorers are very open to social interactions with strangers and foreigners. They have no fear or reservations about having new and stimulating adventures. Global Explorers are informed travelers who do their research before a trip. Flexible regarding transportation options, Global Explorers are particularly enthusiastic about cruises, but also like to vacation in an RV and fly to their destination.

Open to new adventures

Global Explorers consider themselves to be adventurous in both physical activities and social interactions. Of all the Travel segments, Global Explorers are most apt to have this mindset. Adventure travel trips, not surprisingly, have some appeal for Global Explorers.

Rather than sit on the beach and relax, Global Explorers feel it is extremely important to keep busy with many activities while on vacation. Besides physical activities, those in this segment also believe that a good vacation has to provide lots of intellectual stimulation, including diverse cultural activities.

Global Explorers find it absolutely critical to meet new people and mix with the locals while on vacation. They want to experience a country's real culture and will go to great lengths to avoid tourist traps. For Global Explorers, activities such as shopping and casino gambling, enjoyed by Pampered Relaxers, are of little interest.

Seeking the new, different

More than the other Travel segments, Global Explorers want to visit new countries to experience different cultures. Not knowing the language doesn't stop Global Explorers from plunging ahead. Global Explorers are the only Travel segment with no interest in finding a comfortable spot that they can visit year after year. They want to experience new locales.

Packages are appealing

Global Explorers are extremely committed to cruising and find all-inclusive pricing very appealing. Compared to the other Travel segments, Global Explorers are most interested in timesharing as a great way to vacation.

While Global Explorers deny that only the old go on escorted tours, they don't think such tours are safe or comfortable. Nor do Global Explorers consider chartered transportation an appealing way to take a vacation trip.

The people factor

Global Explorers prefer to meet new people and make new friends on a vacation, rather than stick with those they know. They are cool to the concept of vacations as times to visit and enjoy friends and family. Neither do the members of this segment want to spend their vacation time with a group of people they already know, even if such a group provides an additional layer of safety.

Transportation

Global Explorers are very flexible in terms of their transportation options while on vacation. More than the other Travel segments, Global Explorers like to fly to their vacation spot. They expect more from an airline than just low-cost tickets and a frequent-flyer program.

Although they enjoy flying, Global Explorers also appreciate having a rental car or their own car on a vacation. Both Global Explorers and Highway Wanderers are enthusiastic about using an RV for vacation travel.

Travel info & arrangements

Of all the Travel segments, Global Explorers are the most well informed. They are most apt to read books and articles about travel and to be considered a source of travel information by their friends and family. Of all the Travel segments, only Global Explorers fulfill this role. Brochures and other materials sent to them in the mail are used by Global Explorers to select travel destinations and plan trips. They are the only Travel segment which does so. Travel clubs are another source of information for this segment. Compared to the other segments, Global Explorers, along with Independent Adventurers, are most likely to use the Internet for making travel plans and reservations.

Global Explorers have a positive relationship with travel agents. Compared to the other Travel segments, Global Explorers would be open to using travel agents to provide all of the travel services they require. They view travel agents as really helpful because they have the necessary knowledge about different destinations. And, for their part, travel agents should love Global Explorers, the Travel segment that feels most strongly that it has enough money and time to take vacations.

The type of vacation a travel agent might help a Global Explorer plan would not offer the pampering so important to the Pampered Relaxers. It might be a trip to an exotic locale or large city. As they plan a trip, getting sick, being a crime victim, and eating strange foods are of no concern to them.

Although the plan itself wouldn't have to be very detailed, Global Explorers do demand some sort of itinerary; they aren't into spontaneous get aways. Trips shorter than a week are considered by those in this segment to be real vacations.

INDEPENDENT ADVENTURERS

Those in this segment hold highly Romantic views on vacations, which they see as spontaneous events enjoyed in pristine natural areas. When Independent Adventurers arrive at these undiscovered places, they don't plan on encountering any crowds. They are, however, enthusiastic about traveling with multiple generations of their family. Searching for a pure and unique travel experience, Independent Adventurers admit that costs are a consideration. Airlines frequent flyer programs attract Independent Adventurers who dislike group travel and yet need to save.

Destinations

Independent Adventurers want to go on a vacation to a place of great natural beauty where they will not encounter crowds of people. Once they find this beautiful — and as yet undiscovered spot — Independent Adventurers would like to return to it often.

Avoiding all packages

Given the Independent Adventurers' commitment to avoiding large groups of people, we can understand their very negative reaction to packaged travel. Whether timeshare or chartered transportation, organized escorted tour or cruise, Independent Adventurers dislike all types of group travel packages with a profound intensity. For example, Independent Adventurers are the only Travel segment that considers escorted tours just for old people. Such tours — according to Independent Adventurers — are neither safe nor comfortable. In addition, those in this segment don't think of cruises as fun or a bargain.

Purpose of travel

On vacation, Independent Adventurers would like to enjoy fine restaurants, as well as sit on the beach and relax. As the segment most interested in adventure travel, they're also prepared to rough it. A trip to Panama, for example, would seem to suit the Independent Adventurers quite well, combining pristine beaches, sophisticated restaurants, and forays into the rain forest—all in a largely undiscovered locale.

According to Independent Adventurers, a great vacation would leave them feeling refreshed and energized; they're the only segment with these travel expectations. Independent Adventurers also seek authenticity from their vacation, not tourist traps and souvenirs. Of the five Travel segments, only the Independent Adventurers reject the idea of theme parks as fun places to visit while on vacation. Having gambling casinos makes a destination far less attractive to Independent Adventurers.

Considerations of length & cost

When Independent Adventurers go on a vacation they want to stay in a place long enough to really get a feel for it. For them, vacations shorter than a week are just not long enough. Besides the length of their vacation, Independent Adventurers are somewhat concerned about costs. They would like to have a great time, but do not feel they have unlimited funds to do so.

Their concern over cost is reflected in the Independent Adventurers' view of airlines as offering commodity products, with price as the only differentiator. As long as they are getting the cheapest ticket, Independent Adventurers can tolerate being squeezed into a coach class seat in a plane filled to capacity. Another source of cheap tickets is the airlines' frequent flyer programs. Only Independent Adventurers are kept loyal by such programs, which prompt them to go back to the same airline again and again.

Independent Adventurers are somewhat interested in the freedom of using their own car or a rental while on vacation.

But this segment is very much against the idea of traveling in an RV or by train.

Travel info & arrangements

Since Independent Adventurers seek pristine, untouched spots of great natural beauty, it's not surprising that they would find travel agents, most of whom sell packages or cruises to well-visited places, as uninformed. Independent Adventurers seek rare, insider information; it's no wonder that the brochures and other materials sent to them in the mail don't help them decide where to go on a vacation. Perhaps these sources of information are also not useful because Independent Adventurers, like Highway Wanderers, prefer spontaneous travel and never make any real vacation plans. Compared to the other Travel segments, Independent Adventurers would use the Internet for planning a trip and making reservations.

Where to stay

Staying near points of interest is a consideration when Independent Adventurers select a hotel. Perhaps because of cost considerations or because they are in search of something unique, Independent Adventurers would be the most apt of all the Travel segments to prefer a bed and breakfast.

The people factor

Independent Adventurers are the only Travel segment to identify multi-generational family vacations as very appealing.

Safety concerns

Independent Adventurers aren't worried about eating foods in different countries, and the safety of traveling with a group of people isn't something that Independent Adventurers look for.

ANXIOUS TRAVELERS

The travel experience for those in this segment is filled with potential dangers and unpleasantness. In attempts to control their wide-ranging fears, Anxious Travelers travel with others, avoid encounters with strangers, and plan to the last detail. Anxious Travelers see travel agents as highly knowledgeable and useful in planning a trip. Travel experiences for those in this segment are highly restricted in terms of activities. While cost considerations tend to limit their travel, Anxious Travelers prefer to take several short trips rather than one long one.

Safety concerns

Anxious Travelers are beset with a wide variety of safety concerns. Before visiting a place they consider how safe it is; if they are going to visit a big city they worry about their personal safety. Busy places with lots of people unnerve them. Only those in this segment worry about getting sick on a trip and eating foods in different countries. They would feel very uncomfortable traveling in a country where they don't know the language. To help contain their almost overwhelming fears, Anxious Travelers look to a travel company, such as American Express, with many overseas locations to help them in case they need it.

Planning: an antidote to fear

Aggressive planning is another way in which Anxious Travelers attempt to contain their fears. Only they of all the Travel segments find it extremely important to have detailed travel plans. Anxious Travelers have to know exactly where they will be each hour of each day of their vacation. The idea of a spontaneous trip on the spur of the moment without a travel plan is entirely foreign to the Anxious Travelers' mindset.

Stretching each dollar

Compared to the other segments, Anxious Travelers are most concerned with the cost of a vacation. When planning their vacations, Anxious Travelers search for the best bargains. Putting their own enjoyment aside, Anxious Travelers have to care how much a vacation costs.

The Anxious Travelers' twin concerns of fear of the unknown and overwhelming travel costs that will outstrip their resources are resolved in the organized escorted tour. Only this segment favors this format and believes that tour buses are both safe and comfortable for vacation travel. They, along with three other Travel segments, deny that only old people go on such tours.

Heavily scheduled escorted tours map out where Anxious Travelers will be every minute. In addition, faced-paced itineraries keep Anxious Travelers from getting bored, something this segment tends to do.

Anxious Travelers believe that vacationing with a group of people affords them a measure of safety. Besides organized escorted tours, Anxious Travelers also consider chartered transportation a smart way to take a vacation trip.

Activities

Anxious Travelers do not see themselves as risk takers; you won't see them on adventure travel trips. Taking in a Boston Celtics game or any other sports event isn't something Anxious Travelers look forward to on a vacation. Gambling casinos actually lessen the appeal a destination for Anxious Travelers. While they like to meet new people when they travel, they will be those on the escorted tour bus — not the locals they may encounter.

The Anxious Travelers' well-planned holiday includes cultural activities, such as museums. Their hotel should be located near points of interest. They enjoy fine dining, not meals prepared in a hotel room's kitchenette.

High expectations of service

Although far less than the Pampered Relaxers, Anxious Travelers also demand quality service and would be upset if they weren't treated as they think they deserve.

The time factor

While Anxious Travelers have no problem getting enough time to go on a vacation, they prefer taking several short vacations through the year, rather than one long one.

Transportation

Anxious Travelers enjoy flying to their vacation destinations, and things other than the price of the tickets are more important to them in selecting an airline. These possible considerations include an airline's safety record, food, and service. Another transportation option that only Anxious Travelers view positively is train travel. In contrast, this segment does not think using an RV for vacation travel would be fun, nor is renting a car while on vacation a positive for this group.

Travel information

Travel clubs such as AAA serve Anxious Travelers as good sources of travel information and reservations. This segment views travel agents as knowledgeable sources of information and necessary in planning a successful vacation. For Anxious Travelers, travel agents know enough about different destinations to be helpful to them.

Chapter 7

TARGETING CRUISING'S BIG WAVE

Filling the ships

Wider and taller than anyone could have imagined, cruise
ships in ever-increasing numbers ply the seas like monolith-
ic multi-layered wedding cakes. Build them and certainly
they will come seems to be the motto of members of Cruise
Lines International Association (CLIA). CLIA members, who
represent 95 percent of the cruise capacity marketed from
North America, plan to build 47 new ships between 2000 and
2004. These ships will be added to the 145 already serving the
North American market and the hundreds of new ships built
worldwide during the '90s.

The question: where will the cruise industry find the people to fill these new and existing ships?

It is true that the number of North Americans taking a
cruise each year has grown from 4.5 million in 1993 to 5.85
million in 1999. Still the industry seems frustrated that it has
only a 5% share of the total amount spent on vacation trips
costing $1,000 or more. Today only one in ten Americans 25
or older with a household income of $25,000 or more has
taken a cruise. "What the industry needs," notes Jack Sever-

son, executive travel editor at the *Philadelphia Inquirer*, "is more first-time cruisers, not only to swell the ranks necessary to fill the new berths coming on line, but also to then swell the ranks of the repeaters."

Mature a hot growth area

While young adults are eyed as one growth area by the cruise industry, CLIA reports that the percentage of those from the 25 to 39 age group who expressed interest in future cruising remained flat from 1992 to 1998 (44% to 43%). In contrast, prospects among baby boomers and younger seniors 40 to 59 grew from 35% to 41%. Another growth area for the cruise industry is also dependent on the mature market. Among those families with children who had previously cruised, interest in cruising grew from 26% in 1992 to 31% in 1998. Many of these families are baby boomers with children or grandparents traveling with grandchildren.

Based on 1999 CLIA figures, we estimate that North American cruisers generated $7.6 billion in revenues. The bulk of that amount, $5.6 billion, was contributed by those 40 and older. These current expenditures on cruises by the mature market, CLIA's own projections regarding growing interest among those 40 to 59 in cruising, and the explosive growth projected in the population of baby boomers and their elders solidifies them as the cruise industry's best target for the next 20, if not 30, years.

Played against this encouraging scenario is the apparent expectation among cruise industry executives that everyone should go on a cruise. They frequently complain that only 11% of Americans have ever taken a cruise. While satisfaction is high among those who have cruised, the pressure is on to convince new prospects of the benefits and fun of cruising. If only the remaining 89% would try it, surely they would like it, or so CLIA members believe.

Breaking out the market

Our data show that among those 40 and older, 6% have cruised in the past five years but don't intend to do so over the next five years; 53% have not cruised in the past five years and don't have plans to do so over the next five years; 23% have not cruised, but would like to, and 18% have cruised and plan to do so again within the next five years. Taken together, these last two groups constitute 41% of the U.S. 40 and older population and present the cruise line industry with its greatest opportunities.

These two groups are highly receptive to cruising: attracting them and addressing their needs will be relatively painless and cost-effective. In contrast, expensive, long-term missionary work will have to be done to convince someone, regardless of their age or affluence, who does not want to cruise to do so.

Real competition: attitudes

Competition, according to those in the cruise industry, is the land-based vacation. Our Travel segments tell a different story. The real challenge for the cruise industry is dealing with each segment's entrenched perceptions of leisure travel. Three of our five Travel segments are not receptive to cruising, and it will be very difficult to change their attitudes. The cruise industry will have to alter these three segments' deeply rooted motivations about vacation travel, an exceedingly expensive proposition.

Consumers receptive to cruising are concentrated almost totally in two of our five psychographically based Travel segments: the Pampered Relaxers and Global Explorers. But while both segments are committed to cruising, they have entirely different expectations of travel and the cruise experience. Looking at these two segments in aggregate would submerge these very real and critical differences. Attitude questions regarding "interest in cruising" would produce an undifferentiated mass, not the material for targeted marketing.

Two segments dominate

Together Pampered Relaxers and Global Explorers make up 44% of those who have never bounded up the gang plank of a cruise ship, but would like to do so within the next five years. Global Explorers are above average in their interest in cruising. Although 25% of the 40 and older population, they are 28% of those who have never cruised, but would like to do so. The number of receptive non-cruisers among the remaining three Travel segments is average or below average when compared to their occurrence in the overall 40 and older population.

If we take a different perspective and look at the composition of each Travel segment by those in the 40 and older population who have never cruised and don't intend to and those who haven't, but plan to do so in the next five years, the importance of the Pampered Relaxers and Global Explorers becomes clearer. Far more than is the case with the other Travel segments, substantial portions of both the Pampered Relaxers (40%) and Global Explorers (42%) who have never cruised would like to do so in the next five years. Their interest in cruising is grounded in the favorable attitudes these two segments have toward it. They like what cruising has to offer and are the industry's best targets. Whether or not they have actually taken a cruise, two-thirds of each of these two Travel segments strongly agree with the idea that going on a cruise would be fun, as compared to only one-third of each of the remaining three Travel segments.

It isn't surprising, then, that fewer Highway Wanderers, Independent Adventurers, and Anxious Travelers are found in the group that hasn't cruised, but would like to. Of the Independent Adventurers in the total 40 and older population, only about a quarter (28%) of those who have never cruised would like to do so; the rest aren't interested. Virtually identical percentages are seen among Highway Wanderers and Anxious Travelers.

The very best targets

Whether a cruise line is targeting receptive potential cruisers or experienced cruisers who plan to cruise again, Pampered Relaxers and Global Explorers are the segments to pursue. Among those who have taken a cruise in the last five years, Global Explorers represent 40% of the cruises taken, although they are only 25% of the 40 and older population. While Pampered Relaxers account for 25% of the cruises taken, they are just 15% of the 40 and older population. Together these two segments account for two-thirds of the cruises taken over the past five years by those 40 and older.

Most frequent cruisers

Added to the profile of Pampered Relaxers and Global Explorers as the two primary cruising segments is the fact that our data also show them as the most frequent multiple cruisers. Of the total 40 and older population, 24% have cruised over the past five years. Among these cruisers, 65% have taken one cruise, 28% have taken two or three cruises, and 7% have taken four or more cruises. As they do in the other categories, Pampered Relaxers (36%) and Global Explorers (39%) dominate those who are frequent cruisers, defined as those who have taken four or more cruises in the past five years.

Two different profiles

From a variety of perspectives it is evident that both of these two Travel segments like to cruise. But because their fundamental attitudes toward travel are very different, their expectations of cruising also differ. The chapter on our Travel segments details each segment's expectations regarding leisure travel. Pampered Relaxers stress pampering, impeccable service, and indulgence. Their focus is on themselves, more than on a shared experience. They do not see a vacation as the time to extend themselves intellectually or exert themselves physically.

In stark contrast, Global Explorers are driven to seek out new cultural and intellectual experiences while on vacation. They enthusiastically embrace new people, foods, and experiences. Global Explorers, who would like to stretch and grow during a vacation, emphasize intellectual stimulation as very much a part of the leisure travel experience they are seeking.

Source of growth

Recognizing the importance of these two very different, but highly receptive, segments, cruise industry executives should focus on them as engines for growth. Relevant messages should be communicated to each segment in their preferred media. In addition, cruise experiences should be created specifically for each segment. In short, every aspect of marketing, from product development to travel agent support to customer relationship management (CRM), should be directed at Pampered Relaxers and Global Explorers.

Length of cruise differs

Attempts to attract Pampered Relaxers who have never cruised, but intend to do so, should focus on the shorter cruise. More Pampered Relaxers in this group (83%) have taken one or more short vacations one to four days long in the past 12 months, as compared to Global Explorers (67%). In contrast, far more Global Explorers (42%) who are receptive non-cruisers have taken at least one or more long vacations of more than 10 days in the past 12 months as compared to Pampered Relaxers (19%).

One reason for the preference among Pampered Relaxers for shorter vacations is the fact that more receptive non-cruisers among them are still working full time (78%) as compared to Global Explorers (67%). In fact, more Global Explorers don't work at all (19%) as compared to Pampered Relaxers (10%) in this group. Much of the phenomenal growth in shorter cruises, which the industry regards as the entry-level cruise experience, is no doubt attributable to the Pampered Relaxer segment. According to CLIA figures, the number of shorter cruises, defined as those two to five days long, grew by 506% from 1980 to 1999.

Differences in the length of vacations taken over the past 12 months flatten out between the Pampered Relaxers and Global Explorers who have cruised and intend to cruise again. A possible explanation is the fact that for both these Travel segments in this group the percentages of full time workers is almost the same (62% and 65%). For example, over the past 12 months 53% and 56% of previous cruisers in these two Travel segments had taken a vacation more than 10 days long.

Museums or the beach

A trio of activities appeal to virtually the same percentages of both Pampered Relaxers and Global Explorers who tell us that they will cruise in the future, regardless of whether or not they have cruised in the past. These activities include shopping, nightlife and entertainment, and gambling. Interest in nightlife and gambling is of even greater interest to previous cruisers than to receptive neophytes.

Some activities clearly appeal to far more Global Explorers than to Pampered Relaxers who are planning to cruise again or try it for the first time. On their next vacation, far more Global Explorers plan to include activities such as observing nature, taking in native and ethnic activities, hiking, going to a zoo, and attending cultural events or concerts. More Global Explorers (31%), for example, plan on being a part of a community festival on their next vacation as compared to Pampered Relaxers (11%). More Pampered Relaxers than Global Explorers are planning to golf on their next vacation, sit on the beach, and enjoy a spa.

Given the differences in the activities in which they plan to participate during their next vacation, specific types of cruises can be targeted to each of these two segments. A three-day cruise focused on a luxurious ship-based spa would appeal to Pampered Relaxers, as would a golf clinic. In contrast, a cruise to Alaska which offers the opportunity to observe whales, view a Native American celebration, and take a hike would be perfectly structured for Global Explorers.

Creating the message

Once a cruise has been designed with a specific segment in mind—whether for Global Explorers or Pampered Relaxers—messages have to be crafted that are relevant to that segment. Luxurious pampering, sybaritic inactivity, service fit for royalty, and a sensual, indulgent experience should be conveyed in messages relevant to Pampered Relaxers. At this time, cruise lines appear to be targeting Pampered Relaxers far more than Global Explorers. Royal Caribbean's "coming your way" campaign a few years ago seemed to address Pampered Relaxers with enticements of "perfection," including the "perfect lobster" served by a smiling waiter, "total rejuvenation," a "sparkling ship," and "an island all your own."

In contrast, messages reflecting the discovery of new worlds, the exploration of nature or perhaps a spiritual dimension, an expansion of one's universe, of seeing things for the first time, appeal to the Global Explorer. Holland America's 1996 advertising campaign asked "When was the last time?" and then described experiences in nature. This campaign could have been positioned to attract Global Explorers.

Reliance on travel agent

A major difference between receptive non-cruisers and receptive experienced cruisers is in the two groups' use of a travel agent. Of those who have cruised and will do so again, 71% say they have used a travel agent in the past 12 months. In this group, the numbers of Pampered Relaxers and Global Explorers who use a travel agent are above average. CLIA reports that 90% of those who have cruised in the past five years consult a travel agent.

In contrast, our data shows that only about half (54%) of those who haven't cruised, but plan on doing so, have used a travel agent for any travel-related purchase over the past 12 months. This percentage is higher than that of the 40 and older population overall, 42% of whom have used a travel agent in that time span. Pampered Relaxers and Global Explorers who are the most receptive non-cruisers are just average or below average in their use of a travel agent. Since the travel agent remains the source of 90% of all cruise sales, the lack of contact between receptive non-cruisers and a travel agent poses a major impediment to increasing sales among potential new cruisers.

Another dark cloud on the cruise sales horizon is the fact that the decline in the number of travel agencies is accelerating. In 2000 the Airlines Reporting Corporation (ARC) projected that the number of travel agencies would decrease by 5.5%, compared to a historical average of 3.5% and a 4% decline in 1999. The vulnerability of this channel of distribution is further underscored by the fact that only 64% of all travel agencies reported making a profit in 1999, a decrease from 76% in 1997. Small- and medium-sized travel agencies, responsible for 79% of all leisure travel sales, may not have the financial resources to keep their doors open.

To this threatening scenario is added the fact that the Travel Industry Association of America (TIA) reports a decline in reliance on a travel agent as the number of Internet reservations has increased. This insight is echoed by a Bear Stearns report in early 2000 predicting a decline of 25% in the number of travel agents as a result of increasing Web bookings.

Identifying the segment

Given the importance of each prospect who walks into a travel agency office, it is extremely important that the prospect be accurately identified as either a Global Explorer or Pampered Relaxer. It's easy for a travel agent to determine the length of cruise desired or the prospect's budget. What's critical is to accurately identify the prospect's attitudinal or psychographic segment. Doing so will allow the travel agent to pitch the cruise experience using messages relevant to that segment. Why stress viewing wildlife to a Pampered Relaxer who only wants to lie in a deck chair by the pool?

Improving direct marketing

As the number of travel agents continues to decline, the increasing use of direct marketing by cruise lines may become not only a necessity, but also a responsive marketing channel. In fact, the untapped market of receptive non-cruisers may well be reached more effectively through direct marketing. As we've pointed out, far fewer of those who have never cruised, but are interested in doing so, use a travel agent compared to those who have.

Cruise lines have not always been successful in their past attempts at direct marketing when that has entailed bypassing the travel agent. For some years the now-defunct Renaissance Cruises used a contrarian strategy and went straight to the consumer using direct mail, promotional e-mails, and even cold calling. A more conventional example of the use of direct marketing by the cruise industry was Seabourn's "bid to distinguish itself from its better known big sister, Cunard." Paired with print ads, this early 2000 direct marketing campaign targeted both Seabourn's current and potential cruisers.

Considering that cruise lines may very well be heavily dependent on direct marketing in the future, it is important to note that our data shows that there are significant differences among our five Travel segments and their reaction to travel-related direct mail. It is clear that Global Explorers and Pampered Relaxers who are receptive to cruising have very different reactions to such offers as compared to the overall 40 and older population. While only 7% of the 40 and older population opens travel-related offers and reads them carefully, it's something 25% of Global Explorers tell us they do. While 38% of the 40 and older population opens travel-related offers and skims their contents, it's something done by almost half of the receptive, but non-cruising, Pampered Relaxers (49%).

A total, integrated profile

The most effective direct marketing campaigns develop comprehensive profiles of those in their databases. These holistic profiles would include a psychographic segmentation, such as our Travel segments; behaviors; demographics, and geodemographic coding. This type of razor-sharp targeting reaches prospects who are both qualified and receptive. Once models are developed, finding prospective cruisers can be as straightforward as reaching past ones.

The quest for new and repeat cruisers can begin with geo-demographics. For example, CLIA's research shows that 63% of all cruise days are generated from 17 states. Historically, states in the South Atlantic, Middle Atlantic, and Pacific Census Divisions have been most productive in terms of cruise sales. Among those who have cruised and will cruise again in these Census Divisions, our data tracks that from CLIA. The organization's data show that the South Atlantic Division generates 31% of total cruise days from all age groups, by far the greatest percentage of all the Divisions. Our data reveal that 24% of those 40 and older living in the South Atlantic Division have cruised and also intend to cruise again.

But the geodemographic approach, while highly useful, is still wasteful. Among households with pre-tax incomes of $50,000 and above only 30% will be non-cruisers interested in taking a cruise over the next five years. If 100,000 brochures describing a cruise are mailed to these households, only 30,000 will reach receptive targets. How much better to mail 50,000 pieces to Global Explorers or Pampered Relaxers who have incomes of $50,000 and above and know that 72% or 36,000 will reach both qualified and receptive targets.

The need to apply robust psychographic segments to a direct marketing database is seen in the fact that cruise line sales aren't generated equally among our Travel segments within a Census Division or any other geographical area. For example, in the Middle Atlantic Census Division, the second most productive Census Division for cruise lines, Global Explorers (40%) and Pampered Relaxers (27%) are the majority of receptive, experienced cruisers. In contrast, Independent Adventurers in this Census Division are only 5% of this group.

Testing new waters

In their drive to acquire new cruisers, we suggest that the cruise industry test Census Divisions that have not drawn large numbers of cruisers in the past. The Middle Atlantic Census Division remains slightly above average in its population of receptive non-cruisers. But others, such as the Mountain, East South Central, and East North Central Census Divisions, are above average in their levels of receptive non-cruisers and will be even more productive if targeted by our Travel segments. For example, among those in this group living in the Mountain Census Division, which includes such states as Arizona, New Mexico, and Colorado, exists a large population of interested Global Explorers (35%).

The combination of geodemographics, behaviors, and psychographics results in such precise targeting that it is possible to reach a far higher percentage of receptive potential cruisers, even in Census Divisions that have been previously regarded as marginally productive. Attitudinally we know that the Pampered Relaxers and Global Explorers are very open to cruising. The barriers that have kept them from cruising in the past have to better understood and addressed, but consumers in these segments are already motivated to cruise.

Considering that Global Explorers and Pampered Relaxers who have never cruised, but plan to do so over the next five years, have an average pre-tax household income of $56,000, any impediment to their taking a cruise is probably not financial.

Internet reaches potential cruisers

Another channel for reaching Pampered Relaxers and Global Explorers who are potential cruisers is the Internet. Jupiter Media Metrix predicts that consumers will buy $63 billion worth of travel online by 2006, compared with $18 billion in 2000. Given the 38% increase in new vessels over the next four years, Vicki Freed, senior vice president at Carnival Cruise Lines, believes the cruise industry must find "additional ways to fill ... ships .... we've no choice but to also invest in Internet solutions as a result of all the new product being launched." The need to develop sales channels such as the Internet is underscored by the previously discussed decline in the numbers and influence of travel agents.

Similar percentages of both receptive cruisers and non-cruisers have computers in their homes and access to the Internet. For example, among receptive non-cruisers 23% have Internet access and 20% subscribe to an on-line computer service. Among those who have cruised in the past and plan to do so in the future, 19% have a multimedia computer, while 33% have a non-multimedia computer in their homes.

Commitment to the Internet appears higher among receptive non-cruisers, 19% of whom regularly access the Internet, as compared to 14% of those who have cruised and plan to cruise again. Regardless of their level of access, only one in five of those receptive to cruising spends one to 10 hours on the Internet weekly.

Rethinking print media

Besides direct marketing and the Internet, potential cruisers historically have been targeted through major travel magazines. While these publications provide editorial support, they deliver only small percentages of the target Travel segments cruise lines should covet. Both 5% of the 40 and older population and receptive non-cruisers are subscribers or regular buyers of *Travel & Leisure*. This magazine also attracts 7% of receptive Global Explorers.

An alternative to placing ads in travel-related publications is to select more general magazines that attract a large number of persons receptive to cruising. Although not focused on specific travel-related editorial, *Reader's Digest* counts 37% of receptive, non-cruising Global Explorers among its subscribers or regular buyers. In this situation, the value of travel-related editorial support to an advertising campaign has to be weighed against the delivery of large numbers of receptive potential cruisers.

Editorial content in magazines suggests, informs, and convinces. In the case of *Reader's Digest*, its readers already include large numbers of receptive Global Explorers. Those in this segment are already informed and convinced of the enticements of cruising.

Need for improved marketing

The fear of travel generated by the events of September 11, 2001 has been added to the cruise lines' other marketing obstacles, intense competition and a declining economy among them. How the public's heightened fear of travel will affect its plans to cruise will not be known with any degree of accuracy for months. Immediately after the attacks, the World Travel & Tourism Council predicted a 10% to 20% drop in U.S. tourism. While two cruise lines, Renaissance and American Classic Voyages (AMCV), declared bankruptcy shortly thereafter, a month later cruise ships were sailing at almost capacity. While prices on cruises were lower at that time, they were expected to rebound.

Faced with this complex scenario, it's evident that the cruise industry needs to apply insights from a psychographic segmentation to new marketing programs. Integrating all facets of a marketing campaign using such a segmentation strategy would result in an increase in the acquisition of new cruisers and the retention of experienced ones. With marketing dollars in short supply, cruise lines need to use each dollar efficiently by targeting their most receptive segments.

REFERENCES

Cruise Lines International Association. *The Cruise Industry: an Overview* 2000.

Severson, Jack. "Scrambling to attract first-time cruisers." *Philadelphia Inquirer* 4 October, 1998.

Zbar, Jeffery D. "Carnival sets sail to out race resorts." *Advertising Age* 6 March, 1995.

Shoup, Mike. "Booming cruise-ship population shrinks the discount-berth rate." *StarTribune* 26 October, 1997.

Sanfilippo, Michele. "Travel marketers see major role for agents despite poor forecasts." *Travel Agent* 15 May, 2000.

"2000 Travel Weekly US Travel Agency Survey." *Travel Weekly* 12 December, 2001 www.TWCrossroads.com.

Fredericks, Alan. "Do the math." *Travel Weekly* 12 July, 2001.

"Seabourn sets sail on lone voyage." *Precision Marketing* January 2000.

Beirne, Mike. "Upping the ante." *Brandweek* 10 September, 2001.

Chapter 8

THE FINANCIAL SEGMENTS

SELF-RELIANT SAVERS

Self-reliant Savers are highly positive about their financial futures and that of the U.S. While not very sophisticated or knowledgeable investors, those in this segment are fixated with avoiding debt. Relying on themselves rather than seeking advice from others, Self-reliant Savers are careful about the basics in dealing with their finances and investing. They are the most comfortable of the segments in using technology in their financial transactions.

No need to use credit

Whether paying their bills or saving for the future, Self-reliant Savers believe they have enough money. With sufficient resources, they don't need to use credit for many purchases and are highly averse to doing so. One of their major goals is staying out of debt. Even if they wanted something very much, they wouldn't tap into their home's equity or purchase it with a credit card. If Self-reliant Savers find it necessary to buy something on credit or with a loan, the interest rate charged is far more important to them than the ease of getting the loan.

Self-reliant Savers are adamant about restricting the number of credit cards in their wallets, which they find is a good way to control their use of credit. Those in this segment don't view frequent flyer miles and other perks offered by credit card companies as incentives for them to make a purchase. For Self-reliant Savers it's fiscal stupidity not to pay the balance on their credit cards completely each month.

Comfortable with technology

Self-reliant Savers are the most comfortable of the Financial segments in using technology to complete financial transactions. They prefer using debit cards rather than writing checks and like using a computer to pay bills and transfer money. But even with their willingness to use a computer to complete financial transactions, Self-reliant Savers aren't ready for a cashless society that depends entirely on electronic transactions.

Some concerns amid enthusiasm

Self-reliant Savers stand out in their extremely positive views not only on their future, but also that of the U.S. At the same time, they still wonder whether they will have enough money for retirement. More than the other segments, Self-reliant Savers worry about their investments and also procrastinate about making decisions concerning them.

Their combination of positive views on their finances and the economy, worry about insufficient funds for retirement, and procrastination may tempt Self-reliant Savers to take big risks in order to see greater returns more quickly.

Going it alone

While Self-reliant Savers believe they need advice in making investment decisions, they are not willing to pay for it. They have little trust in financial advisers and view them as

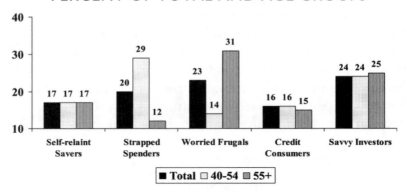

FINANCIAL SEGMENTS: PERCENT OF TOTAL AND AGE GROUPS

Figure 4: *At a statistically significant level, a lower percentage of Strapped Spenders exists among those 55 and older as compared to those 40 to 54. At the same time, a higher percentage of Worried Frugals exists in the older population as compared to the younger.*

opportunists just out to sell their products and not there to give good advice. If Self-reliant Savers do buy financial products from an adviser, it has to be someone with whom they have a personal relationship. This segment's other option is to research financial products on their own and rely on the conclusions they draw about their investments.

Support in retirement

Self-reliant Savers realize they won't reach their financial goals, including a comfortable retirement, unless they plan. As they consider retirement, Self-reliant Savers aren't counting on Social Security or a pension for much support. Instead, they are building a nest egg with tax-deferred savings, such as IRAs and 401(k)s.

Investment strategies

Perhaps because Self-reliant Savers tend to use income from their investments for current living expenses, they, of all the Financial segments, have the greatest aversion to paying taxes and the greatest need to get the highest return on their savings. Self-reliant Savers are interested in tax-free financial investments, such as municipal bonds, and safe investments, such as U.S. government bonds.

Using their investments

Rather than deplete their assets enjoying their retirement, those in this segment are the only ones concerned with conserving some of them. Self-reliant Savers, for example, aren't interested in buying a new house. Unlike all of the other Financial segments, Self-reliant Savers are committed to leaving as much money as they can to their relatives and favorite causes.

STRAPPED SPENDERS

There just isn't enough money each month for Strapped Spenders to save or even meet basic needs, perhaps because, as those in this segment concede, they are spending too much. With insufficient funds, Strapped Spenders are forced to use credit, and they're not paying off their balances completely each month. Strapped Spenders worry about how they will live through retirement, but, at the same time, they fantasize about what they will buy when they retire.

Awash in debt

Compared to the other segments, Strapped Spenders admit they are not doing a good job staying out of debt. Their fondness for carrying many different kinds of credit cards increases the likelihood of incurring debt. Strapped Spenders admit that perks, such as frequent flyer miles, lead them to use a credit card to buy things. Strapped Spenders aren't fazed by the negative impact of high interest rates on their financial well-being. After running up a balance on their credit cards, paying them off at the end of the month isn't a goal of theirs.

In applying for a loan, Strapped Spenders are more concerned with how easy it is to get, rather than the interest rate they will be charged.

Not able to save

Strapped Spenders tell us that their households live from paycheck to paycheck. Even if they increase the amount of money coming in, it is always insufficient. It's not surprising, then, that Strapped Spenders don't see how they can save any money. Unable to save and leading desperate financial lives, Strapped Spenders recognize the solution to their problem: they should be spending less and saving more.

While finding it difficult, if not impossible, to save, Strapped Spenders also have some major purchases in mind. They clearly expect to sell the house in which they currently live. Far more than the other segments, Strapped Spenders want to build a new house in a warm climate.

A pessimistic view

Strapped Spenders view both their financial prospects and those of the U.S. as highly negative. Those in this segment are extremely concerned that in their older years they won't have enough money to live on. Unable to save and fearful of the future, Strapped Spenders are also frightened of making poor investment choices. Whatever investments they have made are a source of worry and discomfort for them. Facing a situation that terrifies them, Strapped Spenders aren't willing to take big risks with their investments—even when the prospect of making more money appears.

Fragmented investment strategies

Strapped Spenders don't have a cohesive investment strategy. While they tell us they see the importance of diversification, they aren't specific about what they would invest in. They have no interest in government bonds. If they were going to invest in a certificate of deposit (CD), those in this segment wouldn't try to ferret out the best interest rate.

Strapped Spenders realize they need help in making investments and are willing to pay for advice. While they think it is important to research various options before investing, one imagines the difficulty Strapped Spenders would have in doing so. Unsophisticated investors, Strapped Spenders tell us they don't understand investment terms. Regardless of their openness to paying fees, getting advice, or doing research, when they select investments Strapped Spenders follow their friends' advice. Certainly, direct marketers and telemarketers should avoid Strapped Spenders, a segment not at all receptive to buying investments or insurance through their channels.

Doubtful they will survive retirement

Strapped Spenders know they should be planning for retirement. While they don't have an immediate need for investment income, Strapped Spenders do recognize an eventual need for such resources. Those in this segment are convinced that without planning they won't reach their financial goals, one of which is to leave the people they care about as much money as possible. So far, however, Strapped Spenders feel that they have not saved adequately for retirement, and they recognize their precarious position.

Beyond their recognition of the need for planning, it is, however, difficult to ascertain what will support Strapped Spenders in their retirement. They don't see Social Security providing a major amount of support when they retire. Nor are they depending on tax-deferred savings, such as IRAs or a 401(k), or a traditional pension to get them through their last years. In short, Strapped Spenders do not view any of the traditional sources as providing them with income in retirement.

Open to technology

The money that slips through the fingers of Strapped Spenders is perhaps somewhat less than real to them. Strapped Spenders are the most open of all the segments to making a deposit into an automated teller machine (ATM). Compared to the other Financial segments, Strapped Spenders are also the most enthusiastic about a cashless society dependent solely on electronic transactions.

WORRIED FRUGALS

Those in this segment are terrified of being in debt. With insufficient incomes, they teeter on the edge of a financial abyss. Unable to save, they don't think that there is much they can do to improve their financial situation and aren't interested in learning more about their options. Worried Frugals are, however, open to paying for financial advice. The application of technology to financial transactions frightens them.

Unable to save

Worried Frugals are fearful of their futures. They hardly have enough income to get by from month to month. Whatever they have is not enough. The shortfall they experience makes it impossible for them to save. And if they do manage to put a bit aside, it is for short-term goals rather than for things that are far in the future.

Avoid credit

Worried Frugals are totally committed to staying out of debt. They wouldn't tap into their home's equity even if they needed or wanted something. One way Worried Frugals avoid debt is by not having a collection of credit cards. Those in this segment think it is smart to pay off credit-card debt at the end of each month, and if they had to get a loan the interest rate charged would be of considerable importance to them.

Handling investments

Tax avoidance is a major part of the Worried Frugals' investment strategy. Because they are dependent on investment income to live on now, it's no surprise that Worried Frugals would shop around to find the best rates.

Worried Frugals struggle with financial terms and don't enjoy reading detailed information or articles about investments, financial matters, and the economy. Instead of becoming informed themselves or turning to friends and business associates, Worried Frugals are at least open to relying on financial advisers. And they are willing to pay fees for such advice.

Worried Frugals want their financial advisers to sit down with them face-to-face and would avoid buying investments or insurance over the phone or through the mail. Those in this segment aren't interested in keeping up with the latest developments in financial products. They probably expect their adviser to do so and clearly expect frequent contact from him or her.

A point of no return

At this point in their lives, Worried Frugals aren't concerned with financial planning for retirement and don't see planning as essential in reaching financial goals. Sources of support in retirement that Worried Frugals count on include Social Security and a pension. Tax-deferred savings such as IRAs or 401(k)s are not part of the Worried Frugals' retirement package.

Counting on these two sources of financial support, Worried Frugals aren't concerned about having enough money to survive retirement. At the same time, those in this segment see a rather dismal financial future ahead of them. Worried Frugals, concerned about ending up old, poor, and homeless, are the least willing of the segments to take big risks with their money.

Avoiding technology

Worried Frugals are most resistant to new technology. Making a deposit into an Automated Teller Machine (ATM) scares them, and they prefer to write checks rather than use a debit card. Making greater use of a computer in their financial transactions isn't something Worried Frugals are planning on: they have no interest in using a computer to pay bills, invest, save or transfer money. They have a strongly negative reaction to living in a cashless society in which all transactions are done electronically.

Staying put

Of all the Financial segments only Worried Frugals don't plan on selling their current residence, and they feel strongly about not doing so. Those in this segment have no interest in moving to a warmer climate in their retirement years.

CREDIT CONSUMERS

Credit Consumers think it is a good idea to have multiple credit cards. When taking out a loan, they aren't concerned with the amount of interest they would be charged. Credit Consumers are naïve investors who believe they will enjoy multiple sources of retirement support. They feel comfortable limiting the types of investments they hold. Although they have sufficient money to live on, saving remains a challenge for Credit Consumers.

Open to credit

While Credit Consumers tell us that they try to avoid debt, only those in this segment think it is a good idea to have several VISA or MasterCard cards. In addition, they believe that having a wide variety of credit cards is a smart move. Credit Consumers are more interested in getting a loan quickly and easily than in the interest rate they will have to pay.

Perhaps because of their openness to credit, Credit Consumers find saving a challenge. Credit Consumers feel that they have enough money to live on, but as they look at their check books and credit-card statements, they realize that they should be saving more and spending less.

Saving for retirement is an important goal for most people. And while Credit Consumers count on the widest variety of sources of financial support in retirement — Social Security, a pension, tax-deferred savings plans, and the equity in their house—they are doing little to save for that goal. Credit Consumers worry about having enough money for retirement, but they don't act to remedy the situation.

A dim view of future

Of all the Financial segments, Credit Consumers have the most negative view of their own financial futures and that of the entire U.S. economy. But even while envisioning a grim future on their horizon, Credit Consumers aren't worried about their investments. The unconcerned Credit Consumers also have a head-in-the-sand approach to seeking financial advice.

They realize that they are not knowledgeable regarding investments, but they don't seem to be interested in doing anything to correct their ignorance. On one hand they don't want to assimilate investment information themselves, and, on the other, they don't see a benefit in paying for financial advice. While recognizing the importance of planning in reaching their financial goals, Credit Consumers give no evidence that they are either capable of such planning themselves or willing to pay for it.

Taking no risks

The Credit Consumers' lack of concern regarding their investments and their disinterest in professional advice may be related to the fact that they are conservative, risk-averse investors whose portfolios lack diversification. Only those in this segment invest where they are guaranteed not to lose any money, favoring investments such as bonds guaranteed by the U.S. government. Credit Consumers don't see any benefit to investing in other countries or in owning a variety of investments. While finding the best rate of return on savings is important to this segment, tax avoidance is not part of their strategy.

No interest in technology

Credit Consumers are willing to make a deposit using an ATM, but they find little else about new technologies helpful to them in their own investing and saving. Credit Consumers aren't planning to increase their use of a computer in managing their money. They prefer writing checks to using a debit card. A cashless society relying on electronic transactions isn't one Credit Consumers look forward to.

Investment objectives

Credit Consumers absolutely deny any need for their investments to generate current income. They are also adamant in having no interest in leaving money to the people or causes they care about when they die. Credit Consumers tell us frankly that they intend to enjoy their money while they live and have no intention of passing on whatever they have accumulated. One of the things Credit Consumers will be spending their money on is a house in a warm climate, something which is of great importance to them.

SAVVY INVESTORS

Those in this segment see a bright financial future ahead for themselves—and for the U.S. They are the most sophisticated and confident of investors. Savvy Investors are unique in that they alone enjoy reading information about the economy and investment products. While willing to pay for a financial planner's insights, they don't think they need help in selecting financial products. Savvy Investors feel comfortable about using money, both in spending and investing it.

Bullish on U.S., themselves

Savvy Investors, even more so than Self-reliant Savers, are brimming with enthusiasm about their financial futures and that of the U.S. This supreme confidence in the positive financial rewards they will enjoy in the years ahead is a major distinguishing characteristic of the Savvy Investors. Those in this segment are comfortable with both investing and spending money. Unlike the other segments, Savvy Investors don't view dealing with their investments as a burden. If they decide to buy or sell an investment, they move forward confidently, unhampered by second thoughts about making a mistake.

Absorbing financial information

Highly involved with their finances, Savvy Investors enjoy learning more about financial products and issues. Because they understand financial terms, Savvy Investors actually relish reading about financial services and the larger economic picture. Even if articles are very specific and detailed, Savvy Investors find them enjoyable. It isn't surprising that the friends and family of those in this segment consider them to be highly knowledgeable about financial products and services. Savvy Investors, however, don't have the same confidence in their friends and family and wouldn't follow their investment advice.

Reading financial information is part of the research Savvy Investors conduct before investing their money. When it comes time to invest, Savvy Investors tell us that they gravitate toward the investments they have read about.

Financial advisers, one source of many

While they do considerable research on their own, Savvy Investors also consider it a wise move to pay for the advice of a reliable financial adviser. They believe that investment advisers can help them stay on top of the latest investment developments. But when it comes to the actual selection of financial products and services, Savvy Investors believe they have little need for such help.

Savvy Investors would like to sit down with their financial adviser face-to-face. They have no interest in buying investments or insurance over the phone or through the mail. Financial salespeople are wasting their time in phoning Savvy Investors—even if their excuse is to keep them up to date on new investment possibilities.

Reaching investment goals

Of all the Financial segments, Savvy Investors have by far the greatest commitment to financial planning: they see it as the only way to reach financial goals. All of their saving and planning, however, is not motivated by a desire to leave as much money as possible to their children or to favorite causes.

Savvy Investors will reach their investment goals by taking a variety of actions. Taxes are to be avoided, but not because Savvy Investors are dependent on investments to provide them with current income. Finding the highest return for their savings is important, even if it means taking considerable time to shop around. Savvy Investors consider it important to invest in a variety of instruments, one indication of their high level of sophistication. They believe a diversified portfolio should include international investments, and they are the only Financial segment with this perspective.

While the Worried Frugals are terrified of running out of money in retirement and ending up on the street, old and homeless, Savvy Investors vehemently deny any such concern. Savvy Investors are convinced they will have sufficient money to live on as they grow older. Perhaps because of this conviction, Savvy Investors can take a more moderate perspective on investing. The fear of an impoverished old age doesn't motivate them to grab for a fast return: they aren't willing to take big risks to realize higher gains. Savvy Investors are moderate investors, committed to investing for the long-term.

Whatever happens to Social Security, it isn't anything Savvy Investors are counting on to provide them with a substantial amount of support in retirement. Savvy Investors don't expect to tap into their home equity, perhaps with a reverse mortgage. They are counting on a pension to help fund part of their retirement.

Savvy Investors haven't been dreaming of buying a new home, but they can envision selling their current house. The fact that those in this segment would like to spend their retirement in a warm climate makes them natural targets for homebuilders such as Del Webb.

Comfortable with money

Overall, staying out of debt is a major goal for Savvy Investors. But if they really want something, they take out a loan or charge it on their credit card, but not before shopping for a low interest rate. Confident that they can pay off debt, it becomes a transient event. Savvy Investors admit the allure of perks, such as frequent flyer miles, increases their use of credit cards, and they see the benefit of having many different kinds of credit cards. However, they also strongly believe in paying off credit-card balances completely at the end of the month.

Achieving a balance

Savvy Investors like where they are in terms of saving and spending. At this point, they don't think they should be doing more of one than the other. Savvy Investors absolutely don't think that they are just scraping by in terms of their household incomes, and they believe they have enough money to be able to save and invest.

Using technology

Technology doesn't intimidate Savvy Investors. For example, making a deposit using an automated teller machine (ATM) isn't a problem for them. In the future, Savvy Investors plan to make increasing use of a computer in their investing and saving. For all of this openness to technology, however, Savvy Investors do not crave the advent of a cashless society.

Chapter 9

ATTITUDES DEFINE AFFLUENT SAVVY INVESTORS

No need for separate programs

The best targets for financial services and related purchases are Savvy Investors, one of our Financial segments. Regardless of sex, those who are affluent within this segment are the prime target for bankers, stockbrokerage firms, and real estate agents. Recognizing the importance of the female component of the affluent market, several financial firms have developed separate—and unnecessary—marketing programs for them.

Whether male or female, Savvy Investors share the same attitudes and motivations toward investing and other issues surrounding the management of money. This means that advertising messages and images and the products and services they sell can be targeted to Savvy Investors—regardless of sex.

The similarities between affluent male and female Savvy Investors extend beyond attitudes to many demographic measures, as well as to a host of behaviors. Success in marketing to the mass affluent who are 40 and older rests not in creating different programs for males and females, but in thoroughly understanding Savvy Investors, without regard to sex.

Defining the mass affluent

Because of their numbers, financial companies are particularly interested in boomers and their elders in the "mass affluent" category. Since those 40 and older comprise 72% of the U.S. population with household incomes of $75,000 and above, the attention given them by these companies is not surprising. We define mass affluent as those couples with incomes of $75,000 or more and/or investable assets of $200,000 and above and singles with an income of $50,000 or more and/or assets of $100,000 and above. As we have defined them, the mass affluent are 29% of the 40 and older population.

Of the five Financial segments described in Chapter 8, Savvy Investors make up the majority of mass affluents. While they account for 24% of the total 40 and older U.S. population, those in this segment are 46% of the mass affluent. But the use of only an average demographic, such as income, to define this market results in the inclusion of all five Financial segments.

Targeting affluent female Savvy Investors

When financial services companies market their services to a mythical average affluent woman, the attitudes and motivations of the knowledgeable Savvy Investor are submerged and co-mingled with those of Worried Frugals and Strapped Spenders. Such averaging forces us to market to the middle, moving our focus from our most receptive prospect, the Savvy Investor. The products and advertising that result from this homogenized viewpoint are relevant only to a nonexistent average customer.

Besides flattening out real differences, averaging also conjures up differences where none exist. Defining the mass affluent market — or any market — by averages has resulted in some incorrect assumptions. One of these is that mass affluent females are — on average — different than males — on average — in how they view money and its uses. An example of this misleading thinking is seen in a RoperStarch study that concluded that "women have less confidence in their knowledge of saving and investing than men."

From Oppenheimer Funds to Charles Schwab & Co., Morgan Stanley to Salomon Smith Barney, firms are creating print and television advertising targeting women, offering financial seminars just for women, and creating marketing brochures and educational materials that address what they perceive to be women's needs. For example, in marketing to women, American Express Financial Advisors partnered with cosmetic companies to present entertainment events combining fashion with financial information.

Take aim on the average

Certainly affluent women with disposable dollars to invest are the targets of these financial institutions. In the past, such firms focused on wealthy women with $500,000 and more in assets. Now they've widened their scope to include the mass affluent with perhaps $100,000, or even slightly less, to invest. In doing so, they should be targeting Savvy Investors, who are, as we have seen, almost half of the mass affluent market. But the fact that Schwab and Morgan Stanley have created separate programs for women suggests that they are marketing to an *average* mass affluent woman, not the Savvy Investor.

This assumption is underscored by the way in which they describe their female market. Carrie Schwab Pomerantz, who now heads a program for Charles Schwab & Co. marketing its services to women, believes that "women feel differently and learn differently about investing." Pomerantz says that Schwab is "trying to speak to women in terms relevant to their lives and in language that's appealing to them."

But, as we have pointed out, separate marketing programs for affluent females, largely Savvy Investors, are unnecessary. Even *Equity*, a short-lived magazine supplement for women distributed to subscribers of *Worth*, was envisioned as a "way to showcase inspirational female role models," according to Alison Parks, chief operating officer of Worth Media, "rather than presenting financial information specifically for women." Parks notes that those at *Worth* "believe good financial information to be unisex." This position was echoed at the launch of *Equity* three years ago by Steve Swartz, then president of *SmartMoney*, a competing publication, who noted that he didn't "see why a woman's needs" in "a professional white-collar audience ... are any different than men's."

Writing in one of her columns, Jane Bryant Quinn, the noted financial journalist, revealed her dislike of financial advertisements and books based on the need to treat women "as a breed apart." She finds this position condescending and is "sick" of it. "Who besides women," she asks, "are told they need help because they're emotionally impaired?" Quinn then refers to several studies which come to similar conclusions: there is, she points out, "no difference in investment patterns by sex."

Equal numbers of both sexes

Among those 40 and older, the total affluent sample as we have defined it is composed of virtually the same numbers of males (51%) and females (49%). In considering only affluent Savvy Investors, slightly more males (49%) than females (44%) are in this sophisticated segment. Similar levels of representation by both sexes in the Savvy Investor segment support our view that there is no need for separate marketing initiatives for affluent males and females in this psychographic segment.

As we describe them in the chapter on our Financial segments, Savvy Investors know how to use money, seek out sources of information on financial issues, and are confident in their diversified investment choices. Males and females in the Savvy Investors segment share the same attitudes and motivations toward financial concerns and investing.

Demographic differences

There are some differences between affluent men and women in our sample. For example, the median age of the mass affluent in the 40 and older population is 52. But affluent female Savvy Investors are younger, with a median age of 50, as compared to males in this segment, who have a median age of 58.

Almost half of affluent female Savvy Investors are single. Nine out of ten affluent male Savvy Investors are married (86%), as compared to only half of the females (51%). Although affluent female Savvy Investors have a lower median age than their male counterparts, far more of them are widows. The death at earlier ages of males in the U.S., as compared to females, contributes to this situation. Compared to females, mature males arriving at a single status through death or divorce have a larger pool of persons of the opposite sex available to them and, thus, a greater opportunity for remarriage.

But regardless of whether their affluence was created by a now-deceased spouse or parent—or themselves—Savvy Investors, whether male or female, currently feel highly competent to manage their own finances. In fact, doing so is something they relish.

Current household income

Affluent male Savvy Investors enjoy the highest pre-tax median household income ($108,869) of all the Financial segments; affluent female Savvy Investors are second with a median income of $99,762. It is true that the household income of affluent male Savvy Investors is 9% higher than that of females. One possible explanation for the lower household incomes of affluent female Savvy Investors is their dominant single status. In contrast to males, their household incomes more often reflect the earnings and financial resources of just one person.

Work, a source of income

Another factor contributing to the higher household incomes enjoyed by male Savvy Investors is that more of them are working full-time (79%) as compared to females in this segment (64%). In contrast, one in four affluent female Savvy Investors works part-time (25%) as compared to one in ten males (10%). Not working at all or working part-time obviously has a negative impact on income.

Impact of retirement

One in five of the affluent sample (21%) has retired with no intention of returning to work, as have male (23%) and female (20%) Savvy Investors. Female Savvy Investors retirees have also retired at a younger median age (50 versus 59) as compared to their male counterparts. From a variety of perspectives, early retirement can also affect female affluent Savvy Investors' current incomes.

The issue of retirees returning to work after retiring or perhaps never fully retiring is a topic of intense interest deserving fuller exploration in its own book. We can only note here that our studies show 30% of affluent retirees returning to work, either full or part time, although they have retired at least once with no intention of working again. And another 30% of the affluent sample 65 and older, as well as the same percentage of Savvy Investors, tell us they have never retired.

After retiring and returning to work, fewer affluent Savvy Investors of either sex were employed in professional, technical, management or executive positions or as business owners as compared to their pre-retirement occupations. For example, while no affluent Savvy Investor males were employed in clerical or service positions before retirement, 8% were working at these jobs afterward. As for affluent female Savvy Investors, more of them became homemakers

(28%) after retirement, a four-fold increase compared to their pre-retirement (7%) status.

Education boosts income

Despite the fact that many of them are widows, the affluent female Savvy Investor market should not be viewed as composed predominately of women who have inherited their wealth. It is apparent that affluent female Savvy Investors have contributed significantly to the generation of their own assets, a position supported by their very high levels of education. Far above average percentages of affluent male and female Savvy Investors (73% and 67%) have a four-year college degree or more compared to the affluent sample as a whole (63%) and to the total 40 and older population (33%).

As highly educated women, affluent female Savvy Investors worked prior to retirement or are currently working in well-paying jobs. Three-quarters (75%) of affluent Savvy Investor females work or worked in a professional or technical capacity, as a manager or executive, or as a business owner. It is true, however, that more affluent male Savvy Investors (87%) are in these types of positions or were so if they are now retired. Other differences in occupation between affluent males and females in the Savvy Investor segment include the fact that a small percentage (7%) of female Savvy Investors currently work or have worked as homemakers, just as a small percentage of affluent male Savvy Investors are skilled craftsmen (3%) or in the armed forces (4%).

Taking care of business

That self-employment leads to riches is supported by a number of researchers. Writing in their book, *The Millionaire Next Door*, Thomas J. Stanley and William D. Danko note that "self-employed people make up less than 20 percent of the workers in America but account for two-thirds of the millionaires." According to Stanley and Danko, the net worth of a household in which the head of the household is self-employed is almost five times greater ($248,100) than one in which the head of the household works for someone else ($52,400). Among the super affluent, defined as those with a net worth greater than $3 million, almost half (46%) own a business which is their primary source of wealth.

Whether male or female, among affluent Savvy Investors in our studies, virtually one in three owns his or her own business (both 32%) or is married to someone who does. This percentage compares to only 18% of the 40 and older population who own their own business.

These businesses are typically very small, with 64% employing only one or two persons, including the entrepreneur. Our studies of the 40 and older population support the link between self-employment and higher financial rewards. Those who are self-employed have a far higher median net worth ($179,575) as contrasted to those who work for someone else ($108,023).

Getting an early start

While about one in four (24%) of the total 40 and older population began investing in stocks and bonds when they were under 30 years of age, 26% of those who are affluent did so. At the same time, 30% of male affluent Savvy Investors started at this age, as did 29% of females. The median age at which male affluent Savvy Investors began saving for retirement on a consistent and continuing basis is 33, while that of their female counterparts is 34. Our studies do not support the idea that affluent female Savvy Investors were late in investing in stocks and bonds or in creating retirement savings. There is no need to encourage female affluent Savvy Investors to take responsibility for their financial futures: they've been doing so for decades.

What drives investment

The majority of affluent female Savvy Investors (60%), as well as their male counterparts (66%), seek growth as their primary investment objective, typically in the form of large company stocks. While one in five of these affluent male

Savvy Investors (20%) seek aggressive growth, that goal is shared by slightly fewer affluent females in this segment (16%). The need to create separate marketing programs for affluent female Savvy Investors is not evident, considering the fact that growth is the investment objective of the majority of both genders.

It is true that about one in ten (12%) of the affluent population as we have defined it seek tax-free income, and affluent female Savvy Investors are average in this respect (12%). At the same time, fewer males (6%) have tax-free income as a primary investment objective. Considering the fact that more affluent female Savvy Investors are working only part-time as compared to males, their need for supplementary income is not surprising. Their need for income is also driven by the fact that far more of them, as compared to males, are single and dependent on only one paycheck, their own.

Considering the risk

In assessing the risk level with which they are comfortable, the overwhelming majority of both affluent male and female Savvy Investors are committed to a medium risk for a medium return (76% and 77%). At the extremes, however, slightly more males (16%) than females (12%) would take a high risk for a potential high return. And, conversely, fewer males among the affluent Savvy Investors say they prefer to take the barest minimal risk (2%) as compared to females in this category (5%). Again, these slight differences in the risk-tolerance profiles of male and female affluent Savvy Investors are not sufficient to warrant specific marketing programs for females.

Advice and its uses

Just under a third of both male and female affluent Savvy Investors have paid a professional to develop a written, long-range financial plan as part of their retirement planning (30% and 29%). But while Savvy Investors are 44% of the total affluent 40 and older market, they are 50% of those who have paid to have such a plan written for them.

In terms of making investment decisions, to where do male and female affluent Savvy Investors turn? When respondents were asked to select their one or two primary sources of financial advice from a field of 17 possible sources, the following were the top choices of more female affluent Savvy Investors: full-service stockbroker (35%), financial planner paid through commissions (21%), do not use an adviser (21%), financial magazines (18%), and their spouse (14%).

In contrast, the prevalent selections of male affluent Savvy Investors were: do not use an adviser (42%), full-service stockbroker (31%), financial magazines (27%), financial newsletters (16%), and a financial planner paid through commissions (15%). While the top five sources of advice between males and females is remarkably similar, it is true that far more male affluent Savvy Investors do not use an adviser (42%) as compared to females (21%).

A lack of trust

The higher percentage of male affluent Savvy Investors who do not use an adviser stems from their lack of trust and respect for professional financial advisers. Affluent male Savvy Investors eschew their services because they're convinced they can make more money by going it alone (29%), a point of view shared by far fewer affluent females in this segment (13%). Other reasons more male affluent Savvy Investors give for avoiding a paid adviser as compared to females include a lack of trust, the unreliability of advice, self-serving advice, and a general distrust of financial advisers.

Given their lack of trust in professional advisers, it's not surprising that when asked how they arrive at investment decisions, 43% of affluent male Savvy Investors say they do so without the help of an investment adviser. In contrast, only 25% of their female counterparts take this position. Female affluent Savvy Investors are more likely to either follow suggestions made by their investment adviser (26%) or to rely on a variety of sources in making investment decisions, including advice from their adviser (36%), as compared to males (17% and 32%).

The lower level of reliance which some male affluent Savvy Investors have toward financial advisers in contrast to some females can be better understood when we examine the Lifestyle segments into which some of these affluent Savvy Investors can also be classified.

The distrust some male affluent Savvy Investors feel toward financial advisers can be linked to the fact that almost a third of them (29%) are also Threatened Actives, one of our Lifestyle segments. Those in this segment resent any external force exerting control over their lives. Because of this, it isn't surprising that Threatened Actives are the only Lifestyle segment opposed to the use of financial planners. Besides resenting any intrusion or change in their lives, Threatened Actives are also distrustful and fearful people.

In contrast to affluent male Savvy Investors, females are disproportionately in the Financial Positive segment (39%), another of our Lifestyle segments. Those in this segment have been planning for an early retirement for years and have no intention of working after retiring. Financial Positives feel successful, confidant, and very financially secure. They are convinced they have reached this position by following the advice of trusted financial planners and investing carefully. In everything they buy, Financial Planners are concerned with obtaining a good value.

Investments in retirement

From a field of 21 options, affluent male and female Savvy Investors express some differences in their investments for retirement. More affluent female Savvy Investors, for example, count on bond mutual funds (30%) than do males (25%). While the same percentages of males and females in the affluent Savvy Investor segment will rely on a variable annuity (both 21%), more females (23%) as compared to males (16%) will have a fixed annuity in retirement. Considering their longer lifespans, buying a fixed annuity seems to be a wise move on the part of affluent female Savvy Investors.

While more males say a SEP-IRA and a Keogh, retirement plans typically associated with a small business, will provide financial support, a similar percentage of both males and females will rely on a 401(k) (50% and 53%). Among affluent Savvy Investors, males (25%) more than females (20%) are counting on work in retirement to provide them with income.

Social Security's role

The role Social Security will play or currently plays in the retirement plans of the total U.S. 40 and older population is under debate. Our studies underscore the fact that Social Security's contribution to the financial support of the total 40 and older population is in sharp contrast to that of those who are affluent. We ask respondents to apportion what percentage of their financial support in retirement will come from a total of seven sources, ranging from Social Security to an employer-provided pension, an inheritance from parents or relatives to non-tax sheltered investments or savings.

In our studies, 32% of those in the total 40 and older population and 60% of the affluent envision that Social Security will provide, or is currently providing, them with somewhere between 1% and 20% of their support. Another 26% of the total 40 and older population and 25% of the affluent group believe Social Security is providing or will provide between 21% and 40% of the funds they will need in retirement. For the majority of the affluent, Social Security plays only a supplementary role in providing retirement support.

A slightly higher percentage of female affluent Savvy Investors (64%) as compared to the total affluent sample (60%) believes Social Security will provide 1% to 20% of their retirement funds. More affluent female Savvy Investors than the affluent as a whole relegate Social Security to a minor role in their financial support in retirement.

Minimal support from Social Security

But even more male affluent Savvy Investors (82%) are counting on Social Security to generate only a minimal amount of support, ranking it in the 1% to 20% range among the sources considered. A possible reason for this disparity is that more affluent male Savvy Investors than females are continuing to work, despite their higher median age. That far more affluent female Savvy Investors are single also means that they can rely on only their own income and assets and have a greater need for Social Security.

The result of these behavioral and demographic differences can be seen in the higher median net worth ($533,332) of male affluent Savvy Investors as compared to their female counterparts ($458,259). It is also true that females have a longer life expectancy and, whether affluent or not, will live longer on average in retirement than males. According to figures from the U.S. Centers for Disease Control and Prevention, females now 50 can expect to live to 81.8 years, as compared to 77.9 years for males. There is, then, a greater chance that the retirement savings of females will dissipate before they do.

Politicians and others should expect many affluent, educated female Savvy Investors to express their displeasure if reductions are threatened in Social Security benefits. Identification with a particular political party will, no doubt, color their views on Social Security. Virtually one in three (31%) female affluent Savvy Investors identifies herself as a Democrat, far more than her male counterparts (19%). Any discussion of receiving prescription drug benefits through Medicare would be of particular interest to female affluent Savvy Investors, 17% of whom take three or more such drugs daily.

The promise of inheritance

Stockbrokers, trust officers, and others have been waiting for baby boomers to inherit an estimated $14 trillion (in 1999 dollars) by 2050. Jagadeesh Gokhale, an economic adviser to the Federal Reserve Bank in Cleveland, and Laurence J. Kotlikoff, a professor of economics at Boston University, argue that "inheritances are unlikely to augment boomers' retirement resources significantly."

Gokhale and Kotlikoff take this position because, compared to the 1960s, inherited wealth must now be distributed among more siblings. These researchers note that many of the resources of the elderly are annuitized, which means that when the recipient dies, the income flow ceases. Compared to past generations, current retirees are also spending down their assets at a far faster rate. There will be less to divide among more siblings. In analyzing data from the Federal Reserve's *1998 Survey of Consumer Finances*, Gokhale and Kotlikoff find that "the vast majority of households (92 percent) reported receiving no inheritances."

Our studies show that whatever the hype surrounding vast potential inheritances, baby boomers themselves realize that the amount they will inherit will not be very large. When we asked what percent of their retirement support would be furnished by an inheritance from a parent or relative, 73% of affluent 40 and older consumers said none. While 15% of these affluents look forward to an inheritance supplying 1% to 10% of the funds they will need in retirement, only 11% look forward to an inheritance supplying 11% or more of these needs.

Perhaps because they provide more care to an elderly parent or relative as compared to males, 15% of affluent female Savvy Investors count on 11% or more of their financial needs in retirement being supplied by an inheritance as compared to only 10% for affluent males in this segment, a 50% increase.

Credit card favorites

VISA and MasterCard have succeeded in attracting virtually the same percentages of male and female affluent Savvy Investors. For example, 86% of male affluent Savvy Investors have a VISA card compared to 83% of females. American Express, however, has attracted more Savvy Investor males (41%) as compared to females (33%). Perhaps male affluent

Savvy Investors believe the American Express card has more prestige and offers more travel benefits. Although over the past 12 months, both male and female affluent Savvy Investors have made similar numbers of average business trips (3.2 and 3.9) requiring an overnight stay in a hotel or motel.

On the other hand, department store credit cards are carried by more female affluent Savvy Investors (68%) contrasted with males (48%). This is not surprising since females, rather than males, are prime department store shoppers. As we have also previously noted, 39% of female affluent Savvy Investors are also Financial Positives. Those in this segment have a very high regard for prestigious department stores such as Neiman Marcus, Nordstrom's, and Saks Fifth Avenue.

Not in my wallet

Attempts to induce affluent Savvy Investors to slip yet another credit card into their wallets encounter great difficulties. Three-fourths of male and female affluent Savvy Investors (76% and 78%) report that their most common response to credit card offers they receive in the mail is to toss them unopened into the trash or recycling. While 1% of both genders admits to reading credit card solicitation carefully, almost one in five opens them and only skims their contents.

Whatever the type and number of credit cards held by those 40 and older and by affluent Savvy Investors, they have succeeded in controlling their non-mortgage debt. About a third of both male and female affluent Savvy Investors (35% and 33%) have no non-mortgage debt, such as credit card balances and car loans. Twenty-nine percent of those 40 and older in the general population have debt of this kind. Among affluent Savvy Investors who have debt other than their mortgages, males have a median debt of $15,351, while females have $11,261.

Home ownership an asset

More of those in the affluent 40 and older population own their own homes (98%) as compared to those in the total 40 and older population (87%). Homeownership continues to be a major component of net worth. A study by Harvard University's Joint Center for Housing Studies shows that "well over half" of homeowners regardless of age "with incomes between $60,000 and $99,000 a year . . . have more real estate equity than stock."

The importance of home equity increases in retirement, when it can become a way of accessing needed cash through refinancing, a home equity loan, or a reverse mortgage.

Regardless of sex, affluent Savvy Investors are virtually identical in every real estate-related issue we track. Virtually the same percentages of both affluent male and female Savvy Investors own their homes (98% and 99%). Median home values of both male ($231,850) and female ($205,881) affluent Savvy Investors are higher than that of the affluent group as a whole ($188,364) and those of the other Financial segments. The median value of houses owned by affluent Savvy Investors of either sex also far exceeds the median September 2001 sales price of an existing home ($148,100).

Mortgage debt similar

While 43% of the total 40 and older population owes nothing on a mortgage, only 28% of the affluent sample is living mortgage free. Affluent Savvy Investor males and females are average (26% and 28%) in the percentages of them who owe nothing on their mortgage. A factor contributing to the high rate of mortgage debt among the affluent is that they have resided in their homes for fewer years. While the total 40 and older population has spent a median of 12 years in their homes, the affluent sample has spent 10. Again, affluent Savvy Investors of either sex are average on this point.

Although affluent Savvy Investors of both sexes own homes with the highest valuations, their mortgage debt is only in the middle of the range for those affluents in the Financial segments. Affluent Savvy Investors of either sex are quite similar on this point. Only a mortgage payment or two separates the median mortgage debt of affluent male and female Savvy Investors: $64,757 for males and $66,302 for females.

No plans to move

A study by the Urban Land Institute concludes that 45% of baby boomers "expect to move to other homes in retirement." Our studies show that more than a third (37%) of those in the affluent 40 and older market say they would like to buy a home within the next ten years.

Affluent Savvy Investors make up 46% of those who intend to buy a house in the next decade, with very similar numbers of male and female affluent Savvy Investors (52% and 48%) intending to do so. Savvy Investors are the dominant segment in the home purchase market (46%) among persons 40 and older. While they should be targeted by Del Webb and other developers, their interest in buying a home is only average compared to their size in the affluent market (46%).

Taking the next steps

Rather than create marketing programs based on incorrect assumptions, such as the financial cluelessness of affluent female Savvy Investors, marketers will enjoy greater success if they better understand the attitudinal realities of Savvy Investors, regardless of sex.

By accepting the fact that separate marketing campaigns are not needed in targeting male and female Savvy Investors, marketers can move on to create products that offer this segment real benefits, devise more effective targeted advertising, and embed Savvy Investor attitudes into databases for direct marketing campaigns. Obviously, images in advertising should show both males and females successfully handling their money.

Models incorporating the Savvy Investors' attitudinal profile, as well as demographics and behaviors, can be developed and used to classify entire databases. Being able to do so would benefit mutual fund companies, insurance firms, and banks in both direct marketing and one-to-one sales. Identifying Savvy Investors in a personal encounter, particularly at an early age, would be of great use to stockbrokers and insurance salespersons.

REFERENCES

"Financial Marketers use educational materials, grassroots seminars to sell women on the concept of investing." *Marketing to Women* June 1999.

Lee, Louise. "Brokers are from Mars, Women are from Venus." *Business Week* 4 December, 2000.

Parks, Alison. Telephone interview. November 11, 2001.

"Capital Publishing woos women with new 'Equity.'" *Advertising Age* 16 November, 1998.

Quinn, Jane Bryant. "Selling financial advice to women plays to stereotypes." *Los Angeles Business Journal* 19 February, 2001.

Stanley, Thomas J., and Danko, William D. *The Millionaire Next Door: The surprising secrets of America's wealthy*. Atlanta, Georgia: Longstreet Press, 1996.

Wilcox, Melynda Dovel. "Are you above average?" *Kiplinger's* January 2001.

"The Kiplinger Monitor." *Kiplinger's* January 2001.

AARP Bulletin. November 2001.

Avery, Robert B. and Rendall, Michael S. "Estimating the size and distribution of baby boomers' prospective inheritances." American Statistical Association's *1993 Proceedings of the Social Statistics Section*.

Gokhale, Jagadeesh and Kotlikoff, Laurence J. "The baby boomers' mega-inheritance—myth or reality?" *Economic Commentary* 1 October, 2000.

Harney, Kenneth. "Homeownership is major component of net wealth." *StarTribune* 1 July, 2000.

National Association of Realtors. 10 January, 2002 www.Realtor.org.

"Boomers are changing home building." *StarTribune* 30 June, 2001.

Chapter 10

THE FOOD SEGMENTS

NUTRITION CONCERNED

By far the most health conscious of the three Food segments, the Nutrition Concerned follow-through on their concerns. They are convinced that what you eat influences how you feel. Nutrition Concerned monitor what they eat, avoid restaurant meals, and cook from scratch. Nutrition Concerned are distinguished by their commitment to reading food labels. Searching for new food products containing low-calorie fat substitutes and artificial sweeteners, those in this segment pay attention to advertising.

Commitment to good nutrition

As they've grown older, Nutrition Concerned have become increasingly concerned about nutrition and what they are eating. Only those in this segment are convinced that what you eat influences how you feel. This viewpoint explains why the Nutrition Concerned focus so much of their attention on eating healthfully. They are committed to eating fresh fruits and vegetables and cutting back on their salt intake. They would also avoid eating such things as hormone-treated red meat.

Nutrition Concerned supplement fresh fruits and vegetables with a daily vitamin tablet. This segment is also interested in foods formulated to meet the nutritional needs of older adults. Far more than the other two Food segments, Nutrition Concerned are focused on avoiding fats and eating enough fiber, actions they do more now that they are older.

With high expectations of good nutrition having positive benefits on their health, Nutrition Concerned work to reach their goals by reading labels before trying new food products. The only segment committed to label reading, the Nutrition Concerned know what they are eating.

Monitoring what they eat

To know what you are eating, means you must control what you eat. The Nutrition Concerned is the only Food segment that still cooks most of its meals from scratch. Only this segment considers it important to invest time in cooking regular meals and not skipping meals. And they do this all the time, not just on special occasions.

Controlling what you eat also means passing on many convenience foods. Only the Nutrition Concerned don't find that they are using more convenience foods now than before. Those in this segment have little interest in new convenience foods they could store on a shelf or heat in their microwaves. They are, for example, the only segment that isn't open to purchasing complete pre-cooked meals made from fresh food that could be heated and served at home.

Another way in which Nutrition Concerned control what they eat is avoiding restaurant meals. Overall, those in this segment find it a challenge to stay on their diet while eating in a restaurant. They worry that fast food restaurants don't serve food that is healthy for mature adults. Restaurant meals have little social appeal for the Nutrition Concerned, who would rather offer friends a home-cooked meal than meet at a restaurant.

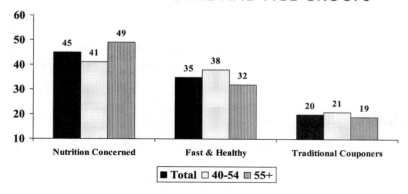

FOOD SEGMENTS:
PERCENT OF TOTAL AND AGE GROUPS

Figure 5: *At a statistically significant level, a higher percentage of Nutrition Concerned exists among those 55 and older as compared to those 40 to 54. In contrast, lower percentages of Fast & Healthy and Traditional Couponers exist in the older population as compared to the younger.*

Brand loyal food shoppers

Sticking to a shopping list when they go to the supermarket is yet another way in which Nutrition Concerned are able to carefully monitor what they eat. No impulse buying here. Those in this segment are looking for new products: ones low in fat or using fat substitutes or artificial sweeteners.

Given their focus on nutrition and new food products, it's important to note that, compared to the other two Food segments, Nutrition Concerned are far more swayed by advertising. They admit that they pay attention to advertising when selecting food products and look favorably on food products endorsed by well-known figures. Nutrition Concerned also tell us that they are increasingly reliant on their favorite brands.

FAST & HEALTHY

Those in the Fast & Healthy segment are interested in convenience foods, new packaging ideas, and restaurant meals. Maturity has meant cooking fewer meals. For them restaurant meals offer both a good value and a place to socialize with friends. Fast & Healthy, although somewhat concerned about nutrition and the impact of food on their health, are spontaneous food shoppers whose overriding focus is on convenience. The microwave is their primary kitchen tool.

Meals on the go

As they have grown older, Fast & Healthy find they are cooking fewer meals and snacking through the day. Their cooking is increasingly limited to the times when they have their family together—perhaps a holiday or family event.

Besides grazing, Fast & Healthy have also turned to restaurant meals and convenience foods. This segment finds restaurant meals to be a good value. Fast & Healthy say they have no problem staying on their diets when they eat at a restaurant. Even fast food meals are considered by those in this segment to be good for older people. With all the benefits of eating at a restaurant, it's easy to see why Fast & Healthy would rather meet friends at a restaurant than go through the bother of cooking a meal.

Fast & Healthy tell us that they have increased their use of convenience foods. Those in this segment are not only committed to convenience foods, but willing to pay for them. The microwave is at the heart of the Fast & Healthy's food preparation. Viewing this appliance as quite safe, they enthusiastically seek new products to heat within it.

These new options could take several forms. Complete, pre-cooked meals bought at a grocery store and ready to warm in a microwave have immense appeal for the Fast & Healthy. Shelf-stable foods that are normally frozen would also be of interest to those in this segment. The Fast & Healthy tell us that all food products should be available in individual or small packages.

Spontaneous shoppers

Fast & Healthy move through the grocery store quickly, paying little attention to a grocery list. They consider one brand as good as another, and, in fact, feel their brand loyalty has decreased as they have grown older. Fast & Healthy wouldn't believe a well-known person endorsing a food product.

Passing interest in nutrition

Those in this segment are most interested in quick ways to quiet their growling stomachs, whether a handful of crackers, a trip to McDonald's, or a TV dinner. But they are also somewhat more concerned about nutrition now than when they were younger. They are trying to cut down on their salt and fat consumption and want to get enough fiber in their diet. Fast & Healthy also have a passing interest in trying to eat lots of fruits and vegetables.

Taking a daily vitamin pill is something they consider to be beneficial, and they would buy food products specially designed for the nutritional needs of mature adults. But they aren't afraid of eating hormone-treated red meat, as are the Nutrition Concerned.

TRADITIONAL COUPONERS

Traditional Couponers eat as they always have. Concerns about eating healthful foods or seeking out new foods for their convenience are not increasing in this segment. Traditional Couponers are least likely to pay attention to what is in the foods they eat. What is of importance to them is saving money through the use of coupons and discounts. As they have aged, they have become increasingly brand loyal and heavy coupon use makes their preferred brands more affordable.

Searching for discounts

The main interest Traditional Couponers have in grocery shopping is being able to use coupons. As they have gotten older, Traditional Couponers have increased their use of coupons for groceries and are enthusiastic about using them. As they age, Traditional Couponers are becoming even more brand loyal and heavy use of coupons is one way they can afford to buy their preferred brands. Knowing the brands they prefer, Traditional Couponers report paying absolutely no attention to advertising.

Those in this segment also search for discounts at restaurants. Believing that restaurant meals are expensive, Traditional Couponers favor restaurants that offer special discounts to people over a certain age. Perhaps related to cost, those in this segment would like it if restaurants served smaller portions.

Minimal nutritional concerns

Any concerns Traditional Couponers had about nutrition when they were younger have, they believe, decreased with age. Now that they are eating more convenience foods and cooking fewer meals, those in this segment have little incentive to demonstrate an interest in nutrition. Compared to the other two Food segments, Traditional Couponers are least likely to pay attention to what is in the foods they are eating or to believe that they can feel better by eating healthful foods. Even taking a daily vitamin pill is of no interest to them.

Recent findings about the importance of increasing fiber or reducing fat in the diet have washed over the Traditional Couponers. Foods made with low-calorie fat substitutes or artificial sweeteners won't be found in their shopping carts. They are trying to cut down on salt, however, and report eating more fruits and vegetables. Those in this segment realize that meals from fast food restaurants aren't healthful for mature adults.

Long-term storage

Traditional Couponers look for food packaged so that it can be stored in a cupboard for a long time. Packaging that allows food normally frozen to be shelf stable also appeals to Traditional Couponers. These foods would then be heated in a microwave. Foods targeting this segment have to be offered in easy-to-open packaging. Only Traditional Couponers report having difficulty opening many kinds of food containers.

Chapter 11

YOU WILL BE WHAT YOU EAT

Food choices distinguish segments

Imagine that on your next trip to your local supermarket you assess the contents of three carts, each one pushed by someone over 40. The first cart is filled with a dozen containers of nonfat yogurt, two giant boxes of shredded wheat cereal, a turkey breast, a box of artificial sweetener, and apples, carrots, and broccoli.

Several low-fat, low-salt frozen dinners, a jar of instant coffee, a tube of frozen biscuit dough, two bags of frozen vegetables, a small box of strawberries, three prepared entrees from the deli, and two cans of Boost take up space in cart number two.

The third cart is loaded with three bags of corn chips, a quart of ice cream, a pound of butter, a sirloin steak, two six-packs of beer, pickled beets in glass jars, a package of bologna, and a box of muffin mix.

Although our Food segments are based on attitudes and motivations, the contents of each cart suggest their representative food choices. The first cart, filled with good-for-you foods, belongs to a Nutrition Concerned. The Fast & Healthy person pushing cart number two has focused on convenience-oriented food items that are also positioned as healthful. Snacks and traditional fare represent many of the food choices of the Traditional Couponer filling cart number three.

Opportunities abound

The food choices made by each of our Food segments, both at supermarkets and restaurants, have tremendous economic impact. New products can be created for the needs and interests of our three Food segments within the aging population. And when the food industry at last understands the food- and health-related motivations of the mature market, these new products will be more successful than those produced over the past four or five years with this market in mind.

Disease and diet linked

The health of our Food segments will be impacted by the food choices they make. The chronic diseases typically seen in maturity, from diabetes to heart disease, are heavily influenced by diet. While heart disease remains our number one killer, diabetes in epidemic proportions is already sweeping the U.S. Today 20% of Americans over age 60 have obesity-linked diabetes. The true costs of those 40 and older snacking on bags of potato chips as they watch their favorite television programs or diving into slices of apple pie topped with a mountain of ice cream at the local coffee shop will eventually be borne by all of us.

In this chapter we examine current trends in food offerings, whether indulgent, functional, organic or traditional, as they are reflected in the attitudes and motivations of our Food segments. The linkage between attitudes and behaviors is frequently questioned, and the relationship is often dismissed as tenuous. We will show, however, that the Food segments' attitudes and motivations are linked directly to what, where, and how they eat.

Instead of generalizations spread across mythical average consumers, we will demonstrate that food-related attitudes are concentrated in each of our Food segments. Each Food segment presents challenges for those producing, distributing, and marketing food. At the same time, the Nutrition Concerned, Fast & Healthy, and Traditional Couponers—each one receptive to specific offerings—point the way for successful foods of the future.

Burgeoning mature population

Both their numbers and expenditures compel food manufacturers and restaurant companies to pay increasing attention to mature adults. Persons 40 and older are currently 43% of the population. Baby boomers, now 37 to 56 years old, will all be 50 and older by 2014. Largely because of the boomer phenomenon, those 40 and older in the U.S. population will increase from 43% to 48% from 2000 to 2025, while those 39 and younger will decrease by 6%. But even in the face of these numbers, food marketers tend to dismiss the mature market as making insignificant purchases or of being so entrenched in its brand loyalties that its members are impossible to convert. Neither position is supported by the facts.

Spending on food eaten at home

As calculated by the U.S. Bureau of Labor Statistics, 1999 average weekly expenditures for food consumed at home by consumer units composed of persons 40 to 64 were $62.97, the highest for any age group. Although not directly comparable, our research shows household weekly median expenditures for groceries at $72.64 for this age group. It is true that food eaten at home for those 65 and older declines to an average $43.40 per week, according to the U.S. Bureau of Labor Statistics, and to a median of $45.81, based on our research. But the lowest of all expenditures for food consumed at home are in consumer units of persons under 25, who spend an average of $35.09 per week.

Smaller households wave of future

The reduced household expenditures for groceries among mature consumers reflect changes in their household composition. Of those 65 and older, only 57% are married, as compared to 73% of those 40 to 64. In addition, fewer than one percent of households 65 and older live with a child of their own who is 18 or younger or with a grandchild.

By calculating expenditures for food consumed at home solely on a per capita basis, rather than by household, a far less dramatic decline in spending on food consumed at home by those 65 and older is revealed. According to the figures stated above, a 45-year-old couple with one child under 18 at home may spend $21 per individual per week on food eaten there. A child-free 65-year-old couple's expenditures might be $22 per person.

If average household size in the U.S. continues to shrink at its present pace, families with children may decline as the food marketers' stellar target. The year 2015 may see households with an average of 1.93 people, rather than today's 2.52. This shrinkage of overall household size should further encourage marketers to value the mature market's exploding numbers, even if many of its households are made up of only one or two persons.

Household composition and size also impacts on the amount each of our Food segments spends on food eaten at home. Fast & Healthy spend the least amount on groceries. These lower expenditures are influenced by the fact that, compared to the other two Food segments, more Fast & Healthy are single. In fact, by the time they reach 65 and older, the vast majority (72%) of Fast & Healthy are not married, and their median expenditures for groceries per week ($43.87) reflect their pervasive single status. But these lower expenditures on groceries are, as we will see later in this chapter, counterbalanced by the Fast & Healthy's high consumption of restaurant meals.

Not entrenched in brand loyalties

U.S. food companies focus virtually all of their marketing budgets on younger consumers or couples with children, dismissing mature buyers as so staunchly committed to specific brands that they will never switch. Nothing could be further from the truth.

In discerning brand loyalty between younger and older consumers, Mark D. Uncles and Andrew S.C. Enrenberg, professors at the London Business School, studied a year's worth of purchasing records from the Market Research Corporation of America's (MRCA) national consumer panel. The authors reviewed multiple products in each of seven categories with sample sizes of approximately 6,000 in each category. They found that the "somewhat smaller number of brands bought by older households is due in part to them buying less often ... compared with ... younger households." Over a longer time period, "older households would buy as often ... [and] then have as wide a repertoire of brands as do younger ones."

The authors conclude that decreases in consumption of a product, such as salad dressing, indicate not an "inflexibility of brand choice behavior," but, rather, the reduced needs of an empty nest. If consumption and brand loyalty are measured not by household, but rather by individuals, mature consumers are no more brand loyal than are younger consumers. This conclusion underscores the fact that it is, indeed, of value to advertise to the mature market.

But beyond this fundamental conclusion, the question of brand loyalty, whether in reference to the mature market or to younger consumers, is a complex one that cannot be dismissed by simple generalizations. Our studies show that variations in brand loyalty exist both across attitudinal segments and in reference to specific products. We define brand loyalty as the self-reported purchase of only one or two brands in a specific category.

Do brands deliver value?

If we accept that brand loyalty in mature consumers does-n't rest on age, their attitudes toward the values and benefits that a brand represents come to the forefront. Each of our Food segments who uses a specific product values brands in that category to a greater or lesser degree. In addition, their loyalty is more or less linked to the degree of their attitudinal involvement with that category.

For example, more of the Nutrition Concerned, focused on eating whole foods and good-for-you foods, buy only one or two brands of hot cereals and non-fat salty snacks, while fewer of them are brand loyal to cola-flavored soft drinks. In contrast, more Fast & Healthy, convenience-oriented grazers, are brand loyal to crackers, cookies, canned soups, and instant coffee, but not to certain brands of wine. Compared to the other two segments, more Traditional Couponers, who pay little attention to healthful eating, are loyal to one or two brands of regular salty snacks and beer, but do not limit their purchases to one or two brands of bagels.

Given its size, food marketers cannot ignore the mature market. Rather they have to encourage brand loyalty in those Food segments who buy more of their products and have the highest involvement with a specific category. At the same time, marketers must create innovative products that target receptive Food segments and address their needs. Doing so will assure a high degree of brand loyalty and repeat sales.

Motivational segmentation needed

The Food segments are also essential in untangling the mature market's apparent contradictions regarding food trends. On one hand we are told that boomers are "intensely interested in living longer, and staying healthier for longer than any other generation" and that "they have figured out that food can play a key role in contributing to a longer, healthier life." The United States Department of Agriculture (USDA) advises us that "Older Americans [defined as those

65 and older] appear to be moving towards dietary guidance and closer to the 1995 Dietary Guidelines for Americans."

But such assessments contradict other realities. How can the boomers' supposed increased interest in eating a nutritious, balanced diet in order to enjoy a long and healthy life exist at the same time that obesity among them is skyrocketing? We used our respondents' self-reported heights and weights to calculate a body mass index (BMI) for each of them. We found that our statistics very closely track those collected by the Center for Disease Control (CDC) in its *Behavioral Risk Factor Surveillance System* (BRFSS), "the world's largest telephone survey that tracks health risks in the United States."

In our studies, 22% of our respondents 40 to 64 are obese. In the BRFSS, 22.9% of those 40 to 49, 25.6% of those 50 to 59 , and 22.9% of those 60 to 69 are obese. Among those 70 and older in the BRFSS 15.5% are obese, compared to 18% of those 65 and older in our studies. Whatever the source of the numbers, it is obvious that as a group those 40 and older are obviously eating too much and exercising too little.

An analysis of consumption patterns for adults over the age of 20 using data from the third *National Health and Nutrition Examination Survey, 1988 – 1994* shows that 27% of daily energy intake is supplied by energy-dense, nutrient-poor (EDNP) foods. Specific age groups favor certain types of EDNP foods. This analysis found, for example, that for those 40 and older, desserts supply 9% of total daily energy intake, while 5% to 6% comes from visible fats, such as butter and salad dressings. Bottomline: the consistent consumption of EDNP foods results in an overweight and yet undernourished population.

The diets of older Americans also have significant deficiencies. While the USDA reports that older Americans are "moving towards" a more healthful diet, it also finds that among those 65 and older "average intakes of food energy, dietary fiber, vitamins B-6 and E, calcium, magnesium, and zinc were lower than recommendations." Their low intakes of dietary fiber suggests that these individuals are not "consuming the recommended servings of fruits, vegetables, and whole-grain foods."

Food choices exist on continuum

Some commentators wonder how an interest in healthful eating among the mature can co-exist with overindulgence and the consumption of empty calories. Their conclusion is to label these trends as "schizophrenic." This simplistic viewpoint fails to realize that food choices are not made from one extreme or another, but exist on a continuum. Very few consumers limit their diet to only celery stalks and dried apricots. At the same time, a diet made up solely of corn chips and ice cream represents another extreme.

When viewed by averages, the mature market is confusing and frustrating for food marketers because the mythical average mature consumer is eating both indulgent and good-for-you foods to a greater or lesser degree. When traditional market research averages very different patterns of consumption across all consumers, these differences are submerged and lost.

Examined by our attitudinally based Food segments, a clearer perspective of food consumption by mature consumers emerges. Rather than dismiss seemingly contradictory food trends as "schizophrenic," an attitudinal segmentation shows that interest in good for you eating by the mature market is largely concentrated in the Nutrition Concerned. While the Fast & Healthy give some lip service to eating fresh vegetables and fruits, convenience is far more important to them. And, of course, Traditional Couponers have no interest in giving up their bacon and eggs for apples and eggplants.

At the same time, while attitudes and behaviors define our Food segments, their food choices do not exist as absolutes. The Food segments demonstrate strong propensities toward making certain food choices over others. The Nutrition Concerned eat far more fruits and fresh vegetables than the 40 and older population as a whole and more than the other two Food segments. And yet the Nutrition Concerned occasionally indulge in cookies.

Eating out, not in

As we discovered in Chapter 10, the Fast & Healthy are attitudinally grazers, noshing their way through the day and seeing little need to prepare meals at home. They are also the most interested in single-serve convenience products and foods that can be eaten on the run. If these foods have a good-for-you gloss, so much the better. Besides snacking when they are at home, Fast & Healthy also eat frequent restaurant meals, which they perceive as sufficiently healthful. As we have seen, the Fast & Healthy satisfy both their nutritional and social needs by eating out.

This segment's motivations to eat out are reflected in their behaviors. On one hand, Fast & Healthy prepare the fewest number of meals at home over a three-day period compared to the other two Food segments. While half of the Nutrition Concerned prepare six or more meals at home over three days (53%), not even one in three of the Fast & Healthy do so (31%). On the other hand, 70% of the Fast & Healthy eat out once within a three-day period, compared to only 57% of the Nutrition Concerned. In fact, virtually one out of every two Fast & Healthy eat out once a day (46%), something done by only one in three (34%) Traditional Couponers and about one in four Nutrition Concerned (28%).

Compared to the other two Food segments, the Fast & Healthy eat far more frequently at restaurants in the fast food, casual dining, and coffee shop categories. Certain demographic factors also stimulate their receptive attitudes toward eating out. Fast & Healthy in the 40 to 64 age group enjoy a higher than average median income ($45,733), almost half of them are married, and more of them work full time (78%), as compared to the other Food segments (72% and 73%).

Choosing convenience

The Fast & Healthy are committed to healthful eating—as long as it is convenient. Their reliance on convenience foods is seen in their heavy use of frozen dinners. About one in four (23%) of the Fast & Healthy eat a frozen dinner at least once a week or more, as compared to about one in ten of the other two segments. In fact, 43% of the Nutrition Concerned say they never buy frozen dinners.

Our data show that one reason the Fast & Healthy are so committed to convenience foods and skip meals is that they are very busy people. Besides work, the Fast & Healthy engage in a number of activities. For example, Fast & Healthy 40 and older are most apt to have gone on three or more short vacations in the past 12 months. Those 65 and older are also more apt to have traveled independently in the last five years than the other Food segments.

More meat and potatoes

The attitudes of the Traditional Couponers are based on a conviction that they want to eat what they have always eaten and that meat is central to virtually every meal. Traditional Couponers, who don't believe that what they eat will influence how they feel, aren't motivated to eat a healthful diet. Their food-related motivations are better understood when compared to our Health segments. One factor that contributes to their attitudes is the fact that 39% of all Traditional Couponers 40 and older are also Optimists, one of our Health segments. At numbers far greater than we would expect by chance, many Traditional Couponers also share the Optimist mind set. In Chapter 12 we described the Optimist's belief that they are in great health and will stay that way. It's no wonder that Traditional Couponers show little restraint in delving into a bowl of mashed potatoes laced with butter.

In example after example, it is clear that the Traditional Couponers' attitudes and motivations toward eating and nutrition are reflected in their food choices. Compared to the Nutrition Concerned, the Traditional Couponer's diet is high in energy-dense and nutrition poor (EDNP) foods loaded with fat, cholesterol, sugar and salt. These EDNP foods displace fresh fruits and vegetables, fruit juices, and frozen vegetables in the Traditional Couponers' diets.

Traditional Couponers are above-average consumers of meat, butter, whole milk, cheese, eggs, salty snacks, hard liquor, beer, and candy. Virtually a quarter of the Traditional Couponers eat meat daily (22%), almost twice as many as compared to the Nutrition Concerned (12%). It is evident that the Traditional Couponers have put the California Beef Council's tagline, "It's what's for dinner," in practice. Traditional Couponers 40 to 64 haven't gotten the skim milk message, with 29% of them drinking whole milk daily, as compared to 21% of this age group as a whole. While about a quarter (24%) of those 40 to 64 use butter daily, more than a third of the Traditional Couponers do so (35%). This percentage zooms to almost half of the Traditional Couponers (49%) in the 65 and older category.

Hard liquor and beer are additional sources of EDNP calories for the Traditional Couponers. Enthusiastic in their consumption of beer, Traditional Couponers are also the heaviest consumers of hard liquor among the Food segments, with 21% of Traditional Couponers 65 and older drinking hard liquor once a week or more. Representing 20% of the 40 and older market, Traditional Couponers are the best target for Frito-Lay and Jim Beam, Land O'Lakes and M & M Mars.

Choosing good foods naturally

The Nutrition Concerned's deep commitment to healthful eating is linked to their attitudes toward staying healthy. Our studies show that a statistically significant relationship exists between our Food and Health segmentation strategies. While Proactives, one of our Health segments, are 33% of the 40 and older population, they are 44% of the Nutrition Concerned. As we saw in Chapter 12, Proactives are convinced that they must take care of themselves and that present actions, such as reducing fat in their diet and exercising, will deliver future health benefits.

More Nutrition Concerned regularly eat fresh fruits and vegetables. Among those 40 to 64, more Nutrition Concerned (64%) eat fresh fruit daily as compared to the Fast & Healthy

(50%), and Traditional Couponers (39%). In addition, more Nutrition Concerned consume fresh vegetables daily. While 78% of the Nutrition Concerned 65 and older eat fresh vegetables daily, only 59% of the Fast & Healthy and 64% of the Traditional Couponers do so. Nutrition Concerned are also over consumers of several other healthful foods, such as hot cereal.

Living a healthy lifestyle

Besides eating a healthful diet, the Nutrition Concerned underscore their commitment to a proactive lifestyle by not smoking and by exercising. While a quarter (24%) of the Fast & Healthy and a third (34%) of the Traditional Couponers currently smoke cigarettes, only 17% of the Nutritional Concerned light up. In terms of exercise, our studies show that 58% percent of the 40 and older population says that it exercises, but not as part of their jobs. That percentage increases to 63% among the Nutrition Concerned.

Not only do more Nutrition Concerned exercise, they do so more vigorously. When we further defined exercise as getting within the range of one's target heart rate and working hard for at least 20 minutes each time, 28% of the Nutrition Concerned exercise four or more times a week at that level as compared to 14% of the Traditional Couponers. While Traditional Couponers favor golf and shuffleboard, hardly fat-burning exercises, Nutrition Concerned prefer jogging and aerobics, despite the fact that they have a higher median age (56) as compared to Traditional Couponers (53).

Enjoying health benefits

Has the Nutrition Concerned's avoidance of cigarette smoking, healthful eating and regular aerobic exercise paid off? More than half of the Nutrition Concerned who are 65 and older (54 percent) rate their current state of health as "excellent" or "very good" as compared to about a third of the Fast & Healthy (32%) and Traditional Couponers (30%). Through a combination of diet and exercise, more Nutrition

Concerned than Fast & Healthy are maintaining a normal weight. For example, among those 65 and older, more Nutrition Concerned have a normal weight (41%) as indicated by their BMI as compared to the Fast & Healthy (33%). At the same time, fewer Nutrition Concerned are obese (16%) as compared to the Fast & Healthy (21%) and to the total 65 and older population (18%).

It's true that more Nutrition Concerned 65 and older take a prescription drug for high cholesterol (17%) to prevent heart attacks as compared to the other two segments (10% and 10%). Compared to the Fast & Healthy in this age group, however, Nutrition Concerned report far lower prescription drug usage for heart rhythm disorders, angina, and blood clots. And fewer of them take prescription medications for sleep problems, anxiety, depression, and osteoporosis.

The food and lifestyle choices made by the Nutrition Concerned have paid off. Data from our studies supports the findings of the University of New Mexico School of Medicine's New Mexico Aging Process study. Begun in 1979, this ongoing, long-term investigation of 300 older adults between the ages of 65 and 93 concludes that the process of aging may be slowed down through behavioral changes. Dr. Philip Garry, an associate with the study, says that "You really can slow aging down through eating well, exercising properly, keeping positive, and staying active." These are all behaviors that the Nutrition Concerned practice. "We don't see much change," Garry continues, "in them [participants in the study] due to aging…they are going on in life like they did when they were much younger."

The challenge of functional foods

Both good-for-you foods, such as tomatoes, low-fat yogurt and whole-wheat bread, and indulgent foods, such as Ben and Jerry's ice cream, Land O'Lakes butter, and Nabisco's Chips-Ahoy! cookies are already available to all buyers, regardless of age. Given this fact, food marketers are devising functional foods specifically targeting an aging population's health

concerns. Unlike spinach, which offers natural health benefits, a health benefit has been added to a functional food. The
Grocery Manufacturers of America estimates that the functional foods market reached $17.5 billion in 2001.

Given our understanding of the Food segments, which segment or segments would be interested in functional foods?
Nutrition Concerned, over consumers of fresh fruits and vegetables, make food choices based upon the knowledge that
"broccoli, cabbage, kale and spinach ... grapes, strawberries,
and blueberries ... are loaded with plant chemicals that can
diminish our risk of developing everything from heart disease
and cancer to diabetes and stroke." Functional foods, which
are processed foods, would have less appeal to Nutrition Concerned than the fresh foods they prefer to cook from scratch.
From their attitudes and past behaviors, we conclude that if
Nutrition Concerned wished to improve their diet still further
they would simply eat another bowl of hot cereal or a plate of
ratatouille.

Traditional Couponers have settled in with a bottle of beer
and a bowl of regular potato chips. Since they are not looking
for health benefits from their food, Traditional Couponers
would not be receptive to the promise of functional foods.

Fast & Healthy best target

The best target for functional foods is the Fast & Healthy
segment. This segment already demonstrates an interest in
functional foods through their heavy consumption of liquid
protein drinks, such as Ensure. While 4% of the Nutrition
Concerned have one or more of these drinks a week, 6% of
the Fast & Healthy do so, a 50% increase. Among Fast &
Healthy who are 65 and older, one in ten (10%) consumes one
or more liquid protein drinks a week, far more than the Traditional Couponers (1%) and the Nutrition Concerned (5%).

In addition, the Fast & Healthy are already self-medicating
to a great degree. While 6% of the Nutrition Concerned 40 and
older regularly take three or more over-the-counter (OTC)
drugs daily, 9% of the Fast & Healthy do so, a 50% increase.

When they reach 65 and older, 15% of the Fast & Healthy take three or more OTC drugs daily. Moving from ginkgo biloba taken in pill form to ingesting it in orange juice would not be a major step for this segment.

As we've seen, the Fast & Healthy have a superficial interest in healthful eating, but require that it be delivered in a convenient format. If their interest in good-for-you eating were more serious, they would increase their consumption of readily available fresh fruits, vegetables, and whole grains. Instead they resort to frozen dinners and crackers.

Of the 19 food properties or ingredients our studies cover, five are of great current interest to food manufacturers: low in lactose, high in calcium, grown organically, has antioxidants, and has live yogurt cultures. In every one of these categories, fewer Fast & Healthy are interested in these attributes as compared to Nutrition Concerned. But, as we've pointed out, the Nutrition Concerned's interest is rooted in obtaining these properties or ingredients in natural, not manufactured, foods.

Best target for functional foods

We've already noted the superficial quality of the Fast & Health's commitment to healthful eating. That this segment's interest in good-for-you foods is lukewarm is seen in both their attitudes and their behaviors. We've noted their lower consumption of fresh fruits and vegetables, their lack of interest in cooking from scratch, and their habit of grazing, rather than eating complete meals. But the Fast & Healthy's very strong commitment to convenience and snacking, combined with the attraction of some potential health benefits easily and quickly arrived at, make them the natural market for functional foods.

Beyond the ingredients in a functional food, what other product attributes are necessary in order to attract the Fast & Healthy? Given their casual eating habits, the Fast & Healthy would be unwilling to commit themselves to a functional food that demands a regimen. Many Fast & Healthy are also looking for a breakthrough product: a quick cure to a specific health problem.

One reason many functional foods to date have failed to achieve their promise has been the necessity of eating them a certain number of times a day or in large quantities. For example, it's necessary to eat two tablespoons of Benecol, a margarine substitute, daily in order to lower cholesterol. Not only must the consumer eat twice as much margarine as the current daily average amount, but the margarine must be eaten three times a day. In the case of Ensemble, the now discontinued line of functional foods from Kellogg, it was necessary to eat at least three servings for three weeks before seeing any reduction in cholesterol levels. In addition, the extensive Ensemble line was based on an old and tired ingredient: psyllium, a soluble fiber.

Besides avoiding a regimen, functional foods would also have to taste delicious. Fast & Healthy aren't willing to sacrifice great taste for a potential future health benefit. Unfortunately, Campbell's Intelligent Cuisine, frozen entrees that were "clinically demonstrated to be useful for those who need to follow therapeutic diets," did not "deliver the taste or variety consumers craved."

The Fast & Healthy would also find functional foods more appealing if they were competitively priced. Only a fast acting and dramatic benefit would lead the Fast & Healthy to stomach the high cost of many functional foods. As we've pointed out, the amount the Fast & Healthy spend on food eaten at home is the lowest of all the Food segments. Benecol costs three to four times as much as regular margarine. Bread from the defunct Ensemble line was priced at an astronomical $7.96 a pound. At these elevated prices, Fast & Healthy may question whether the benefit of a functional food is worth its cost.

Estimating the market

Besides taste, pricing, benefits, and ease of use, estimating the market for functional foods products has also been another significant problem for food marketers. There were high hopes that Benecol and its rival, TakeControl, would become blockbuster products in the margarine market. These expectations were no doubt based on an assessment of the size of the high-cholesterol market which included everyone with high cholesterol as a potential buyer.

The number of persons with high cholesterol ranges from the American Heart Association's estimate of 40 million American adults, about 20% of the population, to new guidelines issued by the National Cholesterol Education Program of the National Heart, Lung and Blood Institute. These guidelines increase those who should be on "cholesterol-lowering diets...to 65 million from the current 52 million ..." While *Advertising Age* described the stakes in offering Ensemble as "potentially huge," Kellogg's investment in these products was also huge. In this instance, Kellogg estimated the market of adults with elevated cholesterol at 95 million—"a full 60% of households."

Our studies show that of those 40 and older only 24% say they currently have high cholesterol or have had it in the past. Of these, 33% are Fast & Healthy, only some of whom would be attitudinally receptive to a functional food used for this purpose, further decreasing the size of the market. Further reductions would result in eliminating those who can't afford such products, as well as those who have the resources to pay for them, but are unwilling to do so. The potential market for functional foods dealing with high cholesterol is then not 20% of the total adult population, but probably closer to a total of 6 million persons. Viewed from the perspective we have laid out, the potential market for such functional funds is perhaps 15% of those who actually have high cholesterol.

Impossible expectations

Overestimates of the potential market for new types of products create impossible expectations which many functional foods will never fulfill. The marketing of functional foods products by major corporations has to date been less than encouraging. First year sales of Benecol and Take Control amounted to 4.5% of total margarine sales according to Information Resources Inc. If blockbuster products were expected, they did not deliver. Due to slow sales, Benecol salad dressings and snack bars have been withdrawn from the market, and Benecol cream cheeses and yogurt, available in Europe, were never introduced in the U.S.

In early 2000 Kellogg abandoned its Ensemble line of psyllium-based functional foods because of weak sales, "barely three months" after it appeared on shelves. The company said it had pulled the Ensemble line "in order to better pinpoint target consumers and determine how best to reach them." Apparently Kellogg was not aware of the Fast & Healthy segment, the best target for such functional foods, before it created the Ensemble line. Rather than test market Ensemble in the South, where the largest population of Fast & Healthy can be found, it unfortunately did so in the Midwest, which has only an average concentration of this key segment.

Reaching the Fast & Healthy will require precision targeting and imagination. They are average or below average in their consumption of all media and use of the Internet. The magazines Kellogg may intuitively have chosen to advertise in, such as *Prevention*, *Modern Maturity*, or *Health*, attract fewer Fast & Healthy as subscribers or regular purchasers as compared to the overall 40 and older population.

We believe such functional foods failures have resulted from marketing without an in-depth understanding of food- and health-related attitudes and the interaction of these attitudes. Tens of millions of dollars have been wasted because of the confounding of attitudes and motivations, gross miscalculations regarding receptive targets, and the lack of accurate targeting. A better target for functional foods are consumers who have the attitudes of both the Fast & Healthy segment, as well as the Proactive Health segment. Described in Chapter 12, Proactives are 33% of the 40 and older population and 28% of the Fast & Healthy. Those who are in both segments would have both the highest level of commitment to taking care of their health and also want foods delivering a health benefit in an easy and convenient way.

Understanding the motivations of the Fast & Healthy, about one in four of whom are also Proactives, is a first step. A psychographic segmentation defining the best attitudinal prospect for a specific functional food is the required second step. Having shed the incorrect assumption that all persons with a certain disease or risk factor will buy their functional foods, marketers should then focus their marketing activities on targeting this best prospect. Positioning, messaging, media, and channels of distribution will all be selected with the target prospect in mind. Only with this highly focused, comprehensive, and motivationally based approach will the marketing of functional foods succeed.

REFERENCES

Shell, Ellen Ruppel. "Bad news about obesity curse only faint shadow amid scientific illumination." *St. Paul Pioneer Press* 14 November, 1999.

U.S. Census Bureau. Current Population Reports, middle series projections.

U.S. Bureau of Labor. *Consumer Expenditure Survey* 1999.

Uncles, Mark D. and Enrenberg, Andrew S. C. "Brand choice among older consumers." *Journal of Advertising Research* August-September 1990.

National Center for Chronic Disease Prevention and Health Promotion. "Obesity trends: Prevalence of obesity among U.S. adults, by characteristics 2000."

McMahon, Kathleen E. "Consumers and key nutrition trends for 1998." *Nutrition Today* January 1998.

Center for Disease Control (CDC). *Behavioral risk factor surveillance system* (BRFSS) 2000.

"Dietary Changes in Older Americans from 1977 to 1996: Implications for dietary quality." *Family Economics and Nutrition Review* 1999.

Kant, Ashima K. "Consumption of energy-dense, nutrient-poor foods by adult Americans: nutritional and health implications. The third National Health and Nutrition Examination Survey, 1988 – 1994." *American Journal of Clinical Nutrition* October 2000.

Greeley, Alexandra. "Nutrition and the elderly." *FDA Consumer* October 1990.

Kant, Ashima K.

Sugarman, Carole. "How are we doing?" *Supermarket Business* September 1991.

Wilkes, Ann Przybyla. "Divergent approaches to snacking." *Snack Food & Wholesale Bakery* March 2000.

Brody, Jane E. "Produce: eating the healthiest." *International Herald Tribune* 4 January, 2001.

Mogelonsky, Marcia. "Functional foods." *American Demographics* February 1999.

Pollack, Judann. "Kellogg takes light approach for Ensemble." *Advertising Age* 19 April, 1999.

Simonson, Scott. "'Functional foods' would mix pharmaceuticals with food." *StarTribune* 25 August, 2000.

Thompson, Stephanie. "Non-Functional Foods." *Brandweek* 7 June, 1999.

Chapter 12

THE HEALTH SEGMENTS

PROACTIVES

Those in this segment are intensely committed to exercise, eating a balanced diet, and avoiding foods high in fat. Proactives are convinced that taking such actions will have a positive effect on their health. They are also unique in their interest in collecting information on how to stay in good health. Proactives trust their doctors and respect the health-care system. They are compliant patients who are concerned with taking a prescription drug as directed.

Working to stay healthy

While one Health segment believes it gets sufficient exercise and another eats a balanced diet, only Proactives see themselves as actively taking both these actions. They are also the only segment avoiding foods high in fats. Proactives are distinguished from the other Health segments by their intense commitment to all three of these actions. It is not surprising, then, that Proactives are very optimistic about staying in good health. At the present time, those in this segment can't think of additional things they can do to improve their health.

At the heart of all the Proactives' preventive strategies is a very strong belief that these actions will have a positive effect. Proactives, for example, don't believe they are fated to get cancer. They can act to shape their health. Proactives, along with Faithful Patients, are committed to getting an annual physical.

Underlying these actions is the Proactives' desire to live as long as they can, even if they are in pain. They are the only Health segment that holds this view.

Using information on health

Proactives also differ from the other Health segments in researching and collecting information on how to stay in good health. While they say they don't understand most of what they hear about cancer, they aren't confused about what actions they must take to avoid getting a serious illness. Compared to the other segments, they are the only ones viewed as experts on health-care topics by their friends.

Trust in doctors

Proactives work with their doctors, whom they trust. Those in this segment are the least apt to seek a second opinion. They want to feel that their doctor is concerned about their state of health, and they believe they have no trouble finding doctors who will listen to them. Proactives view their doctors as knowledgeable about such things as drug interactions.

Prescription medications beneficial

Proactives are convinced that the prescription medications their doctors give them will have a positive effect. Perhaps their increasing concern about over-the-counter drugs has led those in this segment to rely more heavily on prescription medications. As compliant patients, Proactives are careful to take prescription medications as directed.

HEALTH SEGMENTS:
PERCENT OF TOTAL AND AGE GROUPS

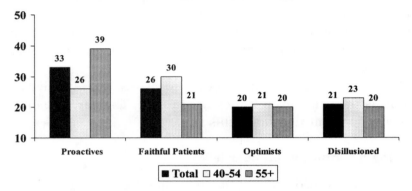

Figure 6: *At a statistically significant level, a higher percentage of Proactives exists among those 55 and older as compared to those 40 to 54. At the same time, a lower percentage of Faithful Patients exists in the older population as compared to the younger.*

The medical system works

For Proactives, the medical system is functioning quite well. Proactives don't blame high medical costs on the system's inefficiencies or on lawyers pursuing medical malpractice cases. They believe that if they needed them, there are government programs that would provide them with acceptable medical care. Proactives respect the system, denying that they would experiment with drugs not approved by the Food and Drug Administration (FDA).

Committed to better hearing

While both Proactives and Faithful Patients, another Health segment, are committed to having occasional hearing tests, the former are far more dedicated to taking care of their hearing. Of all the Health segments, only Proactives don't believe that hearing aids make the wearer look old. They are also singular in thinking that hearing aids are worth their cost.

Sufficient health insurance

Proactives are strongly convinced that they have sufficient health insurance, regardless of the health problems they may face. They are the only Health segment with this view.

FAITHFUL PATIENTS

Those in this segment know what they should be doing to improve their health, but admit they don't take action. Since Faithful Patients don't take responsibility for their health, they are apt to turn to doctors, pharmacists, and medications to help them get better. They are the only segment that says it turns to religion in times of poor health. Faithful Patients are very interested in joining a health-maintenance organization (HMO) which would cover all of their health-care needs.

Not doing what they should

As they age, Faithful Patients have become increasingly concerned with their health. But this concern has not been translated into action. This segment admits that they could do a great deal more to improve their health. Looking back, they wish they had eaten a more healthful diet when they were younger. Faithful Patients don't believe they eat a balanced diet, nor are they frequent dieters. They are very well aware of the fact that they don't exercise enough to stay healthy. When they are sick, Faithful Patients turn to religion, the only Health segment to do so.

Perhaps the Faithful Patients' lack of follow-through regarding healthful actions is related to the fact that they have no desire to live a long life if they are in pain, something the Proactives would willingly accept.

Trusting a medical approach

Since they don't take responsibility for their own health in very basic ways, Faithful Patients rely on doctors, pharmacists, prescription and over-the-counter medications, and

169

surgery to improve their health. Faithful Patients trust their doctors and consider it important to schedule an annual physical. Those in this segment rely on their pharmacist to keep them informed about over-the-counter drugs. Faithful Patients advocate occasional hearing checks for older persons. If eye surgery would improve their vision, they would consider having it.

As do all the Health segments, Faithful Patients want their doctor to show concern about their state of health. While they trust their doctor, Faithful Patients would get a second opinion if faced with the need for a heart pacemaker. They prefer doctors who are specialists and feel very strongly that it is far better to have an eye exam from a medical doctor, or ophthalmologist, than from an optometrist.

Faithful Patients are careful to take a prescription medication as directed by their doctor. Taking these medications, they believe, is far better than having the disease. And Faithful Patients consider prescription medications to be effective. In taking such medications, Faithful Patients are convinced that generic drugs work as well as branded ones.

Selecting health insurance

Faithful Patients are very interested in joining an HMO where all their health care needs would be met for one monthly premium. Although Faithful Patients are somewhat concerned about having sufficient health insurance, they believe they are covered for any medical problem.

While blaming our litigious society and lawyers for high health-care costs, Faithful Patients would be the most prone of all the Health segments to sue a doctor if he or she made a mistake in treating them.

OPTIMISTS

Thanks to good luck, great genes, or infrequent health exams, those in this segment believe they are in terrific health. Optimists think that they rarely get sick. And if they were to get sick, those in this segment would think that there wasn't much they could have done to have avoided the ill-ness. Optimists try to avoid taking prescription medications and see little need for health care delivered by an HMO: after all, they have no health problems.

Good genes, good luck

Other than exercise, there isn't much more that Optimists believe they can do to stay healthy. They aren't, for example, constantly dieting. Even with less than extensive efforts, Optimists are convinced that they will remain in good health.

Those in this segment reveal that they rarely get sick. Even if they are sick, they might not know it: only those in this Health segment don't believe in having an annual physical. If they found out they had cancer, Optimists believe that there was little they could have done to prevent it. Their fatalistic perspective appears to be related to a wholehearted desire to live a full and happy life today and let tomorrow take care of itself. Looking back, they don't wish they had eaten a better diet when they were younger. Looking forward, they have no desire to extend their lives, if it means living in pain.

Their avoidance in knowing the specifics about their health isn't related to feelings about doctors: Optimists trust doctors. They'd get a second opinion, however, before having a heart pacemaker implanted. Those in this segment prefer going to a medical doctor for an eye examination and would consider eye surgery if they were sure it would improve their sight.

Avoiding prescription medications

Optimists try to avoid taking prescription medications and take them only when it is critical. They don't experiment with over-the-counter (OTC) drugs to help them improve their health.

Health-care perspectives

Since Optimists are in such good health, or at least believe they are, they have little need for health care delivered under the HMO concept. While guaranteed health care for everyone isn't something Optimists advocate, they don't see any government programs providing them with good health care. Like Faithful Patients, Optimists view a law-suit-prone society as driving up the cost of health care.

DISILLUSIONED

This segment's greatest concern is having insufficient health insurance. The Disillusioned are highly critical of today's health-care system and feel alienated from doctors. According to this segment, prescription medications are to be avoided if possible. One concern they have is that of harmful drug interactions. The Disillusioned would like to live a long life and act to improve their health. Their interest in achieving good health, however, is thwarted by their lack of access to health care.

Living a long life

The Disillusioned are concerned about living a long life and not just enjoying today. They believe they can take actions, such as eating a balanced diet, that will help them extend their lives and avoid diseases such as cancer. They seek information on how to stay in good health. Their desire for a long, healthy life is impeded, however, by their lack of access to health insurance. Of all the Health segments, the Disillusioned are most concerned about not having sufficient health insurance and worry about how they would cover a medical problem.

Health care in sorry state

Lacking health-insurance coverage, the Disillusioned are sharply critical of today's health-care system. According to the Disillusioned, our health-care system is costly because it is inefficient. What the Disillusioned think we need is guaranteed health care for everyone. For those in this segment, HMOs are a welcome way of getting comprehensive health-care coverage.

Doctors are not to be trusted, say the Disillusioned, who have had difficulty in finding a doctor who will listen to them. They are the only Health segment that believes doctors don't know enough about how various medications interact. As do all of the Health segments, Disillusioned would like to find a doctor who is concerned about their health. While they too would seek a second opinion if their doctor recommended a heart pacemaker, they wouldn't sue a doctor who had made a mistake in treating them.

Avoiding medications

Disillusioned take prescription medications only when they have to and don't experiment with over-the-counter drugs.

Chapter 13

MOTIVATING
HEALTHFUL BEHAVIORS

Transforming knowledge into action

We all know what we should do: quit smoking, exercise regularly, eat plenty of fruits and vegetables, and maintain a normal weight. These healthful behaviors provide an immense pay-off for individuals who enjoy longer, healthier lives. Unfortunately, recent surveys show that mature Americans are not taking care of themselves as they should.

This lack of good health-care habits has several negative results: a lower quality of life, early death, and a higher price tag for health care. A study published in 1999 in the *Journal of the American Medical Association* (JAMA) compared members of a health maintenance organization (HMO) with good health care habits to those with bad ones. Among other things, the study, based on nearly 6,000 HMO members 40 and older, found that smokers cost the organization 18% more than nonsmokers. The study points out that these increased costs are incurred now, not just when these members are older.

On the positive side, persons who exercised at least once a week cost the HMO 4.7% less than those who were sedentary.

Patients in the HMO study with healthful habits had mean annual health care costs 49% lower than those who did not. Such findings are extremely important at a time when annual per capita expenditures on U.S. health care are projected to climb from $4,340 in 1999 to $7,170 in 2008.

The solution posed by this and other research is a series of interventions and health-promotion activities, the success of which depends on the individuals themselves and their motivations. As a study released by the Center for the Advancement of Health notes, merely handing out materials on good health behaviors or on how to combat chronic health problems is "known to be ineffectual." Such tactics do not motivate people to change negative lifestyles and adopt good health-care habits.

In attempting to understand what motivates persons to practice healthful habits, we classified respondents in our database on three criteria: a body mass index (BMI) of 29 or less, whether or not they currently smoked, and whether or not they exercised four times a week or more at an aerobic level. We calculated the respondents BMIs from their self-reported heights and weights. Three groups resulted from this analysis.

Few practice good habits

We found that 6% of the 40 and older U.S. population practices all three of the positive behaviors outlined above, a percentage that parallels the findings of other national studies. We have labeled this 6% as being in our Sound Group, referencing their sound health habits. At the opposite end of the spectrum, we classified 4% of the 40 and older population — who are obese, smoke, and do not exercise aerobically four or more times a week—into our Unsound Group. While Faithful Patients are 26% of the total 40 and older population, those in this segment are 39% of the Unsound Group.

The remaining 90% of the 40 and older population practices only one or more of the healthful habits described above. We have classified this vast middle group of consumers into the Marginal Group, referencing their health-care habits which are, at best, marginal. Three-quarters of those in the Marginal Group received this classification based solely on their lack of exercise, or their lack of exercise combined with obesity or smoking

Demographics aren't enough

Attempts to explain why one group practices healthful behaviors and another does not too often rely on demographics, such as education or income. In 2000, for example, the *Health and Health Care 2010* report, funded by the Robert Wood Johnson Foundation, described a new "top tier" health-care consumer. Consumers in this "securely enfranchised tier" will have "empowerment" as their "primary issue" and will have "the greatest ability to effect change." The authors of this report describe empowered, top-tier health-care consumers as engaging "in shared decision making with their physicians."

The report defines these empowered consumers as having at least two of the following demographics: one year of college education; computer awareness, defined as having a personal computer, and a household income of $50,000 or more.

Boomer stereotypes prevail

Many of those in this demographic group are, according to the report, "baby boomers who will turn 50 during the next decade." Planners may be pinning their hopes of reducing health care expenditures and changing health care on a stereotype of baby boomers. Boomers, more educated and affluent than past generations, are seen as a cohort more committed to healthful habits and self-care. Demographics are once again magically transformed into motivations.

The danger of this distorted view of baby boomers is illustrated by a study of 200 senior executives by Dr. James Rippe, a Tufts University medical professor. If we correlate demographics with healthful behaviors we would conclude that this group's education, income, and access to the very best health care would result in their practicing good health-care habits. But this long-running study shows the opposite: four out of ten of these baby-boomer executives are obese and three-quarters do no real exercise. Demographics aside, these executives are not, as Dr. Rippe says, "paying attention to the basics."

In our studies we see that virtually the same percentages of baby boomers 40 to 55 exercise at an aerobic level four or more times a week as compared to those 55 and older. Attitudinal or motivational segments are far more useful than demographics in predicting levels of exercise: one in three Proactives exercises at this level regardless of age. It is also true that not even one in ten Faithful Patients does so. In fact, the number of Faithful Patients exercising at an aerobic level four or more times a week has actually decreased over the past four years in both age groups.

Using our own data, we pulled a sample by all three aspects of the new "empowered" health care consumer as defined by the Robert Wood Johnson Foundation's *Health and Health Care 2010* report. In our sample all the respondents had the benefits of the requisite high household income, higher education, and a personal computer in the home. If we followed the Report's thinking we would expect those in this rarefied sample to be "empowered" and affecting change in their health care. Instead, only 18% of the "empowered" sample is in our Sound Group, with 2% in the Unsound Group. The vast majority of these "empowered" respondents (80%) are in our Marginal Group. Although enjoying the benefits of our society, the majority of this "empowered" sample is practicing unhealthful behaviors.

It is true that this "empowered" sample contains more persons in the Sound Group (18%) compared to those in the 40 and older population as a whole (6%). We are still faced, however, with the fact that the overwhelming majority (80%) of these "empowered" consumers as defined by the *Health and Health Care 2010* report are in our Marginal Group, practicing some combination of unhealthful habits. The "empowered" consumer profile, based solely on demographics, does not create a strong causal link to positive healthful motivations.

From a motivational perspective, it is difficult to see that the "empowered" consumers we pulled from our pool of respondents based on the criteria from the Robert Wood Johnson report will either begin or increase their practice of good health-care habits. At a statistically significant level, this sample encompasses far more of our Faithful Patients and only average numbers of Proactives compared to the 40 and older population as a whole. As we have previously noted, Faithful Patients enjoy high incomes and levels of education; they know what they should do to take care of their health, but they lack the motivation to act. That the sample drawn by the Report's criteria of "empowered" health-care consumers has no more Proactives (35%) than the total 40 and older population (33%) strongly suggests that the demographic criteria espoused in the Report are actually weak predictors of empowered, "top tier" health-care consumers.

The lack of correlation between demographics and the motivation to practice good health-care habits is also supported by our own studies. Our data show that only 10% of those who have a college degree or more are in the Sound group described earlier. Of those 40 and older with household incomes of $50,000 and above, only 10% are in our Sound Group. Clearly education and income aren't enough to explain the motivation behind healthful behaviors.

Those in the Sound Group are no older or younger than those in the 40-plus population as a whole or the Marginal Group. These three groups have median ages that range from 54 to 55. Proactives in the Sound Group have the same median age: 55. We cannot conclude that Proactives practice good health habits because of some catastrophic health event related to advancing age. Their motivation to practice positive health behaviors is as strong in their 40s as in their 70s and 80s.

With a median age of 51, respondents in the Unsound group have a lower median age than those in the 40 and older population, as well as those in the Marginal and Sound

Groups. In fact, virtually two out of three (63%) of the Unsound group are baby boomers. Once again, the idea that the financial salvation of health care will come from the baby boomers' better health practices appears unfounded.

Whether or not one has health insurance coverage does not appear to be related to the motivation to practice the three basic health behaviors we have focused on in this analysis. While it is true that almost twice as many among the Marginal Group have no health-care insurance coverage (7%) compared to the Sound Group (4%), the overwhelming majority in both of these groups is covered by one or more sources of health insurance.

Attitudes drive good health habits

The demographic explanation addresses just a small part of a puzzle that can be solved only by an in-depth study of motivations. Attitudes, far more than demographics, such as a high income or a college education, drive good health habits. Members of our Sound Group are overwhelmingly in our Proactive segment (60%), while another 27% are Optimists. Faithful Patients (2%) and Disillusioned (11%) make up the rest of this Group. While these same Health segments make up the Marginal Group, there are deeper attitudinal differences between the segments in these two Groups.

Proactives, for example, in the Sound Group — those who do not smoke, have a normal BMI, and exercise four or more times a week at an aerobic level — are also far more apt to be Internal Health Actives, a segment described in Chapter 15 on the Health Information segments, and also to be Informed Avoiders, a segment profiled in Chapter 17 on our Health Compliance segmentation strategy.

In a nutshell, this means that the Proactives in the Sound Group have all the characteristics of the Proactive segment, but a substantial number of them are also strongly opposed to taking pharmaceutical drugs and will make lifestyle changes to avoid them. Secondly, these particular Proactives are motivated by their own internal drive to be healthy—not by external pressures such as their family or physician. They seek, use, and understand health-related information. In terms of their health care, the locus of control is within themselves. They are already internally motivated to take the actions necessary to preserve their health.

In contrast, Proactives in the Marginal Group are far more apt to also be Trusting Believers, one of our Health Compliance segments, and External Health Actives, a Health Information segment. Simply put, a large number of Proactives in the Marginal Group have totally transferred responsibility for their health to their physician. For these Proactives, the motivation to practice good health habits, to the extent that they are practiced, comes from an external source, perhaps their physician or a family member. Interrelationships such as these among our three health-based segmentation strategies are further explored in our chapter on the Morgan-Levy Health Cube.

Internal motivators strongest

When we compare attitudes toward health with actual behaviors, we conclude that internal motivations which encourage the patient to retain control of his or her health care are most powerful, springing from the health consumer's own internal concept of him- or herself. The Super Segment made up of Proactives who are also Internal Health Actives exemplify this type of motivation. More of these internally driven Proactives don't smoke, stay within the normal range in weight, and persist in exercising aerobically four or more times a week.

In looking specifically at behaviors that impact health and distinguish our three Groups, we examined cigarette smoking, weight, and exercise. Our studies show that 22% of the U.S. population 40 and older currently smokes cigarettes, cigars, or a pipe. This percentage parallels findings from the *1999 National Health Interview Survey* (NHIS) conducted by the Centers for Disease Control. That massive study of almost 31 thousand persons found that 23.5% of all adults in the U.S.

smoke. While smoking is higher among those 25 to 44 (27.3%), it declines to 23.3% among those 45 to 64. A further decline is seen among those 65 and older, only 10.6% of whom smoke.

Examined by our Health segments within each of our three Groups, we see both attitudinal and behavioral differences. By definition, none of the Proactives in the Sound Group currently smokes. In contrast, while 22% of the U.S. 40 and older populations smokes, 19% of the Proactives in the Marginal Group are still doing so. Above average levels of smoking are seen in the Faithful Patients (25%) in the Marginal Group, more of whom currently smoke cigarettes than any of the other Health segments in this Group.

Our data show that in the U.S. 40 and older population, 34% are of normal weight, another 39% are overweight, and 22% are either obese or severely obese. Again by definition, all Proactives in the Sound Group are necessarily of normal weight. Proactives in the Marginal Group do better than the Group overall at maintaining a normal weight; however, 20% of them are obese.

While 62% of the U.S. population 40 and older says that they exercise apart from their job, by definition all of those in the Sound Group do so. Furthermore, among those respondents who exercise outside their job, all of those in the Sound Group, again by definition, exercise four or more times per week at an aerobic level, as compared to only 23% of the 40 and older population as a whole and 29% of the Marginal Group. Half of those in the Sound Group are convinced that they get enough exercise, something to which only 18% of the Marginal Group would agree.

But within the Marginal Group there are important differences between the Health segments. More Proactives exercise aerobically four or more times a week or more than the other Health segments. Although Proactives are 40% of the Marginal Group, they are 52% of those who exercise at this level.

Ignoring activities that could require a large financial outlay, such as golf, tennis, or a health-club membership, our studies show wide differences in how frequently both groups participate in various types of exercise. Differences in the rates of participation between the Sound and Marginal Groups in such low-cost activities as aerobic walking and weight lifting are substantial.

There are dramatic differences in levels of participation among those who jog or walk leisurely. While one in five (21%) of those in the Sound Group runs or jogs three times a week or more, fewer than one in ten (8%) of the Marginal Group does so. Leisurely walking, an activity almost half (47%) of the Sound Group does three or more times per week, is something done by only a third (33%) of the Marginal Group. Far more Proactives in both the Sound (52%) and Marginal (43%) Groups do leisurely walking as compared to the other Health segments.

Reducing number of physician visits

Do the positive behaviors of the Sound Group result in lower outlays for their care? Those in the 40 and older population, as well as those in the Marginal Group, make an average of 3.5 physician visits annually. In contrast, members of the Sound Group make an average of 2.4 physicians visits each year. If those in the Marginal Group could be motivated to improve their health care habits, the number of physician visits they make would be reduced.

Based on our own data we calculate that those 40 and older make 407 million physician visits annually. Using costs for physician visits found in the American Medical Association's 1998 Socio-Economic Statistics, we estimate that moving patients currently in the Marginal Group to the Sound one would result in savings of between $4.7 and $8 billion annually. This range results from whether costs are computed on a new patient visit or one for an established patient.

Differences also exist between the Health segments in the Sound and Marginal Groups on the number of physician visits made each year. While those in the Sound Group make an average of 2.4 visits to a physician, Proactives are slightly higher (2.5 visits) on this point as compared to Optimists (2.3

visits). Optimists, as we have noted, consider themselves to be in good health and avoid doctors.

The Marginal Group, which makes 3.5 visits annually, includes Proactives making an average 3.9 physician visits and Optimists who make 1.9 visits. Faithful Patients, however, make physician visits at an extremely high rate, an average of 4.3 per year. Considering the fact that Faithful Patients represent 27% of the Marginal Group, their high level of usage has enormous financial implications. However, since Proactives, as opposed to Faithful Patients, are far more receptive to wellness strategies, initial attempts to change harmful behaviors should focus on the former segment. And the target for such efforts is large: Proactives are almost a third (32%) of the Marginal Group.

Drug consumption concentrated

Who is taking the $90.6 billion in pharmaceutical drugs we Americans now consume annually? Can good health habits reduce expenditures on pharmaceutical drugs which have grown 84% between 1993 and 1998? Discussion surrounding programs to provide prescription drug benefits paints a picture of vast masses of mature consumers in desperate need of such assistance. Our data shows that high consumption of prescription pharmaceutical drugs among those 40 and older is focused on a relatively small population distinguished by the number of drugs they take and by their attitudinal segment.

Of those 40 and older in the U.S. population, more than one in three (36%) do not take a pharmaceutical drug. While those in the Marginal Group are average on this point (35%), more in the Sound Group do not take any pharmaceutical drug (43%). Whether due to avoidance, in the case of Optimists, or inability to pay, in the situation of the Disillusioned, half of those in these two Health segments in the Sound Group do not take a pharmaceutical drug.

Virtually the same percentages of the total 40 and older population, as well as the Sound and Marginal Groups, take between one and two drugs. This situation may be explained by the fact that healthful behaviors cannot reduce the incidence of conditions such as rosacea or glaucoma which must be treated with a prescription drug. Whether within the total 40 and older population or any of our designated Groups, 1% use a prescription drug for rosacea and 1% or 2% use a drug for glaucoma.

Considering diseases caused at least in part by negative health behaviors, we see a different pattern. Among those who take five or more pharmaceutical drugs daily, far more of them take such drugs for conditions or diseases largely caused by unhealthful behaviors, as compared to the total 40 and older population and to those who take only one or two drugs per day. These diseases include diabetes and high blood pressure. Seven percent, for example, of the total 40 and older population reports taking a prescription drug for diabetes, as do 5% of those who take one or two drugs a day. But 31% of those taking five or more drugs take a prescription drug for diabetes.

Striking differences also exist between our Groups and also among the Health segments in terms of taking five or more drugs daily. Within the Sound Group less than 1% takes five or more drugs per day as contrasted to 8% of the Marginal Group. And in the Marginal Group more Faithful Patients (12%) take five or more prescription drugs per day than any of the other Health segments. The Faithful Patients' belief that renewed health will come from pharmaceutical drugs — as opposed to healthful behaviors — is reflected in their high level of usage.

When mean expenditures for prescription drugs to reduce high cholesterol or treat diabetes are over $2,000 per patient annually, it is easy to see that a migration of the mature population from the Marginal to the Sound Group could easily result in yearly savings of billions of dollars. At their current levels, pharmaceutical drug benefits do not lead consumers, and most particularly not Faithful Patients, to practice the healthful behaviors that could reduce their reliance on such drugs.

Increasing reliance on drugs

Given the current benefits structure, companies providing prescription drug coverage will see continuing increases in expenditures for pharmaceutical drugs. We base our conclusion on their enrollees' health-related behaviors and their classification into certain of our Health segments. Among those 40 and older who receive their health care coverage from a managed care organization (MCO), only 7% are in the Sound Group. Among those who have an indemnity health insurance policy, 7% are also classified in that Group. Given these percentages, it appears that MCOs have not done a better job than indemnity health insurance plans in either attracting greater numbers of those who practice healthful behaviors or in motivating their enrollees to practice such behaviors. If MCOs had succeeded in these two challenges, we would be seeing a higher percentage of their members in the Sound Group.

Faithful Patients opt for MCOs

For a variety of reasons, it will be difficult for MCOs to motivate the Sound Group's healthful behaviors among their enrollees. One reason is that they have succeeded in attracting Faithful Patients in disproportionate numbers. While Faithful Patients are 26% of the 40 and older population, they make up 30% of those 40 and older in an MCO. In addition, regardless of what type of health insurance coverage they have, 94% of Faithful Patients fall into our Marginal Group. Those in this segment know that they should exercise regularly or stop smoking, but they are not motivated to take care of themselves. Faithful Patients rely on physicians and pharmaceuticals, rather than good health habits, to make them well. The provision of prescription drug benefits, something many of them receive or can afford, encourages them in this attitude.

Simply giving a Faithful Patient information is not sufficient. Many Faithful Patients are professional information seekers, constantly adding to their health-related knowledge, but never acting upon it. While 33% of the 40 and older have a college degree, 34% of the Faithful Patients have attained this level of education. They are sufficiently educated; they are just not motivated to practice good health-care habits.

Conversely, while Proactives are 33% of the 40 and older population, HMOs have succeeded in attracting only average numbers of them (33%) of them as enrollees. In contrast, 38% of those 40 and older who have indemnity health insurance are Proactives. Proactives not only know what they must do to stay healthy, but they are also more likely to do so. Proactives are not dependant on their source of health-care insurance for guidance, information, or motivation in taking care of themselves.

From six food properties, for example, more Proactives than any of the other Health segments in the Sound Group had on their own reduced sugar, calories, cholesterol, and caffeine. They tied with the Disillusioned in having reduced fat in their diets on their own initiative. The differences between the Proactives, the 40 and older population, and the other Health segments in the Sound Group on the issue of self-imposed fat reduction are dramatic. Of the total 40 and older population, 53% have reduced fat in their diet on their own, as compared to 83% of the Proactives in the Sound Group, but only 65% of the Optimists.

Our data supports the idea that to achieve the greatest payback, wellness programs, regardless of their sponsor, should focus on Proactives in the Marginal Group. Proactives are attitudinally receptive to taking care of their health. As we have seen, in some areas Proactives in the Marginal Group show higher rates of positive health behaviors than the Marginal Group as a whole or the other Health segments within it.

REFERENCES

Health Care Financing Administration (HCFA). *National Health Expenditures Projections: 1999 to 2008.*

Pronk, Nicolaas P., Goodman, Michael J., O'Connor, Patrick J. "Relationship between modifiable health risks and short-term health Care Charges." *Journal of the American Medical Association* 15 December, 1999.

Center for the Advancement of Health (CFAH). *Health behavior change in managed care: A Status Report* January 13, 2000.

Robert Wood Johnson Foundation. *Health and health care 2010* 23 February, 2000.

Kane, Mary. "Fat Cats." *St. Paul Pioneer Press* 27 March, 2000.

Center for Disease Control (CDC). *National health interview survey* (NHIS) 1999.

American Medical Association (AMA). *Socio-economic Statistics* 1998.

Steinberg, Earl P., Gutierrez, Benjamin, Momani, Aiman, Boscarino, Joseph A., Neuman, Patricia, and Deverka, Patricia. "Beyond survey data: A claims-based analysis of drug use and spending by the elderly." *Health Affairs* March-April 2000.

Chapter 14

THE BEST HRT TARGETS

Menopause market heats up

Over the next ten years, 21 million U.S. women will enter menopause. That's four women each minute for the next decade. If each of these 21 million women go on hormone replacement therapy (HRT) for just one year, pharmaceutical companies would generate estimated sales of $5 billion by 2010. Our research shows that 34% of women 50 and older are currently on hormone replacement therapy. From 50 to 65, when taking HRT is highest, we find that 44% of U.S. women are on this regimen, while another 11% are past users.

Compliance and retention issues

Today's mature woman can expect to spend 20 to 30 years in menopause. Typically, however, she will take HRT for the relief of symptoms such as hot flashes, not for its long-term benefits. After one year 40% of women have stopped taking HRT altogether. With 35% of HRT users reducing their pre-scribed dosage, compliance is also an issue. Other patients don't take HRT every day as prescribed, using it only when their symptoms are particularly troublesome. In one study, 54% of HRT users were non-compliant after one year.

Pharmaceutical companies and physicians who believe in the efficacy of HRT for menopausal women seek to increase the numbers of women who accept HRT, as well as raise the level of compliance and retention among current users. For pharmaceutical companies, an improvement on any of these measures means an increase in sales and profits. For physicians, today's low rate of retention could mean that they will be treating more patients in the future for such diseases as osteoporosis.

An immense market

The phenomenal size of the HRT market is brought home by the number of prescriptions written for Premarin, the dominant estrogen medication. *Pharmacy Times*, drawing on data from IMF Research, reports that in 1999 Premarin was "for the eighth year in a row" the prescription drug for which most scripts were dispensed. Premarin was also eighth in terms of "new prescriptions dispensed in 1999 and 17th in revenue."

Pharmaceutical companies marketing HRT have much to gain from improved messaging and targeting of their most receptive prospects. The size of the potential market for HRT will increase dramatically over the next ten years as baby boomer women enter menopause. But unless objections to HRT are met, the percentage of women on HRT could remain stable.

DTC advertising has impact

The need to deal with competitors, as well as convince more menopausal women to accept HRT, no doubt influenced Wyeth-Ayerst Laboratories, manufacturers of Premarin, to increase its direct-to-consumer (DTC) advertising expenditures to $37 million in 1998, a jump of 230% over 1997. The promise of HRT is captured in recent advertising from Premarin which features Lauren Hutton running along a beach, fit, beautiful, and safeguarding her health. An emphasis on the benefits of Premarin to counter osteoporosis is seen in the brand's current advertising in which Hutton reveals she shrank an inch before going on HRT.

The tens of millions of dollars spent on DTC advertising for HRT have, no doubt, contributed to increased sales. From 1982 to 1992 HRT use doubled in the U.S. Our own studies on the U.S. mature market show that the percentage of women 50 to 65 on HRT—the peak years for using this therapy—has increased from 34% in 1995 to 44% in 1998.

Among women 50 and older, we find that 34% report being on HRT, 10% say they have used HRT in past, but do not use it now, and 56% have never been on HRT. Viewing menopausal women in aggregate, as a class which can be dealt with as an "average," will lead pharmaceutical companies to less than optimal DTC media and messaging strategies and physicians to less than successful treatment and patient communication. In contrast, tailoring messages and programs to the two dominant attitudinal segments among menopausal women using HRT will help both pharmaceutical companies and physicians to increase a particular woman's acceptance of HRT, her satisfaction with treatment, and her commitment to it.

Two Health segments dominate

Our studies show that among women 50 and older who are currently on HRT, almost three-quarters (73%) are in just two of our Health segments: Proactives (44%) and Faithful Patients (29%). Compared to their incidence in the population of women 50 and older, Proactives are 10% and Faithful Patients 26% more apt to be on HRT. While Optimists are 16% and Disillusioned women 22% of the 50 and older female population, they represent only 12% and 15% of those on HRT. Together these two segments represent only 27% of current HRT patients 50 and older.

Demographics not sufficient

Far more than demographics, attitudes discriminate between our two Health segments that make up the majority of mature women on HRT. At least on a few of the 35 demographic measures we regularly collect as part of our studies, we find that Faithful Patients and Proactives are very similar. In the population of women 50 and older who are on HRT, Proactives have a median age of 61, as compared to Faithful Patients with a median age of 59. A third of both Proactives and Faithful Patients are married. The median pre-tax household income for both Proactives and Faithful Patients on HRT is $35,000. But despite these similarities, there are differences.

One demographic difference between these two segments is the percentage who have a four-year college degree. One third of women 50 and older on HRT have a four-year college degree or more, something fewer Proactives have (28%), but more Faithful Patients (36%). These highly educated Faithful Patients, who know what they should do to take care of their health, are, as we have seen, the least motivated to do so.

Locating the Health segments

Our studies confirm what other research has shown: HRT use varies by census region. Among women 50 and older, 15% in the Northeast and 27% in the West take HRT. But HRT use also differs by our Health segments within each Census Region. Proactives are 48% of those 50 and older on HRT in the Northeast, but only 40% of those in the South. Optimists are just 2% of those on HRT in the Northeast Census Region, but 18% of those in the South. Given these fluctuations, the composition of segment-specific communications, whether from pharmaceutical companies, managed care organizations (MCOs), or physicians, must be adjusted for regional populations that differ in their attitudes toward health and well being.

Attitudes differ by segment

What really differentiates Proactives and Faithful Patients, the majority of the HRT market, are their vastly different attitudes toward health. These attitudes and motivations parallel each segment's health-related behaviors and their concerns about menopause. The massive attitudinal differences between these two segments as HRT patients has implications for pharmaceutical companies selling HRT, the MCOs that insure them, and the physicians who treat them.

As described in detail in Chapter 12, Proactives, unlike Faithful Patients, are singular in their commitment to good health and motivated to eat healthful foods, exercise, and stay informed about health-care issues. We have also noted that Faithful Patients are well aware of the healthful habits they should practice, but they avoid taking action. Those in this segment believe that if they become ill, their doctor and the prescription drugs he or she dispenses will affect a cure.

Behaviors correlate with attitudes

The attitudes that define our Proactives and Faithful Patients segments parallel their health-related behaviors. More Proactives and fewer Faithful Patients on HRT exercise and eat a healthful diet. Compared to all women 40 to 55 on HRT, 69% fewer Faithful Patients report that they exercise at an aerobic level four times a week, something done by 15% more Proactives. Whether it's aerobic walking or using exercise equipment, three times as many Proactives on HRT as Faithful Patients perform such activities three times a week or more. In fact, only nine percent of Faithful Patients on HRT believe they are getting enough exercise to maintain good health.

It's not surprising that 29% of Faithful Patients 40 to 55 on HRT are obese compared to 20% of all women in this age group. While 36% of women 50 and older take three or more prescription drugs daily, 44% of Faithful Patients on HRT do so, compared to only 37% of Proactives who are HRT users in this age group. While Faithful Patients find it difficult to reject unhealthful behaviors, they realize the toll being extracted on their health. Among women 50 and older, 41% consider their health to be excellent or very good, but only 26% of Faithful Patients on HRT hold this view. In sharp contrast, 63% of

Proactives on HRT rate their health as excellent or very good, a 142% increase as compared to Faithful Patients.

Drilling down the attitudes

We wanted to further refine and enrich our understanding of the attitudinal differences that distinguish Proactives and Faithful Patients who take HRT from those in these segments who do not. To do this we created a Super Segment by over-laying three of our other attitudinal segmentation strategies, Lifestyle, Health Information, and Health Compliance, on Proactives and Faithful Patients in both groups, those who take HRT and those who don't.

Attitudinal differences regarding aging differentiate those Proactives and Faithful Patients now taking HRT from those in these segments who have never done so. Those currently on HRT are disproportionately in our Financial Positive segment, one of our Lifestyle segments. Financial Positives have a very realistic view about the effects of aging. When they look in the mirror, they see every wrinkle. They don't think that they look as young as they did 30 years ago, and they recognize the implications of living in a youth-oriented culture.

Of all the Lifestyle segments, Financial Positives are the most interested in plastic surgery. In terms of behaviors, significantly more Financial Positive females use facial creams of all types. For companies such as Estée Lauder and Lancôme selling treatment products, Financial Positive females are overwhelmingly the segment to target. In contrast, those Proactives and Faithful Patients who have never taken HRT are more apt to be Threatened Actives, a Lifestyle segment that accepts aging and is satisfied with its current appearance.

Proactives make lifestyle changes

Women in our Proactive segment who take HRT are also far more apt to be Informed Avoiders, a Health Compliance segment extremely dedicated to gathering health-related information and making lifestyle changes before taking a prescription drug. While Proactives are the dominant segment in the HRT market, we've previously noted that compared to their incidence in the population of women 50 and older, proportionately fewer Proactives, but more Faithful Patients, are on HRT.

Faithful Patients on HRT are disproportionately Resentful Compliers. Those in this Health Compliance segment have a tendency to be compliant, while, at the same time, resenting the fact that they are taking a medication. Resentful Compliers, described in Chapter 17, don't believe they have a disease or condition unless they can see or feel the symptoms.

Our Disillusioned and Optimists Health segments are concentrated in the group of those who have never taken HRT. To further understand these Disillusioned and Optimists, we overlaid our Health Information segments. We found, for example, that Disillusioned who have never been on HRT are disproportionately Confused Compliants. Considering themselves to be sick people, Confused Compliants are motivated to practice healthful behaviors. Confused about what to do regarding major diseases, those in this segment rely on their doctors.

One third of Optimist women who have never been on HRT are also Self-directed Positives, one of our Health Information segments. Because of their inclusion in this segment, these Optimists would act to retain all control for health-related decisions, while having little or no real knowledge of their options. This Super Segment of Optimists who are also Self-directed Positives are not making informed health-care choices.

Two out of three Proactives who have been on HRT, but are no longer on it, are also Trusting Believers, a Health Compliance segment. Those in this segment are more apt to rely very heavily on their physician for direction. They would tend to go along with what are essentially their physician's decisions regarding their health care. In addition, a second group of Proactives who are no longer on HRT are also over represented in our Fearful Listeners segment, a Health Information segment. Those in this segment are anxious patients. If something happened while they were taking HRT that frightened them or if they heard negative things about HRT, this Super Segment of Proactives who are also Fearful Listeners would find alternatives, including nontraditional remedies.

Attitudes affect reaction to menopause

All women will go through menopause, whether surgically or naturally induced, and the vast majority of these women are candidates for HRT. At the present time, our studies show that HRT use declines with age. In their 50s, 44% of women take HRT, a percentage that decreases to 34% among women in their 60s. The level of HRT usage further declines to 28% of women in their 70s, and, by the time they reach their 80s, only 13% of them are on HRT. Why do some women go on HRT, while others avoid it? And why do those who do take it stop?

Going on HRT

Hot flashes, night sweats, and the cessation of menstruation lead most women to recognize that they are peri-menopausal, if not menopausal. The mature woman's awareness of her choices in dealing with menopause comes from the information she searches out or receives. Pharmaceutical companies, MCOs, and physicians all serve as conduits for this information, shaping both its content and its delivery.

In our studies we ask our respondents about 20 sources of health-related information they may have used in the last 12 months. For women 50 and older, a doctor or nurse is by far the main source of health-related information (55%). After these medical professionals, more women 50 and older on HRT had sought information from health-related articles in newspapers, articles in general-interest magazines, articles in health-specific magazines, and relatives and friends, in that order. Reliance on a doctor or nurse for health-related information is 25% higher among Faithful Patients in this group, the highest of all the Health segments.

Information sources differ by segment

Each Health segment prefers specific sources of health-related information. Being able to target relevant messages to receptive Proactives and Faithful Patients in their preferred media is critical to DTC pharmaceutical advertisers. For example, while 40% of women 50 and older have gotten health-related information from articles in health-specific magazines in the last 12 months, many more Proactives on HRT (52%) have done so. An article in a general-interest magazine on a health topic was used by 36% of women 50 and older, but 48% of Proactives and 40% of Financial Positives on HRT.

A newspaper piece on health was relied on as a source of information by 44% of women 50 and older in the past 12 months, by 53% of Proactives, but by only 46% of Faithful Patients on HRT. Because Faithful Patients are more difficult to reach using mass media as compared to Proactives, it is important that their physician take an active role in providing them with information. Faithful Patient attitudes and behaviors underscore this need.

Each health-specific magazine attracts women in our Health segments in greater or fewer numbers. Magazines provide profiles of their readership in demographic averages, but what is equally—if not more—important is knowing their readers' specific psychographic segments. *Health* not only reaches women 50 and older who have never used HRT (13%), but it also counts 17% of Proactives in this group. While *Prevention* is subscribed to or regularly purchased by 14% of those who have never taken HRT, it attracts 23% of Faithful Patients, but far fewer Proactives (9%). In contrast, *Cooking Light* counts 8% of all 50 and older women as subscribers or regular purchasers, but 20% of Proactives on HRT.

More never users use Internet

The Internet is touted in the media as a primary source of health-related information, yet our studies show that only 17% of younger mature women 40 to 55 have used it in the past 12 months for this purpose. Nineteen percent of those who have never used HRT, but only 12% of those currently on HRT, use the Internet as a source of health information. The above average reliance on the Internet by those who have never used HRT can be explained by a number of factors, both attitudinal and demographic.

Importance of DTC advertising

In 2000 the pharmaceutical industry spent $2.27 billion on DTC advertising for hormone replacement therapy and a myriad of other prescription drugs. According to our studies, 42% of women 50 and older say they ignore DTC advertising, while the remainder of this population pays attention to it. Such advertising has served, for example, to make some women (13%) aware of a disease they didn't know existed.

More Faithful Patients, whether or not they have ever used HRT, take in DTC advertising for health information as compared to Proactives. For example, among never users of HRT, 66% of Faithful Patients, as compared to 51% of Proactives, pay attention to DTC advertising. Given the attitudes of Faithful Patients toward counting on prescription drugs to make them well, it is not surprising that more of them tune into DTC advertising.

Concerns regarding menopause

Whatever a menopausal woman's Health segment, she will only absorb and use health-related messages relevant to her. Messages must relate to a woman's own psychographic views of health, disease, and wellness, and her concerns regarding menopause.

How a woman reacts to going into menopause is based on her perception of the changes occurring in her body. While half the women 40 to 55, a population that includes both per-imenopausal and menopausal women, report they have menopausal symptoms, 22% fewer of those who have never used HRT report such symptoms. Among those who have never used HRT in this age group, one in five reports having menopausal symptoms but doing nothing about them, a rate which is even higher among Faithful Patients.

HRT motivations differ

We investigated ten concerns about menopause and found that among women 40 to 55 one in three is concerned about breast cancer as a result of menopause, but almost half (47%) are worried about heart disease. The primary concern that surfaces in our studies among the total population of women in this age group is osteoporosis (58%). DTC advertising for HRT typically stresses its protective effects on bones, a strategy which entails long-term use and would increase retention.

Mature women clearly have gotten the message about osteoporosis, but are they sufficiently motivated to go on HRT and stay on it for several years in order to protect their bones? Are concerns other than the silent and initially symptomless osteoporosis better motivators?

While osteoporosis is the top concern for all groups, other major worries also surface among other populations. Among women 40 to 55 on HRT osteoporosis is the main concern, followed by menopause bringing a higher risk of heart disease and changes in mood and behavior. Beyond preserving their bones, women who were never on HRT are most perturbed about changes in mood and behavior and hot flashes. More past users of HRT are also worried about hot flashes and dry skin and wrinkles.

Aging concerns more Faithful Patients

Within these groups differences exist between Proactives and Faithful Patients. When compared to all women 40 to 55, more Faithful Patients on HRT than Proactives have concerns about menopause. And these concerns cover both aging and disease. For example, dry skin and wrinkles are a greater worry to 29% more Faithful Patients and 2% fewer Proactives as compared to all women 40 to 55. Changes in body shape disturb 23% more Faithful Patients, but 3% fewer Proactives.

Seven percent more Faithful Patients and 14% fewer Proactives are concerned about osteoporosis as compared to women 40 to 55. While 24% more Faithful Patients are anxious about breast cancer, it worries 17% fewer Proactives. Compared to the female 40 to 55 population as a whole, 36% more Faithful Patients on HRT, but only 29% of Proactives are concerned about heart disease as a result of menopause. The Proactives' lower rates of concern on these conditions may be linked to the fact that far more of them exercise, as compared to Faithful Patients, and they also eat more healthful diets.

In contrast, 46% more Proactives 50 and older on HRT, but 39% fewer Faithful Patients express concern about menopause linked to a higher risk for Alzheimer's disease. These types of differences between the primary two Health segments using HRT dramatize the uselessness of reporting average rates of concern across an entire population. Such averaging fails to account for very real attitudinal differences and does not facilitate targeted communication focused on them. The result: irrelevant messages are too often delivered to non-receptive patients.

Trying HRT

Studies have concluded that almost half of menopausal women have had a prescription for HRT written for them, whether they filled it or not. Our own studies show that among U.S. women 50 and older, 44% have been given a prescription for HRT that they have filled and tried. Of the 44% who have tried HRT, 34% of those in this age group continue to use it, while 10% have stopped altogether.

Staying with the regimen

As we have previously noted, the percentage of mature women staying on HRT through their 60s and 70s decreases with each decade so that by their 80s slightly more than one woman in ten is still on HRT. Whether baby boomer women now in their 40s and 50s will choose to stay on HRT longer than their aunts and mothers is an open question. Will more of them see HRT as a long-term strategy to ward off osteo-porosis long after their hot flashes are gone? How will these current users react to studies on HRT suggesting increased rates of cancer after long-term use? Will baby boomers turn to other options?

Our decade-long studies on the health of boomers and their elders show that the percentage of women 40 to 49 and 50 to 59 in each of our Health segments has remained stable in size over the years. Even as baby boomers have crossed over into their 50s, the percentages of women in the Proactive and Faithful Patient segments have not increased. Given the con-tinued concentration over the past ten years of HRT users in these two Health segments, we see no reason to believe that baby boomer women will embrace HRT at higher rates than their older sisters.

Turning to natural remedies

Mature women, and particularly Proactives who are past users of HRT, may turn in increasing numbers to natural remedies to deal with menopause. Twice as many past users of HRT 40 to 55 tell us that they use a natural remedy, such as herbs, vitamins, or calcium, in dealing with menopausal symptoms as compared to never users and current users. In particular, one in three Proactives, regardless of their past or present use of HRT, uses natural remedies in dealing with menopause.

Among the total population of females 40 to 55, 22% use herbal remedies several times a month or more for diseases or conditions not limited to menopausal symptoms. Given their incidence in the population of females 40 to 55, Faithful Patients and Disillusioned are only average in their use of herbal remedies at this level of frequency. Optimists are under consumers, while Proactives who are 30% of this population are 34% of those using herbal remedies at this level.

Improving total health

Pharmaceutical companies and MCOs can do much to reinforce the healthful activities of Proactives, while helping physicians motivate Faithful Patients to take better care of themselves.

Besides DTC advertising and custom-published magazines, manufacturers of HRT drugs can sponsor exercise-related events and develop exercise modules for physicians treating menopausal women. In targeting Faithful Patients, pharmaceutical companies can develop nutritional counseling programs which physicians can administer.

In treating menopausal women in the two dominant attitudinal segments, physicians can make choices regarding the services they offer and how they configure their practice. Clinicians should also modify what and how they convey information to these two very different types of patients. For example, the Faithful Patient is a better candidate for a practice which diagnoses and treats all aspects of the menopausal woman's health in an integrated fashion. Such a practice will be better equipped to motivate Faithful Patients who require instruction, support, direction, and reinforcement from their physician before they will change behavior.

In contrast, the Proactive patient—who is already committed to wellness, exercises, watches her diet, and keeps informed on health-care issues—is a more suitable candidate for a practice offering a less comprehensive and structured program. In dealing with the Proactive patient, clinicians will have to provide less intensive guidance and monitoring.

Physicians working with the growing number of menopausal women can structure more successful programs, services, and communication by targeting specific attitudinal segments. What each type of menopausal patient needs and wants is submerged and lost in a practice structure focused on the so-called, but non-existent, "average patient."

REFERENCES

Carroll, Linda. "Many Menopausal Women Do Not Take HRT Consistently." *Medical Tribune* August 1996.

Faulkner, Dorothy L., Young, Christopher, Hutchins, David, and McCollam, Jill Schwed. "Patient noncompliance with hormone replacement therapy: A nationwide estimate using a large prescription claims database." *Menopause: The Journal of The North American Menopause Society* 4 (1998).

"Leading National Advertisers." *Advertising Age* 27 September, 1999.

Wysowski, D.K., Golden, L., Burke, L. "Use of menopausal estrogens and medroxyprogesterone in the United States, 1982 – 1992." *Obstetrics Gynecology* 85 (1995).

Competitive Media Reporting (CMR) news release. "Ad spending up by 13.3%; Fourth quarter growth lags at 6.1%," March 20, 2001.

Brett, K.M., Madams, J.H. "Differences in use of postmenopausal hormone replacement therapy in black and white women." *Menopause: The Journal of the North American Menopause Society* 2 (1997).

Keating, N.L., Cleary, P.D., Possi, A.S., Zaslavsky, A.M., Ayanian, J. Z. "Use of hormone replacement therapy by postmenopausal women in the United States." *Annals of Internal Medicine* 130 (1999).

Chapter 15

The Health Information Segments

UNINVOLVED FATALISTS

Those in this segment have a fatalistic view of their health: they feel there is little they can do to improve or preserve it. Perhaps because of this viewpoint, Uninvolved Fatalists say they pay little attention to health information. They have a short-term perspective and have little concern for their health in the future. Although confused over health information and lacking confidence in making health-related decisions, Uninvolved Fatalists still view themselves as in charge of their health.

Fatalists to the core

As their name implies, Uninvolved Fatalists are fatalistic about their health. This pervasive fatalism affects every aspect of how they deal with their health, including whether or not they pay attention to health information. In their view, they will get sick no matter what they do. Uninvolved Fatalists believe there is nothing they can do to avoid diseases such as cancer.

Short-term perspective

Linked to the Uninvolved Fatalists' doomed view of their health is a short-term perspective. They focus on living life to the fullest now and not on the consequences of their actions. Making changes now so that they can be healthy in the years ahead is simply not a concern of theirs. They aren't thinking about living a long life.

Cost a factor

The cost of medical services also restrains Uninvolved Fatalists from getting the treatments and care they need. Whether because of a lack of commitment to better health or insufficient resources, only Uninvolved Fatalists do not go in for regular check-ups from their doctor.

Vanity doesn't motivate

Unlike the other Health Information segments, Uninvolved Fatalists are not invested in their appearance. They aren't concerned about looking as young as possible and don't even care about looking good. Information about feeling and looking good is of no interest to those in this segment.

No interest in health information

With fatalistic and short-term perspectives about their health, Uninvolved Fatalists tell us they aren't interested in knowing about health or how to stay healthy. They are certainly not going out of their way to collect information about how to stay in good health. Even while being bombarded with health information, they don't pay attention to it.

The form or even source of health information won't change their lack of interest. Uninvolved Fatalists are oblivious to health information from the government. Health information on a television or radio show doesn't get their attention either. Even an authority such as Dr. C. Everett Koop, a former surgeon general, would not cut through the Uninvolved Fatalists' lack of interest in health information. And

HEALTH INFORMATION SEGMENTS: PERCENT OF TOTAL AND AGE GROUPS

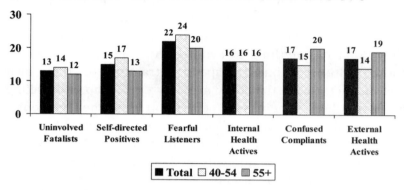

Figure 7: *At a statistically significant level, higher percentages of External Health Actives and Confused Compliants exist among those 55 and older as compared to those 40 to 54. At the same time, a lower percentage of Self-directed Positives exists in the older population as compared to the younger.*

health messages from the experts won't motivate them to change any destructive behaviors. Uninvolved Fatalists know that their friends don't see them as knowledgeable about health care.

If they do read something about health and disease prevention, Uninvolved Fatalists are skeptical of it. It's only when they hear health information from many different sources that they may begin to believe it. And even then they are confused about what they should believe, particularly on what they should do to avoid a major disease.

Uninformed and confused, Uninvolved Fatalists see themselves as tentative in making choices about their health. When faced with making an important health decision, Uninvolved Fatalists are least apt to think through their alternatives and decide on a solution that makes the most sense to them. Instead, those in this segment would go by gut instinct in making major health-care choices.

Not making changes

Uninvolved Fatalists are procrastinators about doing things to improve their health. Even when they decide to do something about their health, they don't follow-through. They feel they don't do anything to avoid getting sick or to improve their health. Too busy to spend extra time on their own health, they reveal that they are very caught up with taking care of others. Their own perception that they currently enjoy good health could also encourage Uninvolved Fatalists to do nothing to benefit their health in the future.

Fatalistic, confused, and with no long-term perspectives on their health, Uninvolved Fatalists won't bother trying a new health idea. While Uninvolved Fatalists avoid doing things, such as exercise, that might improve their health, they continue other activities, such as eating high-fat foods, that they know might damage their health. Even reducing the stress in their lives isn't something they are willing to do.

Only a very strong argument would make an Uninvolved Fatalist even consider making health-related changes. Perhaps some unfortunate experience would serve as a wake-up call because Uninvolved Fatalists say they will only change after life teaches them a hard and nasty lesson. Yet this scenario seems doubtful: after an illness Uninvolved Fatalists tell us they try to forget everything about it.

They run the show

Another impediment to the Uninvolved Fatalists improving their health is that they believe they are in charge of their own health care. At the same time, those in this segment don't think they will know what to do to take care of their health-care problems. Uninvolved Fatalists admit that they are non-compliant and don't follow their doctor's instructions. While they take a passive position and don't argue with their doctor, they don't consider that he or she is always right.

For an Uninvolved Fatalist, the best person to guide them regarding their health is themselves. When a doctor tells them they must quit smoking, a nurse advises them to loose weight, or they get any other advice that suggests they change what they are doing, they resent it.

SELF-DIRECTED POSITIVES

Those in this segment believe they are very smart people blessed with exceptionally good health. Because they have only a few vices, Self-directed Positives anticipate enjoying good health in the years ahead. Perhaps because of an optimistic view of their health, Self-directed Positives have little interest in health information. Those in this segment believe they are in charge of their own health care. Although they don't seek out health-care information, Self-directed Positives are supremely confident they will know what to do when faced with a health-care decision.

They are in charge

Self-directed Positives very strongly believe that they are the best persons to decide how to live a healthy life. Their health, they feel, is in their hands. They don't seek the counsel of friends and family before making a health-related decision. Resentment wells up in Self-directed Positives when someone tells them what they should do to take care of their health.

Convinced that they are very bright, Self-directed Positives see themselves as being able to handle any health-related problem. Besides this inner confidence, Self-directed Positives also believe they have the financial resources to handle any health situation. When they have to make a decision regarding their health, Self-directed Positives believe they act in a very confident manner. After a decision has been made, those in this segment don't procrastinate, but instead follow-through. Part of their motivation in doing so is that Self-directed Positives feel they don't have the time to get sick.

Luckily for them, those in this segment think they never get sick and view their bodies as being in very good shape. They are, in fact, so healthy that they doubt that they will ever get cancer. The good health Self-directed Positives enjoy now, will, they think, last for a long time. After all, they tell us, they have only a few vices. But even if their lives are cut short, Self-directed Positives really aren't worried about it. They are fixated on living a full life now.

Not interested in health information

Since they believe they are currently in such good health, it isn't surprising that Self-directed Positives ignore health information, whatever its source or format. A thread of skepticism about health information also winds through the attitudes of Self-directed Positives. But whether presented in the mass media or a government pamphlet, Self-directed Positives stress that they don't pay attention to health-related insights. Even if health information is presented on a favorite radio or television show, Self-directed Positives don't register interest in it. This lack of interest isn't related to a feeling of confusion regarding health information. Self-directed Positives say they understand what they hear about cancer and don't feel confused about how to avoid major diseases.

FEARFUL LISTENERS

Fearful Listeners constantly absorb health-related information from a wide variety of sources. They may be motivated to do this because they are pessimistic about their current state of health and believe they are frequently sick. Fearful Listeners want to live a long life, but doubt that they will achieve this goal. They see themselves as procrastinators when it comes to making health-related changes. Feeling in charge of their own health care, Fearful Listeners waffle on complying exactly with their doctor's instructions, and they resent those who advise them to change their habits.

Health information sponges

Fearful Listeners want to know a great deal about health. They are always taking in health-related information they receive from many sources. Whether this health information is from friends and relatives or found in a book or government pamphlet, Fearful Listeners consider all of these sources acceptable. If health information appears on the news or on their favorite radio or television shows, Fearful Listeners pay close attention to it.

Poor health an obstacle

While Fearful Listeners want to live a long life, they aren't sure that they will achieve this goal. They are certain that their health will fail and they will suffer some serious illness in the future. They are especially terrified of getting cancer. Fearful Listeners are pessimistic about the current state of their health, and perhaps their almost frantic efforts to gather health-related information stem from this. They don't consider their bodies to be in very good shape and think of themselves as being sick frequently.

Not making changes

Constantly amassing information about health and, at the same time, pessimistic about the possibility of long-term survival, Fearful Listeners admit that they do not always act to improve or maintain their health. Considering the fact that they believe their health is poor and their bodies are breaking down, it's not surprising that Fearful Listeners say they have little interest in knowing what they must do to *stay* in good health. Regardless of all the information on health that they gather, Fearful Listeners tell us they aren't open to trying new health ideas.

Fearful Listeners admit they are procrastinators, putting off changes that could improve their health. Even when they decide to do something to better their health, Fearful Listeners confess they don't follow-through. If something could damage their health, perhaps eating a massive dish of Ben & Jerry's high-fat ice cream, those in this segment say they would do it anyway.

Fearful Listeners admit they don't do anything special to avoid getting sick, not even reducing stress. They aren't even committed to regular medical check-ups. The health information they accumulate may prompt Fearful Listeners to avoid following their doctor's instructions exactly. They resent someone telling them to change what they are doing; after all, they believe they are in charge of their own health.

Not confident

Although they feel they should direct their own health care, Fearful Listeners don't do so with confidence. All the mountains of health-related information Fearful Listeners collect doesn't turn them into secure health consumers able to handle any problem that might develop.

INTERNAL HEALTH ACTIVES

Those in this segment want to live a long, healthy life. They are convinced that what they do now will help them to attain their goal. Internal Health Actives are willing to sacrifice present pleasures in order to preserve their health for a long time. Interested in health-related information from a variety of sources, they say they act on this information in their everyday lives. Those in this segment are confident about how they handle health-care choices and are not at all confused about making them.

Long-term perspective

Internal Health Actives approach health from a long-term perspective. Rather than living life fully at the present time, they want to live a long life. Those in this segment believe that if they pay attention to health information today, they will be healthy in their old age. In addition, Internal Health Actives are convinced that making changes in their lives now will result in an old age blessed with good health.

Self-directed

Internal Health Actives are convinced their long-term goal will be realized only if they themselves make it happen through everyday choices. Those in this segment believe strongly that they themselves are responsible for their own health; they aren't waiting for miracles. Internal Health Actives have a regular schedule of medical check-ups with their doctor. They aren't willing to sacrifice their own health for that of others. Internal Health Actives aren't fatalists about their health; they don't, for example, believe that getting cancer is inevitable.

Interested in health information

Having accepted responsibility for their health, Internal Health Actives listen closely to a wide variety of sources for information and direction. Rather than resent someone who tells them how they can feel better, they listen. Internal Health Actives don't mind it when someone advises them to change what they are doing.

Information that helps the Internal Health Actives attain their goals of good health and a long life is of interest to them, whether presented on a news program on television or radio, in a booklet from the government, or revealed by a local leader. Those in this segment are not skeptical about information on health and disease prevention and tend to believe most of what they read without having to see it in a variety of sources.

Internal Health Actives want information about what actions they can take to achieve better health. More than the other segments, they focus on learning about what they must do to be healthy. They both ferret out a great deal of information about how to stay in good health and also put it to use.

Not confused

Not confused about the health information they hear and read, Internal Health Actives make health decisions in a very confident manner. They know what to believe, and they understand what they have to do to avoid major diseases. A testimonial to the Internal Health Actives' scope and depth of knowledge about health is that their friends view them as experts in this area.

Making changes

Internal Health Actives act, not procrastinate, on the health information they obtain. Life doesn't have to punish those in this segment in order for them to change a destructive behavior, nor are strong arguments needed to convince them that they must make a change to improve their health.

The enthusiasm Internal Health Actives have for making changes is seen in their willingness to try new health ideas. Internal Health Actives aren't too busy to spend extra time on their health; they make time to improve their health. Conversely, Internal Health Actives say they would stop doing things they enjoy if they aren't healthy. They have reduced stress in their lives. Not surprisingly, they consider their bodies to be in really great shape.

CONFUSED COMPLIANTS

Those in this segment are confused about what they should do to avoid major diseases. They don't seek out health-care information so that they can become knowledgeable consumers. Instead, they rely on their doctor's insights and direction. Confused Compliants don't procrastinate when it comes to taking care of themselves. They believe that such efforts will have a beneficial effect on their health. Confused Compliants would like to live a long life, but do not view their present health as that good.

Not self-directed

Compared to the other Health Information segments, Confused Compliants are least apt to see themselves as very smart. They don't believe they can handle any health problem they may face. Confused Compliants are confused about health care and what they should do to avoid major diseases, especially cancer. Friends of the Confused Compliants do not regard them as informed about health-care matters.

Given their insecurities, it is understandable that Confused Compliants are the least apt to accept the idea that they are primarily responsible for making health-care decisions. They strongly deny that they are the best person to decide how they can live a healthy life. While admitting their confusion regarding health care, Confused Compliants do not actively seek out information on health and admit they are only mild-ly interested in becoming informed. Even if their favorite radio or television show presents health-related information, Confused Compliants ignore it. Whatever health information they are exposed to, those in this segment view it with a skep-tical eye.

Since they refuse to accept personal responsibility for their health, to whom or to what do those in this segment turn? When they or their loved ones are in poor health, one option for Confused Complaints is to turn to religion. Confused Compliants also shift responsibility to their doctor. Those in this segment tell us they do exactly as their doctor instructs, although they feel that he or she isn't always right. But what-ever doubts Confused Compliants have about their doctor, they don't confront him or her on them.

Although the Confused Compliants don't know what to believe about health care, they feel they don't make health-related changes based on instinct. Rather, facts from experts, such as their doctor, motivate this segment to change. And because they rely on expert opinion, not their own, Confused Compliants feel confident when taking action on health-care matters.

Dedicated to improving health

Confused Compliants believe they are making special efforts to avoid getting sick. Concerned about living a long life, they are willing to give up things they know aren't healthful in order to achieve this end. One motivation for doing so is their perception of themselves as being frequently sick. They don't believe their bodies are in good shape. Those in this segment are also motivated to take care of themselves because they have to be able to take care of their family.

Confused Compliants don't procrastinate when it comes to matters about their health. When they decide to do something to improve their physical well-being, they think they do a good job following through on it. Those in this segment say they have regular medical checkups and have reduced the stress levels in their lives. Confused Compliants believe that such actions will have beneficial effects, and, therefore, they feel somewhat optimistic about their health.

EXTERNAL HEALTH ACTIVES

Those in this segment are motivated by external forces to absorb health-related information and take care of their health. A prime reason External Health Actives want to stay healthy is so that they can take care of their families. Weighted with this responsibility, they are concerned with living long, healthy lives. External Health Actives collect an arsenal of health information from a variety of media sources and also from authorities, such as their doctor. Confident health-care consumers, External Health Actives believe their actions will enable them to stay healthy. If these efforts fail, those in this segment turn to religion, another external force, when they are ill.

External motivation

External Health Actives are motivated by external forces to take care of themselves. Because they feel they have to take care of their family, External Health Actives say they make a special effort to stay in good health. Perhaps because of this concern, External Health Actives are worried about living a long life and will give up present pleasures to achieve it. They are willing to listen when someone tells them about actions they should take now in order to enjoy a healthy old age.

Another external force in the care that External Health Actives take of themselves is religion, something they turn to when they or their loved ones are ill. External Health Actives also take care of themselves to preserve their outward appearance: they desire to look young. They are receptive to information about looking good, something that's a goal of theirs.

Interested in health information

Because External Health Actives feel they have to stay healthy, they pay attention to health information. While External Health Actives are open to a variety of sources of information on health, authoritative ones are especially important. A book or government brochure will get their interest. In their view, health information from a local leader, perhaps a local physician or state epidemiologist, can be relied on. External Health Actives also pay attention to health information presented on radio or television programs, whether it is on the news or on one of their own favorite shows. External Health Actives aren't confused by health information; they are confident that they know what to believe.

While they seek to become informed health-care consumers, those in this segment also accept direction from others. They don't consider themselves to be the highest authority in terms of figuring out the best way to live a healthy life.

Faced with a health-care problem, External Health Actives use information to make decisions and don't rely solely on their feelings or intuition. Those in this segment think through all of their options and come up with the one that makes the most sense. The solutions they consider may come from information they themselves have gathered or instructions from their doctor.

Pathways to health

Neither strong arguments nor adversity are needed to convince External Health Actives to improve their health. Once they know what they have to do, they take immediate action. They don't feel they are too busy to take extra time to pre-serve or improve their well-being. Besides having regular medical check-ups, External Health Actives say they have given up unhealthy behaviors, even if they enjoyed them.

While External Health Actives are optimistic about their health, they also acknowledge the possibility that they will get a disease. They believe, however, that the special efforts they have made, such as reducing the stress in their lives, will bring positive results. For example, External Health Actives aren't fatalistic about getting cancer.

Chapter 16

TARGETING DIRECT-TO-CONSUMER (DTC) ADVERTISING

Selling pharmaceutical drugs

Prozac, Prilosec, Zocor, Zoloft, Zyrtec, Zyban, Crixivan and Xenical. As if they were part of a ritualistic incantation, the anti-mnemonic names of pharmaceutical drugs bombard consumers in ever-increasing numbers. In the space of ten years, the number of direct-to-consumer (DTC) advertising campaigns for pharmaceutical drugs has soared. The increase from one to the over 60 DTC campaigns launched in 2000 has been largely fueled by changes in Food and Drug Administration (FDA) regulations.

But DTC advertising is just one influence on the tortuous sale of a pharmaceutical drug, one impacted by the FDA, the nature of the condition or disease, a physician, perhaps a health maintenance organization (HMO), the patient's pharmacist and family, and, of course, the motivations and perceptions of the potential patient him- or herself.

This chapter explores how various aspects of a DTC advertising campaign can be aligned and integrated by targeting

SDG's Health Information segments. While the Health Information segmentation strategy addresses scores of issues surrounding one subject, it does not explore a specific disease or condition. By overlaying a disease-specific psychographic segmentation strategy onto the Health Information segments' motivations, an even deeper understanding would be obtained. We would then know what motivates specific attitudinal segments of patients with a disease or condition to obtain and use health information.

Millions spent on DTC

The reason for targeting a consumer marketing campaign to a qualified psychographic segment rests on escalating expenditures for DTC advertising. According to Scott-Levin, a marketing research firm specializing in the pharmaceutical industry, just $20 million was spent on DTC advertising in 1989. By 1996 spending had increased to $600 million, an average annual growth rate of 62%. In 1997 DTC spending reached the one billion dollar mark. By 2000, expenditures on DTC were $2.27 billion, an increase of 42% over the previous year. If this rate of growth is maintained over the next five years, 2005 would see $13 billion spent on DTC. Based on this projection, and factoring in inflation, it is possible that in 2005 consumers will see and hear five times as many DTC ads as they do today.

While soaring DTC advertising expenditures have paralleled massive increases in prescription drug spending, many questions remain regarding its importance in the promotional mix. How important is DTC advertising among the countervailing influences that press in upon a patient? What is the return-on-investment (ROI) on the billions of dollars pharmaceutical companies have spent on DTC ? As the advertising space becomes increasingly crowded with proliferating DTC campaigns, what can pharmaceutical companies do to make such campaigns more efficient and effective?

Skeptical consumers

These campaigns are being aimed at consumers increasingly burned out on advertising, including the DTC variety. The majority of consumers (64%) in a recent Roper Starch study found all types of "advertising to be a 'nuisance' that 'clutters up' TV," a percentage "up 5 points since 1998." One can only imagine the negative reaction to five times as many DTC advertisements. At the same time, the number of consumers who feel "advertising 'provides useful information' " has "declined 5 points since 1998, to 74 percent...."

Besides consumer burn out on DTC advertising, the effectiveness of such mass media advertising is also being questioned. A study completed by Market Measures Inc. in 1997 found that "90 percent of all direct-to-consumer (DTC) advertising impressions produce no significant results at all .... Consumers are beginning to regard information offered in DTC advertisements with increased skepticism." Two studies completed by CME Health, the health care unit of advertising agency Campbell Mithun Esty (CME), suggest a reason for the lack of effectiveness of DTC advertising. According to CME, "many DTC ads fail ... to forge an emotional link with the consumer target." The agency calls for marketers to "demonstrate they empathize with both the psychological and physical effects of the medical problem."

Targeting attitudinal segments

But demonstrating awareness of the "psychological and physical effects" of a disease or condition in DTC advertising isn't sufficient. The effects of disease are perceived differently by each psychographic or attitudinal segment. Images and messages relevant to a targeted psychographic segment should be crafted and placed in appropriate media. This approach can act to reverse the current downward spiral in mass-media advertising effectiveness. Writing in *American Demographics*, Jeff Howe notes that "Commercials that are relevant to the viewers' psychographic profile and interests, retain an audience, and probably a more receptive one at that."

Certainly the explosive growth in DTC advertising is itself a vote of confidence for communicating with and marketing to consumers in this way. But is DTC advertising cost-effective? Why do some pharmaceutical companies reap greater financial benefits from their DTC dollars than do others? As a rough, imprecise measure, U.S. revenue per advertising dollar spent suggests DTC's level of efficiency. For example, in 1999 the top ten pharmaceutical advertisers generated an average return of $16.46 for every advertising dollar spent. Merck & Company, however, generated $52.89 in sales for every advertising dollar it spent as compared to Pfizer's $4.62. At the same time, Pfizer spent more than four times on advertising in 1999 as compared to Merck.

Calculating the ROI of DTC

With funding from the Association of Medical Publications (AMP), Professor Scott Neslin recently conducted a study on the ROI of four types of pharmaceutical promotions. This comprehensive study found that the overall ROI for DTC advertising was $0.19, with a range of $0.00 to $1.37, "depending on brand size/launch date."

But Neslin's ROI figures are for incremental sales, not profits. Once costs are subtracted, an expensive DTC advertising campaign could actually have a negative return, as in the case of two drugs, Glaxo Wellcome's Relenza and Hoffman–La Roche's Tamiflu. Each pharmaceutical company spent around $40 million in DTC ad campaigns for these drugs over the 1999 to 2000 flu season, according to Competitive Media Reporting. But while combined DTC advertising expenditures for Relenza and Tamiflu reached $80 million, combined sales for these drugs climbed to only $61 million.

No guarantees

But even when a DTC campaign generates sufficient sales to justify its cost, substantial expenditures do not guarantee consistent sales. In 2000 Merck invested $160.8 million in DTC advertising supporting Vioxx, its Cox-2 inhibitor for osteoarthritis, 788% more than the $18.1 million it had spent in 1999, the year it was introduced. In 2000, Vioxx was "the most heavily advertised drug on the U.S. market." According to the Scott-Levin Direct-to-Consumer Advertising Audit, the Vioxx advertisement was seen "by 21% of consumers and correctly identified by 19%." Vioxx "sold well, becoming Merck's second biggest drug after Zocor, a cholesterol medicine." By the second quarter of 2001, however, Merck announced that sales of Vioxx were lower than expected, reaching only $3 billion, rather than the hoped for $3.5 billion.

Nor does DTC advertising guarantee that a new pharmaceutical drug entry will compete successfully against a solidly entrenched competitor. In 1999 Duramed Pharmaceuticals launched Cenestin, challenging Premarin, the leader in the $2.9 billion hormone replacement market. Cenestin was backed by an $8 million campaign aimed at physicians and a similarly funded DTC print campaign targeting menopausal women. The company expected Cenestin to generate $100 million in sales over its first 15 months in the market. Instead, Cenestin reached only $3.8 million in sales in the first nine months it was sold.

Is the magic fading?

The marketing campaigns for several drugs, from Relenza, for flu, to Xenical, for weight loss, illustrate the fact that spending millions in DTC advertising efforts does not guarantee that sales goals will be reached. In reviewing lackluster sales for Xenical, *Advertising Age* suggests that "the DTC ad revolution is entering a new and more mature stage," which the magazine believes to be a "good thing." The magazine notes that the lack of " 'miracle' marketing cures" should result in "smarter, more realistic strategies for the long haul." In our view, these "smarter, more realistic strategies" would include targeting a DTC campaign to a psychographic segment. If a consumer views messages and imagery relevant to him or her, it is more likely that engagement will occur.

Besides the flood of DTC campaigns and their fading ability to produce "marketplace magic," a number of other forces are pushing pharmaceutical companies to more targeted marketing. The torrent of competing drugs, the brief time span during which a drug has patent protection, and Wall Street's expectations that every drug will be a billion-dollar blockbuster places immense pressures on pharmaceutical companies to achieve stunningly successful DTC campaigns.

A usable framework

While one-on-one marketing may someday be applied to drugs tailored to an individual's specific genetic material, focusing on prime prospects by attitudinal segment and related factors represents a way to improve DTC marketing now. Every month new pharmaceutical drugs, some of which represent entirely new classes of drugs, enter the market and are advertised directly to the consumer. Consumers in various attitudinal segments face the task of adopting or rejecting innovative products for diseases or conditions for which they may have been newly diagnosed. A framework for understanding the stages in the acceptance or rejection of a pharmaceutical drug by an attitudinal segment and the role of DTC in its adoption is provided by theories explaining the diffusion of innovations.

These theories are described by Everett M. Rogers in his *Diffusion of Innovations*, first published in 1962. Although many theories exist that attempt to describe the process whereby a technological innovation is adopted, Rogers remains prominent in this field and his work is well known. According to Rogers' theory, a technological innovation passes through specific stages on its way to achieving adoption: awareness, interest, evaluation, trial, and adoption.

The first two stages, awareness and interest, are internal and not identified through behaviors. Applied to the marketing of pharmaceutical drugs, the awareness stage provides consumers with information on the existence of a drug and its benefits and limitations. As currently used, DTC advertising functions at this level. In the second stage, interest, the consumer is engaged at some level by what he or she has heard or seen and considers the information.

It is with the third stage, evaluation, that we see one or more behaviors which demonstrate actual interest in a pharmaceutical drug. At this stage the consumer seeks further information about the pharmaceutical drug and evaluates its merits. For example, a consumer reaches the evaluation stage when he or she goes to a physician and asks for a medication. Filling the prescription for the medication he or she has been given marks the fourth phase, trial. Adoption, the fifth and final stage in Rogers' theory of the diffusion of innovation, finds the consumer continuing to take the medication and committed, for whatever reason, to doing so.

Selecting best targets

Following Rogers' theory, attitudinal segments most receptive to DTC advertising, who seek information, secure and fill a prescription, and then continue to take a drug, are clearly a pharmaceutical company's best targets. Because the diffusion process is facilitated by communication, we are using our Health Information segmentation strategy to illustrate this approach.

In our studies, a detailed 14-part question covers the five stages in the diffusion process. Overall, 52% of those 40 and older say they pay attention to DTC advertising, the first stage in the diffusion process. Their attentiveness to DTC advertising has informed them of a drug's existence and told them something about it.

Of the six Health Information segments, two, Uninvolved Fatalists (39%) and Self-directed Positives (37%), are below average in their attentiveness to DTC advertising. Internal Health Actives, attitudinally dedicated to avoiding prescription drugs, are average in paying attention to DTC ads. Under consumers of pharmaceutical drugs, Internal Health Actives are clearly not prime DTC targets. The three remaining Health Information segments, Fearful Listeners, Confused Compliants, and External Health Actives, are all above average in paying attention to DTC advertising and could be considered as potential targets for a campaign.

Interest, the second stage of the diffusion process, is shown by the consumer's own attempts to secure information about a drug. We ask respondents about six of these types of actions. For example, all of the three last segments mentioned above are average in asking a friend or relative about an advertised drug. Above average numbers of External Health Actives had asked both a doctor and a pharmacist about an advertised drug and had read materials on an advertised drug sent to them by a pharmaceutical company.

In evaluation, the third stage, the consumer requests and is given a prescription for an advertised drug by his or her physician. Filling the prescription moves the consumer to the fourth stage, trial. In our studies, 14% of the 40 and older population received a prescription for an advertised drug and never filled it. A failure to achieve trial is another reason to avoid targeting Internal Health Actives. Twice as many (29%) of those in this segment received a prescription for an advertised drug and never filled it. We believe that this action is one of many that underscores the Internal Health Actives' attitudinal bias toward avoiding prescription drugs as much as possible. The three segments we consider as prime targets, the Fearful Listeners, Confused Compliants, and External Health Actives, are all above average in having moved to trial.

Few reach adoption

From trial few consumers 40 and older reach adoption, the fifth stage. Almost two out of five (38%) of those who had filled a prescription for an advertised drug had subsequently stopped using it. While even more Fearful Listeners (50%) had stopped using an advertised drug, External Health Actives were only slightly below average (37%) in this regard. Advertised pharmaceutical drugs were able to retain far more

Confused Compliants: as compared to the 40 and older population (38%), only about half as many Confused Compliants (19%) had taken an advertised drug and then quit.

Among the 40 and older population who had gotten a prescription for an advertised drug 56% say that they had it filled and were still using it. But more External Health Actives (63%) and Confused Compliants (65%) reported doing so. In contrast, below average numbers of Fearful Listeners (51%) were still taking an advertised drug. The Fearful Listeners' low rate of retention makes sense given their attitudes. Fearful Listeners have a fatalistic outlook about their health. The several attitudes that would lead them to stop taking a drug are discussed in detail in Chapter 15.

Evaluating the segments

Besides their poor record on retention, more Fearful Listeners (11%) lack health insurance as compared to the 40 and older population (7%), thus becoming even less attractive targets.

Fearful Listeners are only average in their enrollment in a Managed Care Organization (MCO). When those in this segment have prescription drug coverage, it provides lower benefits compared to that enjoyed by both the 40 and older population and the Confused Compliants and External Health Actives. For these reasons and others, marketers of pharmaceutical drugs may decide to avoid Fearful Listeners and focus instead on the Confused Compliants and External Health Actives. Of these two Health Information segments, which should be pursued and how should they be approached?

Delving into attitudes

The decision to focus a DTC campaign on either the Confused Compliants or External Health Actives or to develop separate campaigns for each segment should be based on a complete understanding of each segment's motivations. We have already noted that once they begin taking a pharmaceu-

225

tical drug, the Confused Compliants' attitudes predispose them to continue. These attitudes are reinforced by the fact that more than a third of Confused Compliants are also Proactives (36%), one of SDG's Health segments, thus creating a Super Segment. As we've seen in previous chapters, both Proactives and Confused Compliants respect and rely on their doctors and have positive and compliant attitudes toward taking pharmaceutical drugs.

Locus of control

Another Super Segment is formed by Confused Compliants who are also Trusting Believers (44%), one of SDG's Health Compliance segments. Trusting Believers have little interest in health-related information. Their lack of enthusiasm for acquiring such information is demonstrated by the fact that fewer of them (36%) used five or more sources of health-related information over the past 12 months as compared to the 40 and older population (41%). As we will demonstrate later in this chapter, Confused Compliants, and particularly those who are also Trusting Believers, will not be easy to reach through mass media or the Internet.

In creating a strategy to target the Confused Compliants who are also Trusting Believers, marketers must also note a second important attitude at the center of the Trusting Believer mind set. Those in this last segment place the locus of control for their health care with their physician, an insight of strategic importance. This second attitude is evidenced in the Confused Compliants' behaviors. For example, we asked respondents which six things, such as sodium or fat, they had reduced in their diet on a doctor's advice. Compared to both the 40 and older population and the other Health Information segments, more Confused Compliants had reduced four of six food attributes on a physician's advice. For example, while 17% of the 40 and older population had reduced sodium in their diet on a doctor's advice, 24% of the Confused Compliants had done so.

Direct to patient

While a DTC strategy typically creates awareness through mass marketing, a direct-to-patient (DTP) campaign targets patients specifically. Rather than a DTC campaign's focus on a generally defined consumer, the target for a DTP campaign is a patient—someone identified as having a disease or condition that can be helped by the pharmaceutical drug. As a patient, the DTP target also exists within the context of a physician-patient relationship.

As we have noted, a substantial portion of Confused Compliants are also Trusting Believers, a segment transferring responsibility for their health care to their doctor. Thus in this case placing emphasis on a DTP strategy or combining it with DTC makes sense. While some DTC advertising emphasizes the idea of working with the consumer's physician as a "partner," in other cases DTC has been supplanted by a DTP strategy. Eli Lilly & Co., for example, in marketing its Evista osteoporosis drug decided that "the more mass-media approach was not going to drive the brand forward." The new campaign, combining print advertising with a direct-marketing campaign, also stresses the physician's role. This approach is well suited to the Confused Compliants segment.

Current DTP campaigns seem to do little more than shift channels of communication. DTP can be made more effective by focusing on specific psychographically defined patient segments. Ideally, patients and physicians should work together in the administration of a prescription medication. It would be highly useful to know the physician's psychographic segment and the profile of his or her practice, as well as the patient's own segment. A physician's attitudes and motivations toward psychographic patient segments and their communication needs, as well as their diseases, can repel or attract health-care consumers.

Two tendencies

In contrast to the Confused Compliants, External Health Actives are exceptional in their quest for health information.

From 20 sources of health information, 41% of those 40 and older had used five or more sources over the past 12 months. With the exception of the External Health Actives (57%), every other Health Information segment is either average or below average on this question. At the lowest end of the spectrum, very few Uninvolved Fatalists (19%) had sought health information from five or more sources.

The External Health Actives' over consumption of healthcare information is further heightened by their inclusion in Super Segments formed with certain Health and Health Compliance segments. More than half of the External Health Actives (53%) are also in the Proactive Health segment, compared to only a third of the 40 and older population (33%) as a whole. As we've noted, Proactives both rely on their physicians and seek to stay informed on health issues.

Examined by our Health Compliance segments, External Health Actives show two primary tendencies. While almost half of them are also Trusting Believers (48%), who shift control of their health to their doctors, another third of the External Health Actives (36%) are also Informed Avoiders. Informed Avoiders are voracious researchers on health-related topics, prefer lifestyle changes over pharmaceutical drugs, and are committed to retaining control over their own health care.

The fact that External Health Actives are enthusiastic users of over-the-counter (OTC) medications and herbal remedies is, no doubt, influenced by those who are also Informed Avoiders. The External Health Actives' drive for health information and their demonstrated use of multiple sources for such information, makes them far better candidates for a DTC strategy than the Confused Compliants.

Can they pay?

Besides the question of how the two target segments can be reached and motivated, marketers must also consider whether or not these segments can pay for pharmaceutical drugs. Confused Compliants and External Health Actives are either average or below average in the number of them who lack health insurance. The Confused Compliants should be singled out for their far higher participation in managed-care organizations (MCOs) (57%) as compared to those 40 and older (48%). As a result, more Confused Compliants (60%) than those 40 and older (50%) have 50% or more of their drug costs covered by insurance.

Use of prescription drugs

Because substantial numbers of our two target Health Information segments, the Confused Compliants and External Health Actives, are also Proactives and Trusting Believers, we know that a substantial portion of them are extremely positive toward pharmaceutical drugs. And the behaviors of Confused Compliants and External Health Actives parallel these positive attitudes. Among the Health Information segments, Confused Compliants and External Health Actives are the heaviest users of prescription drugs. While 25% of the 40 and older population takes three or more prescription drugs daily, 29% of both Confused Compliants and External Health Actives do so. In contrast, only 16% of Self-directed Positives, a segment we rejected as a target for pharmaceutical drugs, takes three or more pharmaceutical medications daily.

Medicine cabinet competition

Although both segments make heavy use of pharmaceutical drugs, External Health Actives distinguish themselves from Confused Compliants by their exceptionally high use of both over-the-counter (OTC) drugs and herbal remedies. In pursuing this segment, marketers face competition from a variety of medications, not just other pharmaceutical drugs. While 9% of those 40 and older use three or more OTC drugs daily, 15% of the External Health Actives do so. Given their enthusiastic acceptance of OTC drugs, External Health Actives would be ideal candidates for drugs moving from prescription to OTC status. In addition, fewer of the 40 and older population (23%) use herbal medicines, as compared to the External Health Actives (30%).

This segment's attitudes help to explain why they take so many types of medications. We've noted that External Health Actives are heavily motivated to stay well in order to help their families. Those in the Super Segment made up of the third (36%) of External Health Actives who are also Informed Avoiders also wants to control their own health care and avoid prescription medications. In using both OTC and herbal remedies, neither of which require a prescription, this Super Segment achieves all three ends.

Getting a script

The frequency of visits to a physician and diagnostic tests increases the likelihood of receiving a prescription for a pharmaceutical drug. While one third (34%) of those 40 and older has seen a physician once every three months or more, greater numbers of Confused Compliants (41%) and External Health Actives (43%) have done so. These two segments are the heaviest consumers of pharmaceutical drugs among the Health Information segments. In contrast, fewer Self-directed Positives (28%) have seen a physician at this level of frequency. A smaller number of those in this last segment (16%) take three or more prescription pharmaceutical drugs as compared to the 40 and older population (25%) or to any of the other Health Information segments.

Fewer of the 40 and older population (60%) have had a cholesterol test for high-density lipoprotein (HDL) and low-density lipoprotein (LDL) in the past three years as compared to Confused Compliants (66%) and External Health Actives (69%). These two segments are also highest of all the Health Information segments in terms of taking a prescription drug for high cholesterol.

Diseases differ by segment

Marketers may decide to target only one of the two prime segments with DTC advertising, depending on the disease.

Our data show that Confused Compliants and External Health Actives have above average rates of different diseases. These differences are not explained away by typically collected demographics. For example, Confused Compliants and External Health Actives share almost identical median ages: 59 and 57. The two segments are also very similar in their marital status. Slightly more than half of both segments are married (53% and 51%).

In marketing Prozac, a marketer might select the External Health Actives over Confused Compliants. Of the 40 and older population, 6% report taking a prescription drug for depression. This medication is taken by 10% of External Health Actives, but by only 5% of the Confused Compliants. The marketers of Vioxx, a Cox-2 inhibitor for osteoarthritis, might pursue the Confused Compliants. Of the 40 and older population, 12% takes a medication for arthritis as compared to 20% of the Confused Compliants, but only 14% of the External Health Actives.

In the case of other diseases, equal or virtually identical percentages of Confused Compliants and External Health Actives take a prescription medication. That's true for prescription medications for high cholesterol (15% each) and osteoporosis (4% and 5%). In these situations, distinct campaigns could be developed to target each segment. Following this option, media and messages will differ, as will informal sources, such as friends and family, used by each segment for health-care information.

Reaching the segments

In a shift that began in 1998, DTC advertisers have overwhelmingly moved their ads from magazines to television. As we've noted, reaching specific psychographic segments effectively entails using their preferred media. In view of the two target Health Information segments we're considering, it's important to note that both Confused Compliants (33%) and External Health Actives (37%) are close to the 40 and older population (35%) in spending 11 or more hours a week watching network television. The Health Information segment that network television draws disproportionately are Uninvolved Fatalists, 44% of whom watch 11 or more hours of network television. This segment, as we have discussed, is not one DTC advertisers should work to attract.

The situation isn't much improved when specific types of programming on network television, such as soap operas and morning shows, are considered. Among those who watch soap operas a few times a week or more, we find 20% of the 40 and older population, 22% of the Confused Compliants, but 24% of Fearful Listeners. While 38% of the 40 and older population watches morning shows a few times a week or more, fewer External Health Actives (35%), but more Fearful Listeners (42%), do so. As we've previously noted, Fearful Listeners are a less than attractive segment to target because of their low retention rates on pharmaceutical drugs.

Conversely, only average numbers of Confused Compliants (36%) and below average numbers of External Health Actives (32%) spend eleven or more hours a week watching cable television. More Fearful Listeners (39%) watch cable television 11 or more hours per week. Admittedly certain cable channels are better than others in reaching Confused Compliants or External Health Actives. A DTC campaign targeting Confused Compliants would have better success on the Lifetime channel. Of the 40 and older population, 48% view Lifetime programming a few times a week or more, but fully 53% of the Confused Compliants watch this frequently. At the same time, it must be noted that at this level Lifetime also picks up 55% of Fearful Listeners.

Magazines of interest

Given our interest in the Confused Compliants and External Health Actives, is the movement away from magazines and into television a reasonable one? The answer depends on the drug being advertised and the attitudinal segment or segments being targeted. Of those 40 and older, 84% spend one or more hours a week reading a magazine. In terms of heavy readers, which we've defined as respondents spending 11 or more hours a week reading magazines, fewer than one in ten (9%) in the 40 and older population would qualify as such. Slightly more Fearful Listeners (11%) and External Health Actives (10%) read magazines 11 or more hours per week.

Using the Magazine Publishers of America (MPA) definition of a heavy reader as someone reading five or more magazines, more External Health Actives (35%) qualify as heavy readers compared to the 40 and older population (29%). Using this definition, all the other Health Information segments are average or below average in the percentage of them who are heavy readers, with fewer Uninvolved Fatalists (22%) in that category.

Specific magazines

Addressing 60 magazine titles, we ask whether or not the respondent subscribes to the magazine or purchases it regularly. A few of these titles, such as *Better Homes and Gardens*, *TV Guide*, and *Cooking Light*, appeal to equal numbers of both Confused Compliants and External Health Actives. Others, such as *Family Circle* and *Woman's Day*, clearly are subscribed to or regularly purchased by slightly more Confused Compliants as compared to External Health Actives. On the other hand, more External Health Actives subscribe to *Prevention* (12%) as compared to Confused Compliants and the 40 and older population as a whole (9% each). But these percentages pale next to the above-average numbers of Confused Compliants (38%) and External Health Actives (35%) reached through *Reader's Digest*.

Events: making them special

As the field of DTC advertising has become increasingly crowded and competitive, some pharmaceutical advertisers have shifted DTC dollars to promotions and sponsorships. Examples of these tie ins and sponsorships are those between Claritin and Viagra and motor sports events. To achieve their full potential, such sponsorships must be geared to appeal to the targeted psychographic or attitudinal segment.

Both Confused Compliants and External Health Actives are below average in regularly attending sports events, listening to sports programming on the radio, and watching sports on television. In contrast, Self-directed Positives, more of whom ignore DTC advertising and who consume fewer drugs than any other Health Information segment, score highest in tuning into media coverage of sports and in viewing actual sporting events.

Marketers hoping to reach the Confused Compliants should consider sponsoring a show or seminar on do-it-yourself projects for the home. Confused Compliants are highly interested in this type of activity. Sponsorship of a pet show, an educational Elderhostel session, or a fine art or antiques seminar would all be of interest to above average numbers of External Health Actives.

Internet as tool

Recently pharmaceutical marketers have begun placing increasing emphasis on the Internet as a tool for reaching prospective patients, whether through a general health site or one dedicated to a specific drug. As it is currently used, this strategy creates buzz about a prescription medication, as opposed to being the primary focus of an entire DTC campaign. *Advertising Age* notes that "There's a divergence between the drugs companies are promoting online and the health info people really want. Pharmaceutical firms promote baldness cures and asthma treatments. Users seek weight loss and cancer sites."

Although participation in the Internet will inevitably grow, our data shows that the number of baby boomers and their elders currently reached through the Internet is exceedingly limited. In addition, our two target psychographic segments are below average users of the Internet, as well as having below average interest in the Internet and personal computers.

For example, more of the 40 and older population (19%) regularly log on to the Internet as compared to the Confused Compliants (14%). More of the 40 and older population (25%) has great interest in personal computers compared to the External Health Actives (20%). In terms of having a computer and access to the Internet, our two target segments are average on both points. As far as getting health information or advice from the Internet, 3% of those 40 and older say they have used the Internet for this purpose over the past 12 months, while 4% of the Self-directed Positives have done so. Our two target segments, the Confused Compliants and External Health Actives, are actually below average in their use of the Internet to retrieve health information (1% and 2%).

Sources of information

We track 20 sources of health advice used by the 40 and older population over the past 12 months. For this population, professional health-care providers continue to be the most important source of information. Both Confused Compliants (14%) and External Health Actives (11%) are close to average (13%) in having asked a doctor or nurse for health information in the last 12 months. Slightly more Confused Compliants have also received health-care information from a druggist (7%), as compared to the 40 and older population (6%).

After health-care professionals, virtually one in 10 of the 40 and older population has relied on articles in magazines and newspapers and on television programs about health for information. This second tier of health information sources underscores the importance of public relations efforts by pharmaceutical companies in promoting pharmaceutical drugs. Average numbers of both Confused Compliants and External Health Actives have used articles in health magazines for information in the past 12 months.

Our two target segments make only average or below average use of informal sources of health information, such as relatives. And they themselves are only average in informing others about a pharmaceutical drug they have seen advertised. Neither External Health Actives nor Confused Compliants can be counted on to create buzz on a prescription medication.

Questionable imagery

In early Viagra advertising dancing couples suggest sexual intimacy. While many mature consumers may wish to go dancing — as they may wish to have sex — the reality is that dancing is an activity in which only 13% of the 40 and older population ever participates. The far more important question, however, is whether or not the target psychographic segment(s) relates to this image.

Rather than using images in DTC advertising that relate to the interests of their target attitudinal segment, marketers all too often have fallen back on the easy choice: generalized imagery. From gardening to golf, grandchildren to miles, and miles, and miles of sandy white beaches, DTC advertising is cluttered with images that probably don't resonate with the specific psychographic segment being targeted. Such irrelevant images succeed only in turning off the target segment.

Messages that motivate

While we have focused on one or two aspects of the Confused Compliants or External Health Actives, their total profiles are far more complex. To reduce a message directed at the External Health Actives, for example, to "Do it for them" would fail to capture their other important motivations. These motivations can be synthesized into highly precise positions. And they can be expanded upon in newsletters, articles in magazines, patient brochures, and seminars, formats that allow marketers to lay out more detailed messages to both External Health Actives and Confused Compliants.

Creating efficiencies

We began this chapter by noting that not all DTC campaigns have delivered a high ROI, or any return at all. Considering the tens of millions of dollars at stake in both DTC and DTP campaigns, it's critical to arrive at and consistently apply an in-depth understanding of the target segment's motivations. Significant insights will result when attitudes toward health information are overlaid with motivations toward dealing with a specific disease. Coupling attitudinal segments to relevant demographics, behaviors, and media and Internet usage will create the seed bed from which models for database marketing can be built. As we demonstrate in Chapter 27, the inclusion of attitudes into databases will result in the most refined targeting.

REFERENCES

Scott-Levin news release. "Winning strategies in DTC," October 1, 1997.

Petrecca, Laura. "New TBWA/Health joins DTC ad fray with merged unit." *Advertising Age* 16 October, 2000.

Competitive Media Reporting (CMR) news release. "Ad spending up by 13.3%; Fourth quarter growth lags at 6.1%," March 20, 2001.

Appleby, Julie. "Prescriptions up as drug makers spend more on ads." *USA Today* 19 June, 2001.

Grimm, Matthew. "Reality bites." *American Demographics* July 2001.

Campbell Mithun Esty (CME) news release. "RX for prescription drug ads lies in formula used by over-the-counter marketers; CME study finds OTC ads deliver awareness levels 2.5 times DTC counterparts," July 12, 1999.

Howe, Jeff. "Total control." *American Demographics* July 2001.

"Revenue per advertising dollar for 100 leaders." *Advertising Age* 25 September, 2000.

Neslin, Scott. "ROI analysis of pharmaceutical promotion (RAPP): An independent study." *The Association of Medical Publications* (AMP) 22 May, 2001. 10 January, 2002 www.amponline.org.

Goetzl, Davis. "Adios, Newman! Glaxo bids adieu to Relenza effort." *Advertising Age* 30 October, 2000.

"Prescriptions up as drugmakers spend more on ads." *USA Today* 19 June, 2001. 5 September, 2001 www.USATODAY.com.

Scott-Levin news release. February 8, 2001.

Brick, Michael. "Merck painkiller profits less than expected." *New York Times* 23 June, 2001.

Goetzl, David. "Menopause drug Cenestin takes on leader Premarin." *Advertising Age* 31 May, 1999.

"No cure-alls." *Advertising Age* 24 April, 2000.

Beardi, Cara. "Lilly redirects Evista." *Advertising Age* 9 July, 2001.

Freeman, Laurie. "Prescription for profit." *Advertising Age* 15 March, 1999.

"Databank health." *Advertising Age* 16 July, 2001.

Chapter **17**

THE HEALTH COMPLIANCE SEGMENTS

TRUSTING BELIEVERS

Trusting Believers transfer responsibility for their health care to their doctor in whom they have total faith and who, they believe, cares about them as people. This profound faith comes with an enormous expectation: their doctor knows exactly how to cure them. For their part, Trusting Believers exhibit a resilient compliance.

Faith in the doctor

Trusting Believers have a total, complete and unwavering belief in their doctors and in the prescription medications they give them. Their motto could be: "Doctor knows best." Those in this segment follow their doctor's instructions exactly. In essence, they have turned over the management of their health to their doctors. In their view, it's the best way to protect their health: they believe doctors are the best resources for efficacious treatments and prescription medications.

Trusting Believers have concluded that following their doctor's advice is a cost-effective strategy. Doctors already know what to do—why research the topic on your own or second guess the expert? If a doctor prescribes a drug, Trusting Believers conclude they must need it.

A personal relationship

The reliance that Trusting Believers place on their doctor stems from their feeling that their doctor is concerned about their welfare. Perceiving that they have a personal relationship with their doctor leads Trusting Believers to pay a great deal of attention to what their doctor tells them about their health. Those in this segment consider their doctor's advice and consultation to be of great benefit in understanding their medical problems. They are careful to read the information their doctor gives them and want frequent feedback—if not reassurance—about their condition.

Expectations are high

The confidence that Trusting Believers have in their doctor, however, comes with an immense expectation: their doctor must determine precisely what is wrong with them and be able to map out a detailed treatment plan. The physician in which the Trusting Believer has the greatest confidence is apt to be a specialist, not a general practitioner. When faced with a medical problem, Trusting Believers are also open to getting a second opinion.

Unwaveringly compliant

Trusting Believers reveal themselves to be highly compliant in several ways. They don't second guess their doctor and would not stop taking a medication without their doctor's approval. According to them, it is not their decision to stop taking a prescription medication. Nor are those in this segment tempted to stop and start taking a prescription medication depending on whether or not they believe they need it. For them, adjusting the dosage of a prescription is an unwise strategy. Even when they don't see results, Trusting Believers would continue taking a prescription medication.

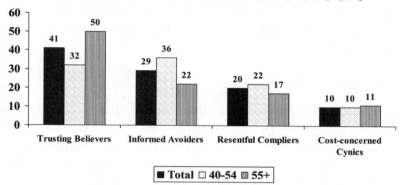

HEALTH COMPLIANCE SEGMENTS: PERCENT OF TOTAL AND AGE GROUPS

■ Total □ 40-54 ▨ 55+

Figure 8: *At a statistically significant level, a higher percentage of Trusting Believers exists among those 55 and older as compared to those 40 to 54. At the same time, lower percentages of Informed Avoiders and Resentful Compliers exist in the older population as compared to the younger.*

Compliance results in good life

Trusting Believers are convinced that if they don't follow their doctor's advice, they won't enjoy good health. For Trusting Believers being compliant in taking a prescription medication will result in being healthy and able to be with their family. Their high commitment to compliance in taking prescription medications also gives Trusting Believers a feeling that they are doing the most for their health. On a practical level, Trusting Believers also want to get the most from their investment in a doctor's advice and prescriptions.

Reliance on prescription drugs

Taking a prescription drug for a medical problem is the first line of defense for Trusting Believers. They wouldn't consider doing something else, such as taking a natural remedy or herb, before turning to a prescription medication. Having to take a prescription medication for the rest of their lives wouldn't deter Trusting Believers from starting the medica-

241

tion. Direct-to-consumer (DTC) advertising has a positive effect on Trusting Believers who feel more secure taking a prescription drug they have seen advertised on television. They do, however, view prescription generic drugs on par with those advertised.

Somewhat involved in care

Although reliant on their doctors to direct their care, Trusting Believers take some responsibility for their health by regularly checking their body for diseases. And they are the only Health Compliance segment that thinks it is a good idea to use a pill case marked with the days of the week to help them remember to take their medications each day.

INFORMED AVOIDERS

Informed Avoiders will do anything they can to avoid taking a prescription medication. They, not their doctors, are in charge of making final decisions regarding their health care. Informed Avoiders do everything they can to be informed about their health-care problems and conditions and use a variety of sources to achieve these ends. Only the Informed Avoiders believe they actually understand what their doctor tells them.

Avoiding prescription drugs

Informed Avoiders are the only Health Compliance segment committed to avoiding prescription medications. They try other things before accepting the idea that they must take a drug. One way they avoid taking prescription medications is through exercise and eating a healthful diet. Their avoidance of prescription medications stems from worry over their long-term side effects, not their cost.

Informed Avoiders are concerned that the cure offered by a prescription medication may be worse than the disease. Those in this segment feel very good about their lives, with the most positive views of all the Health Compliance segments. They are determined to do what they believe is most reasonable in order to preserve this feeling.

In charge of their health

In dramatic contrast to the Trusting Believers, Informed Avoiders believe they, not their doctors, direct their health care. Ultimately, Trusting Believers make the final decisions regarding their health care.

Using health information

If Informed Avoiders have a health problem, they research it. They want to know every detail about their condition or disease, something they don't think takes too much time. Not only do they research their health problems, but, given a prescription, they check it out as well. Once they are comfortable that they have the information to make an informed decision and thoroughly understand all the alternatives open to them, Informed Avoiders then formulate a plan to deal with a health problem.

A variety of sources

Informed Avoiders establish two-way communications with their health-care providers. On one hand, those in this segment don't have a problem being fully open and honest in their discussions with their doctors. At the same time, Informed Avoiders seek out and listen to a variety of experts, while still considering their health to be their own responsibility. If their doctor provides them with materials, they read them and also pay close attention to what their doctor tells them about their health. Informed Avoiders find it helpful to get frequent feedback from their doctors.

For Informed Avoiders, the sources of health-related information may include several doctors: those in this segment are most committed to getting a second opinion about a health problem. And, like Trusting Believers, Informed Avoiders are more apt to rely on the advice of a specialist over that of a general practitioner. Informed Avoiders also see their pharmacist as a good source for information provided by the manufacturers of their prescription medications.

It is extremely important to note that among the Health Compliance segments, only Informed Avoiders believe they understand what their doctor is telling them. This is not surprising: Informed Avoiders are the segment most committed to educating themselves on health issues. The implication, however, is that millions of patients in the other Health Compliance segments feel they don't understand what their doctors tell them, even though they may nod in agreement and ask a few questions.

Monitoring their health

Informed Avoiders pay a great deal of attention to how they feel. More than the other Health Compliance segments, those in this segment consider it important to check their bodies often.

RESENTFUL COMPLIERS

Resentful Compliers are stuck in a series of double binds. They distrust their doctors, but totally transfer responsibility for their care to them. While they don't believe what doctors tell them about their health conditions, they do little to become informed. Their non-compliant behavior is further fueled by their disbelief in having any disease whose symptoms are not seen or felt.

A failure to communicate

Resentful Compliers are trapped in a series of double binds. They have a profound distrust of their doctors, and, at the same time, they regard their doctor as the final decision maker regarding their health. Resentful Compliers also lack a strong commitment to seeking their own information on health issues. With few internal resources, Resentful Compliers say they would feel overwhelmed by a serious health problem.

Resentful Compliers are the only Health Compliance segment that believes doctors don't care about them as people, and they feel this very strongly. Only those in this segment believe that doctors don't really listen to them.

Whether the cause or the effect, the profound lack of trust in doctors exhibited by Resentful Compliers shows up in deeply rooted communication problems. Those in this segment admit they don't understand when their doctor explains one of their medical problems.

While only slightly interested in researching their health issues, Resentful Compliers worry that their own doctors don't understand their health problems as well as they do. And they do not see doctors as informed about the best medical practices.

Doctors, Resentful Compliers believe, are not to be trusted. In discussing their health situation, those in this segment think doctors exaggerate how serious a health condition is. Not only is what doctors say unreliable, Resentful Compliers think their doctor would give them an unnecessary prescription medication. At the same time, Resentful Compliers find it difficult to communicate with doctors honestly about their health.

While getting a second opinion is definitely something Resentful Compliers would do, they wouldn't trust the advice of a specialist over that of a general practitioner.

The lack of trust in their doctors is compounded by the Resentful Compliers' difficulty in believing that they have a health problem if they cannot see or feel its symptoms. If a Resentful Complier were diagnosed with a disease such as high cholesterol, osteoporosis, or diabetes, he or she may very well reject the diagnosis, considering the physician to be exaggerating or misrepresenting the condition. If prescribed a medication for such so-called symptomless conditions, Resentful Compliers would probably think it unnecessary.

It isn't surprising then that Resentful Compliers admit that they do not follow their doctor's instructions. Their conflict and resentment is evident as they question and distrust their doctors' instructions, a situation ripe for the creation of non-compliance. While making their own seemingly uninformed decisions on health, those in this segment still shift responsibility for these decisions to their doctor, the final decision maker.

Open to prescription medication

It wouldn't bother the Resentful Compliers to know that they have to take a prescription medication for as long as they live, nor would they resent taking a prescription medication.

Generally compliant

Resentful Compliers deny that they would alter the dosage on a prescription drug they were taking. Only serious side effects would prompt them to stop taking a prescription medication.

Committed to branded drugs

Direct-to-consumer advertising of pharmaceutical drugs works with Resentful Compliers. Unconvinced that their doctor is aware of the best treatments or drugs, Resentful Compliers help their doctor stay informed by taking him or her advertisements for prescription drugs. They are the only Health Compliance segment with this motivation for doing so.

The value of a brand is not lost on Resentful Compliers. Once those in this segment find a brand of a specific prescription medication they believe works for them, they would resent being switched to another. Resentful Compliers are also the only segment that believes branded drugs are better than generic ones. In fact, they trust some manufacturers of branded drugs more than others.

Bothered by high costs, side effects

While rejecting generics and seeking branded prescription medication, Resentful Compliers are also ferociously resentful about the cost of taking prescription medication. Paying for prescription medication presents Resentful Compliers with a serious financial burden. This situation represents another double-bind in which those in this segment find themselves.

Drug interactions and the long-term side-effects of various medications also trouble Resentful Compliers. But even with these very serious concerns, Resentful Compliers wouldn't be willing to try other alternatives, such as lifestyle changes, before starting a prescription medication.

The shape of some pills bothers the Resentful Compliers, and they find them difficult to swallow.

Minor involvement with health

Those in this segment are willing to check their body for disease, but they don't appear willing to do much more. Whatever health problems they have, Resentful Compliers don't believe they created them and aren't ready to solve them on their own, as are the Informed Avoiders.

Isolated from their doctors, it's probably beneficial that Resentful Compliers feel comfortable discussing their health problems with interested family and friends. They are also open to reviewing materials from a pharmaceutical manufacturer that would help to better understand their health conditions and diseases. In addition, Resentful Compliers view their pharmacist as a source of insights on various prescription medications.

COST-CONCERNED CYNICS

Burdened by the high cost of prescription pharmaceuticals, Cost-concerned Cynics are angry that they must pay for these drugs. If they can, they will choose the generic option. While they consider that they are in charge of their health care, Cost-concerned Cynics believe their doctors care about them. Marginally compliant, those in this segment do little to increase their knowledge about their conditions or diseases.

Driven by costs

If given a choice between two prescription drugs, Cost-concerned Cynics will choose the less expensive option. Those in this segment are completely convinced that prescription generic drugs are every bit as good as branded drugs.

Paying for the cost of prescription drugs imposes a serious financial burden on Cost-concerned Cynics. They, like the Resentful Compliers, are angry that the costs of prescription medications are so high. As a cost-saving measure, those in this segment would break pills apart and take a partial dose.

A strained relationship

One reason frugal Cost-concerned Cynics follow their doctor's advice is because they have paid for it. Those in this segment also believe their doctors have a genuine concern for them. It doesn't take a long-term relationship with a doctor for Cost-concerned Cynics to develop trust in him or her. Ultimately, however, Cost-concerned Cynics, like the Informed Avoiders, are adamant that they — not their doctor — are the final decision maker when it comes to issues that impact their health.

Cost-concerned Cynics have absolutely no expectation that their doctors will deliver certain knowledge regarding their health problems. Nor would Cost-concerned Cynics give greater weight to the advice of a specialist over that of a general practitioner.

Staying somewhat informed

While it is difficult for those in this segment to believe they have a disease if they do not feel or see its symptoms, Cost-concerned Cynics don't want to research their medical problems and do not consider it important to do so. Nor do they need to know the details about any illness they may have or understand exactly how a prescription medication they take will resolve their health problem.

While favoring lower-cost, generic drugs, Cost-concerned Cynics also consider DTC advertising as a source of information about how prescription drugs can help them. In addition, those in this segment turn to their pharmacist for information on the prescription medications they take.

Acceptance of pharmaceuticals

Cost-concerned Cynics wouldn't object to going on a medication, even if it was for the rest of their lives. Doing other things, such as making lifestyle changes, are not realistic options for those in this segment who would prefer to take a pharmaceutical medication for a health condition.

Exhibiting marginal compliance

Even after experiencing serious side effects, Cost-concerned Cynics don't think a patient should stop taking a medication. In several other ways, however, Cost-concerned Cynics show they are non-compliant. Not only would they take partial doses to save money, those in this segment don't see a problem with taking a prescription medication on an occasional basis — when they think they need it. Cost-concerned Cynics don't think they need their doctor's approval before they stop taking a prescription medication.

Problems with shape, packaging

Although most affected by concerns over cost, Cost-concerned Cynics also complain that prescription drug containers are difficult to open. For those in this segment, the shape of certain pills makes them difficult to swallow.

Chapter **18**

COMPLIANCE AND HIGH CHOLESTEROL

The leading cause of death

Harry P. age 57 clutches his chest and falls forward on his desk. His death is painful, but quick. An autopsy reveals three severely clogged arteries. His wife recalls that Harry's last cholesterol test showed a total cholesterol of 280. The unfortunate Harry is but one case that contributes to the pattern seen in large epidemiological studies: high cholesterol tied to an increase in coronary artery disease.

In 1998 almost three-quarters of a million persons in the U.S. died of heart disease. Approximately half of them had high levels of cholesterol. In the U.S., $100 billion is spent annually to treat coronary artery disease. And yet it remains the leading cause of death. Contributing to the immense price tag for the treatment of this disease is the fact that it is frequently linked to other conditions, such as hypertension and diabetes. If patients like Harry could reduce their low-density lipoprotein cholesterol levels, health-care expenditures would be slashed.

Pressure is building for patients, including those with high cholesterol, to take increasing responsibility for their own health care as a way to contain soaring costs. Adopting a healthful lifestyle and taking prescription medications are both recognized as actions patients with high cholesterol can take to reduce their lipid levels. But are patients medicated for high cholesterol actively participating in their own care by reducing their weight and exercising, or are they depending entirely on costly lipid-lowering drugs to reduce their high cholesterol? What can be done to motivate them to increase their involvement in their own care?

The difficulty of inducing patients to make lifestyle changes is compounded by severe problems with compliance and persistency among those taking a drug for high cholesterol, most typically a drug in the statin class. Only two out of five of those being treated with a prescription pharmaceutical for high cholesterol remain on the medication for more than 12 months. Since those with high cholesterol experience no symptoms, must take the drug for the rest of their lives, and have to submit to frequent monitoring, it's not surprising that many of them are less than enthusiastic patients. Which attitudinal segments are most receptive to messages on compliance, and which messages would they consider relevant?

While many patients demonstrate a lack of commitment to making lifestyle changes and taking their high cholesterol medication as ordered, several recent studies also show that large percentages of patients with high cholesterol often go untreated. One study on health maintenance organization (HMO) patients found that fewer than one sixth of them who required drug therapy for high cholesterol actually received it from their primary-care physician. To what extent do the motivations and attitudes of high-cholesterol patients not on lipid-lowering drugs keep them from getting these medications?

Answers to the questions posed above are of obvious interest to several groups. Patients with high cholesterol are concerned about having a heart attack or preventing another one. Physicians want to help patients lower their high cholesterol levels, but also face the reality of prescribing a statin which costs approximately $1,500 a year at a time when

HMO prescription drug expenditures in 1998, the last year for which this figure is available, averaged $211.38 per patient. Non-compliance among patients with high cholesterol also thwarts the physician's ability to affect change.

The attitudes, motivations, and behaviors of high-cholesterol patients are of considerable interest to the pharmaceutical companies manufacturing cholesterol-reducing drugs. Among the top 200 brand-name drugs based on retail prescriptions, drugs for high cholesterol account for 71 million scripts and $6 billion in sales. As baby boomers age, the market for such drugs will explode. Based on our figures, we estimate that sales for statins such as Zocor and Lipitor could soar, with no increase in price or penetration, to $18 billion annually by 2010.

Trusting Believers take drug

Whether one considers maintaining lifestyle changes or taking a prescription medication as ordered or both, compliance is a major block to patients dealing effectively with their high cholesterol. We have, therefore, examined this issue from the perspective of our Health Compliance segments. While Trusting Believers are 41% of the 40 and older population, they are 48% of those who take a drug for high cholesterol. Resentful Compliers and Cost-concerned Cynics, two other Health Compliance segments, are actually underrepresented in the ranks of those whose high cholesterol is treated with medication. Resentful Compliers, for example, are 20% of the 40 plus population, but only 16% of those who take high cholesterol medication.

The percentage of Informed Avoiders, the fourth Health Compliance segment, in the 40 and older population (29%) is virtually identical to those of them who take a prescription medication for high cholesterol (28%). Because Informed Avoiders are committed to lifestyle changes over taking prescription drugs, we could expect even fewer of them to take such a drug. But Informed Avoiders are also highly knowledgeable health-care consumers. They realize that when lifestyle changes alone are insufficient, taking medication is a reasonable choice.

Informed Avoiders largely unmedicated

Looking at those who have seen a doctor for high cholesterol, but don't take a medication for it, we find that Informed Avoiders are more than one in three of this group, as are Trusting Believers. But while Trusting Believers are 41% of the 40 and older population, they are only 37% of those who have seen a physician about high cholesterol, but do not take a prescription medication for it. In contrast, Informed Avoiders are 29% of the mature population, but 37% of those who have consulted with a physician, but remain unmedicated. The result: those who take medication for high cholesterol are dominated by our Trusting Believers segment, while those who have consulted a physician about high cholesterol and do not take a medication are disproportionately Informed Avoiders.

Attitudes differ

The detailed profiles of the Health Compliance segments in Chapter 17 highlight significant contrasts between Trusting Believers and Informed Avoiders. Given the attitudes of Trusting Believers it is not surprising that they are the dominant Health Compliance segment among those taking a prescription drug for high cholesterol. This segment perceives prescription medications as the first line of defense against health problems. While Trusting Believers have transferred the locus of control for their care to their doctors, they maintain high expectations for treatment outcomes. Their doctor will affect a cure. For their part, they will work with their doctor and also take some responsibility for their health.

In contrast, Informed Avoiders will do absolutely everything to avoid taking a prescription medication. Very concerned with the side effects of such drugs, their first option is to make lifestyle changes, hoping their health will improve. In sharp contrast to Trusting Believers, Informed Avoiders retain the locus of control: they are in charge of their own health care. They consider themselves to be knowledgeable health-information consumers. Unlike the other three Health Compliance segments, Informed Avoiders see themselves as truly able to understand health information and equipped to make informed health-care decisions.

Overlays reveal differences

In order to learn more about Trusting Believers who take a medication for high cholesterol, we overlaid them with our Health segments. A disproportionate number of these Trusting Believers taking a medication for high cholesterol are also Proactives, one of our Health segments. This means that to the Trusting Believer psychographic profile we have added the Proactives' attitudes and created a Super Segment. Proactives believe they have sufficient health insurance, a trusting relationship with their doctors, and a commitment to being compliant patients.

Because they are also Proactives, these particular Trusting Believers who take a prescription medication for high cholesterol are also positive toward exercising, eating a healthful diet, and avoiding high-fat foods. Among those who are taking a prescription medication for high cholesterol, Trusting Believers who are also Proactives demonstrate healthier behaviors than only Trusting Believers. For example, among those who are only Trusting Believers 29% are obese, 76% take three or more prescription drugs daily, 63% exercise outside of their work, and just 26% think they are in excellent or very good health.

In contrast, among the Trusting Believers who are also Proactives, fewer are obese (22%), fewer take three or more prescription drugs daily (65%), more exercise outside their work (75%), and more say their health is excellent or very good (36%). It is evident then that Trusting Believers taking a prescription medication for high cholesterol who are also Proactives are practicing more healthful behaviors than those in the Trusting Believer segment alone.

We then overlaid our Health Information segments on Informed Avoiders who have seen a doctor about high cholesterol, but are not on medication for it. The one in three Informed Avoiders who are also Self-directed Positives, one of our Health Information segments, adamantly retains control over their own health care. Informed Avoiders not taking a high cholesterol drug who are also Self-directed Positives believe they enjoy very good health, don't believe they will ever get sick, and are committed to living for today. This Super Segment of Informed Avoiders who are also in this second segment don't seek advice from others; in fact, they resent such advice. They consider themselves to be very smart about making health-care choices and able to handle any health problem. Unfortunately, Self-directed Positives all too often have no sound base of information from which to make health-related decisions.

By overlaying attitudinal or psychographic segmentations it's evident that we can delve deeper into what motivates a particular segment to act. Drilling down into a segment's related motivations enables us to design more effective marketing programs and also do a better job of predicting our target segment's future behaviors.

General state of health

How realistic is it to expect lifestyle changes among those who have high cholesterol? Many of them perceive that they are already in poor health. While 44% of the overall 40 and older population rates its current state of health as excellent or very good, only 28% of those on high cholesterol medication and 32% of those who have consulted a physician about high cholesterol, but are unmedicated, do so. Even fewer Trusting Believers on such medication consider their health to be excellent or very good (26%). Whether they take a medication for high cholesterol or not, those who have seen a doctor about high cholesterol report being less healthy than the mature population as a whole.

Related disease conditions

This perception of poor health is tied to a web of related conditions. The risk for heart disease is compounded among Trusting Believers who take a medication for high cholesterol. Compared to the 40 and older population, more of these Trusting Believers also have high-blood pressure and diabetes. In addition, Trusting Believers are twice as likely to take medication for high-blood pressure and diabetes as the 40 and older population.

Number of prescription drugs taken

Other than diabetes and hypertension, diseases closely linked to high cholesterol, how healthy are those taking a prescription medication for high cholesterol? The number of prescription drugs taken daily can indicate the severity and range of health problems faced. In the overall 40 and older population, 25% take three or more prescription drugs daily, a percentage that increases to 63% among those who take a prescription drug for high cholesterol.

We've noted that Trusting Believers put their faith in medications and are more receptive to taking them than are Informed Avoiders. More Trusting Believers taking medication for high cholesterol also take three or more prescription drugs (76%) as compared to the medicated 40 and older population as a whole (63%). Trusting Believers on high cholesterol medication take prescription medications in numbers higher than the 40 and older population for diseases that include arthritis, general mild to moderate pain, glaucoma, and erectile dysfunction (ED) or impotency.

Weighing in

A lack of vigorous activity and overeating have contributed to an epidemic of obesity among virtually every age group in the U.S. Obesity is currently defined as having a body mass index (BMI) of 30 and above. Those 40 and older are in a particularly difficult struggle to control their weight, the impor-

tance of which is apparent. Obesity is linked to high cholesterol, as well as to high-blood pressure and diabetes.

The Center for Disease Control's *Behavioral Risk Factor
Surveillance System* (BRFSS) for 2000 shows that 22.9% of
persons 40 to 49 and 25.6% of those 50 to 59 are obese. The
obesity rate drops to 15.5% among those who are 70 and
older. From 1991 to 2000 the rates of obesity increased in all
mature age groups. For example, in 1991 only 16.1% of those
50 to 59 were obese compared to 25.6% in 2000.

From our respondents' self-reported heights and weights
we've calculated their BMIs. In our recent studies, more than
one in five (21%) of those 40 and older are obese to severely
obese. Of respondents 40 to 64, 22.1% are obese, while fewer
of those 65 and older (18.2%) are in this state. Our rates echo
those reported by the BRFSS study, "the world's largest telephone survey that tracks health."

Exercise key to weight control

More of those taking medication for high cholesterol (28%),
as well as Trusting Believers (28%) in this group, are obese. A
consistent and life-long commitment to exercise could do
much to prevent obesity and the conditions, including high
cholesterol, to which it is linked. In our studies, 62% of the 40
and older population as a whole reports exercising away from
their jobs, and Trusting Believers are average in this respect.

Compared to the 40 and older population as a whole, however, more medicated Trusting Believers participate in non-
strenuous exercises among the 17 types of exercise we track.
For example, while 16% of the 40 and older population plays
golf once a month or more, 36% of medicated Informed
Avoiders does so. Gardening is something that 62% of the
mature population does once a month or more, as compared
to 73% of medicated Trusting Believers. But fewer medicated
Trusting Believers (14%) participate in swimming once a
month or more as compared to those 40 and older (21%). In
example after example of more vigorous forms of exercise,
fewer medicated Trusting Believers participate. Only 3% med-

icated Trusting Believers run or jog compared to 18% of the mature population, and only 3% of them lift weights or use a Nautilus machine compared to 16% of those 40 or older.

Doctors can influence diet

Besides how much we exercise and eat, what we eat is also a consideration in dealing with high cholesterol. Our studies ask about six food attributes, such as sugar, salt, or calories, that respondents could have reduced on their own or on the advice of a doctor. We find that far more Trusting Believers on high cholesterol medication have reduced these attributes when prompted to do so by their doctor. For example, reducing calories was something that 38% of Trusting Believers on high cholesterol medication had done on the advice of a doctor, but only 32% on their own. While 60% had reduced fat on their doctor's say so, only 40% had done it independently. While 90% had reduced cholesterol on their doctor's advice, only 26% had been motivated to reduce it on their own.

This consistent pattern of behavior parallels the Trusting Believers' attitudes. As we have noted, those in this segment shift the locus of control for their health care to their doctor, rather than assuming this responsibility themselves. This transfer by the Trusting Believer to his or her doctor underscores the importance of open, supportive, and directive communication between the two. We've discussed the Super Segment created by Trusting Believers on cholesterol medication who are also Proactives. While Proactives are dedicated to maintaining healthful lifestyles, the Trusting Believer component of this Super Segment has transferred responsibility for their health care to their doctor. It is unlikely that even these Trusting Believers who are also Proactives will make lifestyle changes without his or her direction and support.

Doctors, who are now seeing more and more patients each hour, will find it necessary to take the time to counsel receptive medicated Trusting Believers who are also Proactives regarding their weight, exercise, and diet. These Trusting

Believers taking high-cholesterol medication could very well be at the contemplation or preparation stage described by Prochaska, DiClemente, and Norcross. Once doctors identify this Super segment of Trusting Believers who are considering making lifestyle changes or who have attempted to make such changes unsuccessfully, they can direct their efforts to those who can best benefit from their guidance.

The unmedicated

Just as Trusting Believers are the largest Health Compliance segment among those who take a prescription medication for high cholesterol, Informed Avoiders dominate those who have seen a physician about high cholesterol, but are not medicated for it. As we saw at the beginning of this chapter, the Informed Avoiders' attitudes and motivations play a major role in keeping them unmedicated for high cholesterol. The attitudes that steer them to lifestyle changes rather than prescription medications combine with certain demographic and behavioral variables to keep more Informed Avoiders from being medicated for high cholesterol.

Income not a factor

The frequently espoused concept that high levels of income and education will necessarily lead to an enlightened health-care consumer committed to healthful living is not borne out by our studies. Our studies clearly show that far more than demographics is at work in influencing health-care choices. Within each demographic pocket, consumers are differentiated by their motivations and attitudes.

When viewed on average, income does not in and of itself distinguish those who are on a drug for high cholesterol from those who are not. While the median pre-tax household income of those 40 and older in the U.S. is $35,000, those who have seen a doctor for high cholesterol, but are not on medication for it, have an annual income of $35,020. The annual income of patients on a drug for high cholesterol is slightly lower at $33,265. Informed Avoiders not on cholesterol medication enjoy a median pre-tax household income of $38,347, the second highest of all the Health Compliance segments, whether medicated or not. It appears that lack of income would not deter most Informed Avoiders from paying for a high cholesterol medication themselves if they wished to take it.

Education does not figure

Neither does education differentiate those who take a medication for high cholesterol from those who do not. A college degree or more has been attained by one-third of the 40 and older population overall, as well as those who do or do not take a medication for high cholesterol. Among those with at least a college degree who have consulted a doctor about high cholesterol, 53% take a medication for it, while 47% do not. Informed Avoiders on medication are the most educated of the Health Compliance segments: 43% of them have a college degree or more. Those in this segment who are unmedicated are average in having a college degree.

Gender influences treatment

Gender does differentiate those taking a prescription drug from those who do not, but simply saying that more males than females take a cholesterol-reducing drug does little to explain the dynamics of the market. While 17% of the 40 and older population has consulted a doctor about high cholesterol, more males (19%) than females (16%) report having done so. Once having seen a doctor about high cholesterol, more males (60%) than females (40%) take a medication for it. It is important to note that Informed Avoiders, the dominant segment among those who do not take a prescription drug for high cholesterol, although they've consulted a doctor about it, skew male.

While the fact that unmedicated Informed Avoiders are predominantly male is interesting, it is even more meaningful to link this demographic insight to their attitudes and motivations. One Super Segment among unmedicated Informed

Avoiders has attitudes revealing a concern and resentment over lack of health insurance. We see that this Super Segment of Informed Avoiders is made up entirely of males. While 7% of the 40 and older population has no health insurance, 39% of male unmedicated Informed Avoiders are uninsured. All female unmedicated Informed Avoiders have some type of health insurance. These females also have far higher median household incomes as compared to males: $47,958 versus $34,551. If females in this segment wished to pay for medication, they could certainly afford to.

Insurance needs examination

Lack of health insurance explains why some Informed Avoiders don't take a prescription drug for high cholesterol. Among those who have health insurance, the type of insurance also influences whether or not those in this segment go on a drug for high cholesterol. To these variables we would add the Informed Avoiders' own attitudes and motivations and the influence of gender to understand why one group of Informed Avoiders doesn't take a prescription drug for high cholesterol.

More female Informed Avoiders who do not take a prescription drug for high cholesterol receive their health insurance from a managed care organization (MCO) (56%) than from any other source. While 27% of all female Informed Avoiders in a MCO take a prescription drug for high cholesterol, 65% of all male Informed Avoiders in an MCO do so. The massive discrepancy that exists between male and female use of a prescription drug for high cholesterol has been observed by others as well. "Compared to men," says Sharonne N. Hayes, M.D., director of the Mayo Clinic Women's Heart Clinic in Rochester, Minnesota, "women are much less likely to be prescribed statins or other cholesterol-lowering medications. We're failing women miserably."

That fewer female Informed Avoiders take a prescription drug for high cholesterol can be due to the interaction of any number of factors, including the attitudes and behaviors of physicians and MCOs themselves. Even if offered a prescription for high cholesterol medication, female Informed Avoiders' own motivations and attitudes may cause them to reject it.

Earlier in this chapter we noted the existence of a Super Segment among unmedicated Informed Avoiders who are also Self-directed Positives. Those in this segment believe they are in very good health, never gets sick, and have faith that it will always stay healthy. Self-directed Positives believe they know everything about health. They want to control their own health-care decisions and resent anyone providing guidance. Uninformed and possibly dangerous decisions about health can result from these attitudes. The preference that unmedicated Informed Avoiders show for alternative therapies over prescription drugs could be one such potentially negative choice.

Alternative medicine used by one segment

From yoga to prayer, massage to meditation, female unmedicated Informed Avoiders use alternative methods to cope with health problems, and they do so at rates far higher than males. For example, among Informed Avoiders who do not take a prescription medication for high cholesterol, 53% of females use relaxation techniques as a way to cope with health problems as compared to 15% of males. While physicians such as Dr. Dean Ornish view relaxation as necessary as diet and exercise in cholesterol reduction, other nontraditional options may not be as useful.

Making DTC relevant

Those attempting to influence patients with high cholesterol must take into account the two very different dominant Health Compliance segments we've discussed. The motivations and attitudes of these segments have implications for the selection of relevant messages and images, effective media, and targeted direct marketing. The regionality of the

Health Compliance segments and their use of a pharmaceutical drug for high cholesterol must also be considered.

For pharmaceutical companies Trusting Believers are the best prospects in terms of increasing compliance and persistency. To date, much of the imagery in direct-to-consumer (DTC) advertising for cholesterol-lowering drugs has been directed at Trusting Believers. How often have we seen 30-second spots for a statin showing grandparents frolicking with their grandchildren and making plans to be a part of their lives for a long time to come? In our studies, we ask about the adoption of a new prescription drug influenced by DTC advertising in 14 separate steps, from awareness through trial and finally to adoption.

Given the dependence of Trusting Believers on their doctors, DTC advertising can't be relied on as the only way to inform this segment about a cholesterol-lowering drug. Slightly more than half (52%) of the 40 and older population reports that it pays attention to DTC advertising. However, 64% of both medicated and unmedicated Trusting Believers do so, the highest percentage among the Health Compliance segments. Our studies show that only 30% of the mature population asks their physician about any advertised drug. But more Trusting Believers have also taken this action (57% of medicated and 50% of unmedicated). These behaviors parallel the Trusting Believers' motivations: an intense commitment to using pharmaceutical drugs to solve health problems.

While the Internet is touted as a source of health information, only 30% of unmedicated Trusting Believers use the Internet at all, for any purpose. More unmedicated Trusting Believers respond to health-related direct mail by throwing it away without bothering to open it (46%) as compared to the mature population as a whole (32%). After all, it's not from their doctor. Pharmaceutical companies will probably find practice-based direct-to-patient (DTP) programs an effective way to attract prospective patients from the Trusting Believer segment and increasing retention of them.

From a different perspective, it will be difficult to attract the attention of unmedicated Informed Avoiders and motivate them to try a cholesterol-lowering drug. Informed Avoiders will resort to a medication for high cholesterol only when they believe they have exhausted lifestyle alternatives. Pharmaceutical companies, however, can increase the Informed Avoiders' awareness of prescription drug options for high cholesterol and provide them with information. DTC advertising could target this segment with decision-making criteria, emphasizing their choices. Images of internally motivated Informed Avoiders surmounting daunting physical obstacles would support these messages. When they are ready, average numbers of Informed Avoiders will take a prescription medication for high cholesterol.

In selecting media for DTC advertising, pharmaceutical companies would benefit from applying our Health Compliance segments to magazine readership. Rather than simply taking an intuitive leap that a particular magazine's readership is receptive — or would ever be receptive — to high-cholesterol medication, an analysis using our Health Compliance segments would deliver a real-world assessment. Using our Simulator media optimization software we find that large numbers of unmedicated Trusting Believers subscribe to or regularly purchase *Reader's Digest* (44%), *Modern Maturity* (28%), and *Health* (18%). Fewer such Trusting Believers subscribe to *Prevention* (10%).

A regional roll out

Because dramatic differences exist between each Census Region regarding the sizes of the Health Compliance segments and other variables, such as demographics and enrollment in an MCO, any campaign targeting Trusting Believers or Informed Avoiders should be set up on a region-by-region basis. Penetration for drugs that combat high cholesterol is highest in the Northeast. This census region accounts for 19% of those 40 and older, but 24% of those on a medication for high cholesterol. Penetration is lowest in the West, where 19% of the mature population resides, but only 14% of those medicated for high cholesterol. One possible explanation for this disparity is that more of those 40 and older in the West receive their health care coverage from an MCO (51%) as compared to the total 40 and older population (40%).

Each Health Compliance segment's use of a prescription drug for high cholesterol also differs from one census region to another. In the Northeast Census Region, Trusting Believers account for 32% of the 40 and older population who have seen a physician about high cholesterol, but only 30% of those on a medication for high cholesterol. In contrast, Informed Avoiders living in the Northeast are 36% of those who have consulted with a physician, but 40% of those who take a prescription medication for high cholesterol. In the South, Trusting Believers are a massive 62% of those on a prescription drug for high cholesterol, while Informed Avoiders shrink to only 15%.

Incorporating our Health Compliance segments, along with demographics and behaviors, into all aspects of marketing allows for precise targeting and greater integration. Everything from media buys to patient information programs, targeted messages to customer relationship management (CRM) can focus on the most receptive customer. Considering the tens of millions of dollars spent each year advertising cholesterol-lowering pharmaceutical drugs, much of it wasted, the approach we advocate would require a relatively small investment and very quickly pay for itself.

REFERENCES

Centers for Disease Control (CDC). "National vital statistics reports," Vol 48, No 11.

Fenster, A.E., Harpp, D.N., Schwarcz, J.A. "The cholesterol story." McGill University. 9 September, 2001 ww2.mcgill.ca/chemistry.

Avorn, J., Monette, J., Lacour, A., et al. "Poor compliance with lipid-lowering medications." *Journal of the American Medical Association* 279 (1998).

Simons L. A., Levis, G., Simons, J. "Apparent discontinuation rates in patients prescribed lipid-lowering drugs." *Medical Journal of Australia* 4 (1996).

Lai, Leanne L., Poblet, Michael, Bellow, Cristina. "Are patients with hyperlipidemia being treated? Investigation of Cholesterol Treatment Practices in an HMO Primary Care Setting." *Southern Medical Journal* 3 (2000).

Hoerger, T. J., Vala, M. V., Bray, J. W., et al. "Treatment patterns and distribution of low-density lipoprotein cholesterol levels in treatment-eligible US adults." *American Journal of Cardiology* 82 (1998).

"Drug cost share of HMOs' total operating expenses continues to rise." *Drug Benefit Trends* 5 (2000).

"Top 200 brand-name drugs by prescription in 1999." *Drug Topics* March 2000.

Centers for Disease Control (CDC). *Behavioral risk factor surveillance system* (BRFSS) 2000.

Prochaska, J. O., DiClemente, C. C., Norcross, J. C.. (1992) "In search of how people change. Applications to addictive behaviors." *American Psychologist* 47 (1992).

McAuliffe, Kathleen. "A better way to lower cholesterol." *More* September-October 2000.

Chapter 19

Overlaying Segmentations: the Morgan-Levy Health Cube

One segmentation doesn't fit all

It seems strange that some major corporations, apparently in their need to simplify what are essentially complex motivations, create a one-size-fits all segmentation. They stretch it to fit almost every product in their portfolio. One car manufacturer, for example, uses a single psychographic segmentation to delve into the motivations of persons buying everything from a truck to a mini van, from an SUV to a four-door sedan.

These all encompassing segmentations unfortunately function like a piece of taffy that's being simultaneously pulled in many directions. It gets so thin it develops holes. Frustrated that the segmentation doesn't work — why would it? — such companies abandon segmentation, muttering angrily of their disillusionment. What doesn't work is their fundamental perception of psychographic segmentation and what it should accomplish.

Multiple segmentations applied

In our view, one of the key benefits of psychographic segmentation is the ability to examine the attitudes and motivations — always complex — of a target market under a microscope. A customer-centric approach dictates that the focus on "one segmentation fits all" be abandoned for a series of segmentations. In addition, when a marketing issue is especially complex or difficult, we believe that the layering of two or more segmentation strategies can yield amazing insights. To the best of our knowledge, Strategic Directions Group is unique in taking this position.

Using the Morgan-Levy Health Cube

Our Morgan-Levy Health Cube, an integration of our three health-related segmentation strategies, Health, Health Information, and Health Compliance, is one example of layering multiple segmentations. These segmentations are described individually in detail in Chapters 12, 15, and 17. Chapters that apply our health-related segmentation strategies to specific diseases or conditions include some insights that result from overlaying one segmentation onto another.

The integration of two or three segmentation strategies makes it possible to drill down ever more deeply into a market's core motivations. A segmentation on general attitudes toward compliance, for example, when interlaced with another segmentation on attitudes toward having diabetes, reveals a far richer view of how to motivate compliance in a diabetic. Of the perhaps 15 or 25 Super Segments created through this hypothetical pairing, we would encounter various combinations of segments of diabetics and their motivations toward compliance. Being able to target discreet Super Segments with this degree of specificity leads us to greater efficiencies: we find the most receptive Super Segments and thoroughly understand the messages that will motivate them.

THE MORGAN-LEVY HEALTH CUBE

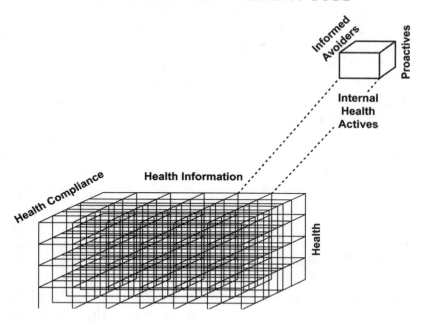

Figure 9: *The four Health, four Health Compliance and six Health Information segments are combined to provide greater in-depth insight into patient motivation. This figure shows how one cell in the Morgan-Levy Health Cube, the Super Segment composed of Proactives (Health), Informed Avoiders (Health Compliance) and Internal Health Actives (Health Information), can be selected as a receptive target for relevant messages and products.*

The combination of our four Health segments, six Health Information segments, and four Health Compliance segments creates 96 Super Segments. Below we explore two applications of the approach we advocate, focusing on the two Super Segments that are optimal targets for them.

A new kind of health club

The generalities abound. Baby boomers and their elders are all taking better care of their health. They are exercising and eating healthful foods. Health clubs must certainly be enjoying an exploding membership. It is true that from 1987 to 1997 health club membership in the U.S. grew by 63.1%, according to American Sports Data, Inc. The International Health Racquet Sports Association (IHRSA) finds that the majority of health club members today are over 35 (55%), "a major shift over the past decade." The Association also reveals that "even before the first baby boomer turned 55, the fastest growing membership segment of the health-club industry was adult men and women over the age of 55. This market segment, in relative percentages, grew four times as fast as young adults 18 to 34, and twice as fast as adults 35 to 54."

The reality, however, is that among those 35 and older in the U.S. population, only 6.4% are members of a commercial health club. Membership attrition at health clubs among groups of all ages is at 37%: every year a health club looses one in three of its members. While it is true that half of those terminating their membership move away, the other half quits because of dissatisfaction with some aspect of their health club.

Services desired by Super Segment

Could their dissatisfaction extend beyond encounters with unfriendly staff or messy locker rooms? Could it be that a portion of these former health-club members did not have access to the services that were of greatest interest to them? Our research suggests receptivity to a new type of health club, one strongly emphasizing preventive strategies for health and wellness and encompassing certain aspects of a medical clinic, a medical library, and a health club.

As we've noted, a purely demographic perspective shows us that 6.4% of those 35 and older are members of commercial health clubs. Examining our attitudinally based Health segments, we see that only 5% of Faithful Patients, who are 26% of the 40 and older population, go to a health club one or more times per week. In contrast, 22% of Proactives, who are

33% of the 40 plus population, do so. Clearly, Proactives, vast over consumers of health-club services, are the psychographic segment to target. But if one examines Proactives who are simultaneously Independent Health Actives, a Health Information segment, and Informed Avoiders, a Health Compliance segment, participation grows even greater: more than a third (36%) go to a health club this frequently.

The motivations and attitudes of this Super Segment made up of those who are simultaneously Proactives, Independent Health Actives, and Informed Avoiders suggests that they would be attracted to this new health club concept. To our perception of Proactives as persons concerned about their health and willing to take care of themselves, we add the inner motivated Internal Health Actives who are driven to stay exceptionally well informed about health matters. They are willing to try new health ideas and aren't too busy to do so. Internal Health Actives take care of themselves today so that they will have a healthy old age. They, like Informed Avoiders, consider themselves to be responsible for their own health care. Informed Avoiders are overwhelmingly dedicated to making lifestyle changes before using medication to deal with an illness or condition. Sufficient exercise and a good diet will result in robust health.

Working for better health

Our new concept health club would offer the exercise facilities of a conventional health club. Additionally, it would be staffed with dieticians and exercise physiologists, nurse practitioners and nutritionists. Its library of reliable printed and electronic materials could be discussed with on-site staff. Special programs could be offered addressing such topics as osteoporosis, bad backs, stress, nutrition and allergies. The health club would offer various software programs so that members can track their progress as they address specific health issues. Trainers and coaches would be available to members desiring support and one-on-one instruction. The health benefits of this new club would be so evident that it would be endorsed by medical organizations and health-related associations as an approved facility for the betterment of one's health.

Given the types of programs and services we have outlined, it is easy to imagine that the look and feel of such a health club would be radically different from the clubs that currently exist: family-oriented clubs, facilities that encourage singles dating, university clubs with Spartan facilities, and hospital-sponsored clubs focusing on rehabilitation, not wellness.

If a conventional commercial health club addresses a direct-mail campaign to Proactives, it would target 33% of the 40 and older population. If it targets the Super Segment made up of those who are at the same time Proactives, Internal Health Actives, and Informed Avoiders, it would take aim at 3.28% of the 40 and older population. In a metropolitan area with a population of 3 million, the 40 and older population would constitute a potential market of 1.3 million or 43% of the total population. Of these, about 42,312 fall into the Super Segment we've described. And of these, perhaps 36% or 15,232 would be interested in a health club offering the services we have suggested. Considering that today the average health club of any type has 2,000 members, our proposed health club has to sign up only one in eight in the target Super Segment.

Higher fees justified

Offering very specialized and desired services and staff, our new club could charge fees that are three or four times that of current commercial clubs, perhaps $225 per month rather than the $57 that is the average adult monthly fee for commercial clubs. Those in our target Super Segment are more affluent than the overall 40 and older population, with a median household income of $47,000 versus $35,000. It's likely that many of them could afford such fees. It would also be possible that membership in such a health club would be covered by a medical-savings account, a managed-care organization (MCO), or an employer. Since the median age of this Super Segment is 54, virtually the same as that of the total 40 and older population (55), those in this segment could potentially remain members for several years.

While we've just examined one Super Segment, that consisting of those who are simultaneously Proactives, Internal Health Actives, and Informed Avoiders, as excellent candidates for a new type of health club stressing preventive health care, another Super Segment in the Morgan-Levy Health Cube is the very best target for pharmaceutical companies marketing statins, prescription medications for high cholesterol.

Selling statins: a billion dollar war

Of the 96 Super Segments in the Morgan-Levy Health Cube, only one is exceptional in its receptivity to statins, such as Pfizer's Lipitor and Merck's Zocor. This Super Segment is composed of Faithful Patients who are at the same time also Confused Compliants and Trusting Believers. These segments are discussed individually in Chapters 12, 15, and 17. In addition, the market for statins is explored in our Chapter 18 on high cholesterol and our Health Compliance segmentation strategy.

Those who are simultaneously Faithful Patients, Confused Compliants, and Trusting Believers are a Super Segment that knows it should exercise and cut down on fatty foods in order to stay healthy, but doesn't follow-through on these health-care initiatives. Furthermore, members of this Super Segment don't seek out health-related information. When given specific health-care information, they don't understand it. If a physician or nurse practitioner were to explain the nature of cholesterol and its potential effects on health, for example, those who are at once Faithful Patients, Confused Compliants, and Trusting Believers would not grasp what is being relayed.

Lacking confidence in themselves as health-care consumers, those in this Super Segment have transferred control over their own health to their physician. Not only do those in this Super Segment have total faith in their doctor, they also view him or her as the dispenser of the magic potions they believe will make them well. Good health will come to them through strict compliance with their physician's orders.

The best target

For pharmaceutical companies selling prescription drugs for high cholesterol, the Super Segment created by layering Faithful Patients, Confused Compliants, and Trusting Believers is the very best target. Combining the attitudes, behaviors, and demographics most favorable to pharmaceutical sales, those in this Super Segment are the most efficient target. Barriers of one sort or another exist in marketing pharmaceutical drugs, and especially statins, to the remaining 95 Super Segments.

We have seen that this attitudinally defined Super Segment has not only transferred responsibility for its health to its physician, it is also highly receptive to prescription drugs. Additionally, all of those in this Super Segment have health insurance coverage from either a MCO or a major medical policy. In contrast, only 78% of the total 40 and older population has such coverage. With a median age of 52, lower than the median age of the 40 plus population by three years, it is possible that those in this Super Segment could remain on a statin for an even longer period.

While our focus here is on high cholesterol medication, we note that shared factors, such as obesity, link several diseases and conditions, including high cholesterol, diabetes, high blood pressure, and erectile dysfunction (ED). Of the 40 and older population, 12% report taking a drug for high cholesterol, but almost three times as many in this Super Segment (34%) do so. While 6% of those 40 and older report being on a drug for diabetes, 31% of our target Super Segment are on such medication. High-blood pressure medication is taken by 28% of the total 40 and older population, but 55% of our target Super Segment does so. A prescription medication for ED is taken by only 2% in the 40 and older population, but by 27% of this Super Segment. Those in this target Super Segment are then not only prime candidates for high cholesterol medication, but also for prescription drugs for high blood pressure, diabetes, and ED.

The one, two punch

Why are so many in this Super Segment, made up of those who are simultaneously Faithful Patients, Confused Compliants, and Trusting Believers, taking so many medications? True, they are ill, but others in the 40 and older population also have these diseases and are never diagnosed, much less treated. In the case of those in this Super Segment, a number of factors result in their getting a prescription, taking it compliantly, and remaining on it. These influential factors include this Super Segment's reliance on their physician; receptivity to pharmaceutical drugs; total access to health insurance, particularly through managed care, and high levels of attentiveness to direct-to-consumer (DTC) advertising.

Slightly more than half of those 40 and older (52%) pay attention to DTC advertising. In contrast, 76% of our target Super Segment do so. To our list of sources of information about health, only 8% of the total 40 and older population checked advertisements on television, radio or in magazines. In contrast, 13% of our target Super Segment relies on such advertising for health information.

DTC advertising, particularly on television, works on this Super Segment for a variety of reasons. Confused about much health-related information, they remain unsophisticated consumers of it. Since it's their physician's job—not theirs—to keep them healthy and give them any necessary information on health, those in this Super Segment have little interest in gathering it for themselves. Given this scenario, it's not surprising that their sources of information on health concerns are overwhelmingly free. Few of them subscribe, for example, to a newsletter on health for which they must pay.

Over consumers of television

Those in this Super Segment are massive over consumers of cable and network television, a medium that delivers health messages in sound bites and 30-second spots. Although they have a median of 14 years of education, those in this Super Segment are not readers. They are under consumers of magazines, newspapers, books, and the Internet. For example, while 16% of the 40 and older population spends 11 or more hours a week reading a daily newspaper, only 5% of our target Super Segment does so.

This Super Segment would have difficulty assimilating the implications of a Jane Brody column on health appearing in the *New York Times*, but will understand the central message of a 30-second television spot on Zocor. If they are flipping through a magazine, a headline in 26-point type in a DTC advertisement will be read, but not a four-page article on reducing fat in the diet. If print is used to target this Super Segment it will demand a high level of spending. And advertising will have to be placed in publications this Super Segment reads, such as *Popular Mechanics* and *Family Circle*, not *Business Week* and *Forbes*.

Close ties to physician

DTC advertising prompts this Super Segment to act out certain behaviors. While 19% of the total 40 and older population has told a friend about an advertised drug, 43% of those in this Super Segment have taken this action. In addition, while 30% of the total population has asked a doctor about an advertised drug, over half (55%) of our target Super Segment has done so. For this Super Segment the physician remains paramount in importance. Those in this Super Segment may bring a DTC advertisement to their physician, but far fewer of them would call an 800-number for information about high cholesterol. Such a call is something that 18% of the total 40 and older population makes, but only 5% of our target Super Segment.

Close ties to physicians are seen in both this Super Segment's attitudes and behaviors. Slightly more than a third (34%) of the 40 and older population tells us that they have seen a physician four or more times a year. Those who are simultaneously Proactives, Internal Health Actives, and Informed Avoiders, the Super Segment that's the market for the new health-club concept, are only about average (32%) on this point. In dramatic contrast, only 8% of the Super Segment composed of those who are at the same time Optimists, Self-directed Positives, and Informed Avoiders see a physician this frequently.

At the other end of the scale is the Super Segment we've been discussing as prime candidates for a statin, those who are Faithful Patients, Confused Compliants, and Trusting Believers. An immense 64%, virtually two out of every three of them, have seen a physician four or more times in the last year.

Multiple diseases

With almost twice as many of them as compared to the total 40 and older population seeing a doctor this frequently, we wonder what brings those in this segment to a clinic. At rates two to four times higher than the total 40 and older population, those in this Super Segment see their physician for diabetes, ED, and high cholesterol. For example, while 7% of the total 40 and older population has seen a physician for diabetes, 32% of our target Super Segment has done so. ED is something that 3% of the entire 40 and older population has had diagnosed by their physician, but 27% of our target Super Segment. While 18% of the total 40 and older population has seen a physician for high cholesterol, a far higher 48% of this Super Segment has done so.

Not only have more of those in our target Super Segment seen a physician for high cholesterol, more of them have been tested for it. Since this Super Segment expects their physicians to assume total responsibility for their care, we assume that testing for high cholesterol was done at the physician's instigation, not their own.

Of the entire 40 and older population, 59% have had their cholesterol tested in the past three years. In contrast, three-quarters of the target Super Segment (74%) have had their cholesterol tested over that time period. One explanation for this difference can be traced to the fact that among those who have health insurance, far fewer of those in the total 40 and older population (37%) are in a plan which provides free cholesterol testing as compared to our insured Super Segment (59%). As we note at the end of this chapter, those in this Super Segment have engulfed MCOs. Given the frequency of their visits to physicians, we assume that those in our target Super Segment are being monitored not only for high cholesterol, but also for their toleration of a statin, if they are taking this medication.

High levels of obesity

What has caused physicians to test our target Super Segment for high cholesterol at levels far higher than the overall 40 and older population? Any physician's initial encounter with a patient in this Super Segment would strongly suggest that they should be tested. Almost one in two (49%) of our target Super Segment can be classified as obese to severely obese, while approximately one in five (22%) of the total 40 and older population is this heavy.

In an initial interview with their physician, one in three of the total 40 and older population can discuss the fact that they exercise aerobically to their target heart rate four or more times per week. In contrast, over half (53%) of the Proactives, Internal Health Actives, and Informed Avoiders, our Super Segment candidates for the new concept health club, exercise this frequently. But this exercise level plummets to only 10% of the Super Segment made up of those who are simultaneously Faithful Patients, Confused Compliants, and Trusting Believers.

Given their high levels of obesity, we conclude that those in this Super Segment take in more calories than they need. Since so few of them burn calories through exercise, it's no surprise that these excess calories turn to fat.

An unwell group

Our target Super Segment's low level of exercise and resulting obesity, transference of responsibility for their health to their physician, and attitudinal receptiveness to taking prescription medications all contribute to their massive use of pharmaceutical drugs. Besides these attitudes and motivations, those in this Super Segment are also sick people who recognize that they are sick. Among the general population 40 and older, 44% rate their health as either excellent or very good. In contrast, only 12% of our target Super Segment does so, the lowest percentage of any Super Segment in the Morgan-Levy Health Cube. The large numbers of them who have been hospitalized as in-patients over the past two years is tangible evidence of this Super Segment's poor health. Of the 40 and older population, 17% have been an in-patient within the last two years, something that has happened to 44% of our target Super Segment.

In the U.S. one in four (25%) of those 40 and older takes three or more prescription medications each day. But this general demographic obscures huge differences in the number of prescription medications taken by certain of the Super Segments. Since a characteristic of the Super Segment made up of Proactives, Internal Health Actives, and Informed Avoiders, our best candidate for the new health club concept, is an avoidance of prescription pharmaceuticals, it isn't surprising that only 12% of them take three to five prescription medications per day and none of them take over five a day.

High consumers of prescription drugs

In contrast, half of the Super Segment consisting of those who are simultaneously Faithful Patients, Confused Compliants, and Trusting Believers take three or more drugs per day, with 37% of them taking over five prescription medications per day. More than any other Super Segment in the Morgan-Levy Health Cube, this target Super Segment is dramatically higher in its consumption of pharmaceutical drugs. We have already seen that those in this target segment are not only over consumers of drugs for high cholesterol, but also of drugs for diabetes, high blood pressure, and ED.

This Super Segment's reliance on prescription pharmaceuticals is counterbalanced by their low level of usage of both over-the-counter (OTC) drugs and herbal remedies. Of the 40 and older population, 9% take or use three or more OTC drugs daily. In our studies, these OTC drugs can include anything from cold remedies to vitamin pills, energy boosters to diet pills. Among our target Super Segment a remarkably low 2%—the lowest of all the Super Segments studied—take this number of OTC medications daily. This Super Segment's belief is centered on their doctor, not on medications they can buy off the shelf. This attitudinal predisposition is also seen in their lack of interest in herbal medicines. Overall, 23% of the total 40 and older population has used an herbal medicine. But a remarkably low 4% of this Super Segment have ever taken an herbal medication, the lowest among the Super Segments we have studied.

From DTC to OTC

Attempts have been made to move currently available statins from prescription to over-the-counter (OTC) status. If this happens, pharmaceutical companies may very well loose their ability to target their best Super Segment, one which is very much centered on the physician. Unwavering in their use of medications obtained by prescription from their physician, our research strongly indicates that this Super Segment would not self-medicate. Those in this target Super Segment would buy an OTC statin only if a physician had initially prescribed the drug and subsequently steered them to the OTC version.

Controlling costs at MCOs

Clearly, pharmaceutical companies should target this Super Segment to increase sales of statins and other drugs with similar underlying causes. From an economic perspective, however, this Super Segment is not one we would recommend for membership in a MCO. But the reality is that MCOs have succeeded all too well in attracting them. Our studies show that 48% of those 40 and older receive health-care coverage from managed care. But an immense 67% of this Super Segment is enrolled in managed care, the highest percentage of any Super Segment.

The result of this Super Segment's attachment to managed care has been escalating health-care costs, specifically pre-scription drug costs, for these organizations. In contrast, if MCOs were more successful in attracting the Super Segment made up of Proactives, Internal Health Actives, and Informed Avoiders, a Super Segment that would do anything to avoid taking a pharmaceutical medication, their drug-related expenses would be dramatically reduced. As it is, only 58% of this Super Segment receives health-care coverage from man-aged care.

References

American Sports Data, Inc. "Analysis of annual nationwide survey of 15,000 households" 1997.

International Health, Racquet and Sports Association. "IHRSA/American Sports Data Health Club Trend Report" 1999.

U.S. Bureau of the Census, unpublished data, Resident population by race and single years of age 1998.

Chapter 20

THE CAR PURCHASE SEGMENTS

ACCESSORIZED AMERICANS

In buying a car, those in this segment would select an American car over a foreign one. Accessorized Americans consider themselves to be experts on cars, doing research before buying. In their view, cars are an investment, one whose resale value has to be preserved. Accessorized Americans want a car that doesn't call attention to themselves and is socially acceptable. While lively acceleration isn't important to them, lots of head and leg room is.

Buy America first

Convinced that American cars are as good as foreign ones, Accessorized Americans believe it is an act of patriotism to buy a Cadillac rather than a Mercedes-Benz. Even considering small cars, Accessorized Americans feel American compacts are as good as their Japanese counterparts. Unless a foreign car manufacturer is already selling a lot of cars in the U.S., Accessorized Americans would worry about the availability of parts.

Informed buyers

Accessorized Americans consider themselves to be experts on cars and don't rely on others' advice in buying one. Before Accessorized Americans buy a car, they have done a great deal of reading on available models. They know how *Consumer Reports* has rated various cars, and they give this information a great deal of weight. They also pay attention to reports on cars from J.D. Powers & Associates. Since Accessorized Americans consider their cars to be an investment, perhaps they believe this research will pay off financially.

A complex purchase

For Accessorized Americans, purchasing a car is a multilayered experience. On one hand they view a car as an investment and are concerned with its resale value. In their attempt to preserve its resale value, Accessorized Americans feel good when their car is clean and polished, the only segment that has this perspective. Accessorized Americans view buying a car as a major purchase; they aren't interested in an inexpensive, although reliable, car.

At the same time, Accessorized Americans also see their car as a statement of where they fit within society. Buying a best-selling car, perhaps a Ford or Buick, suggests to an Accessorized American that he or she has made a socially acceptable choice, one repeated by thousands of others. Buying a unique car, one owned by few others, makes Accessorized Americans uncomfortable. In a similar vein, Accessorized Americans want to drive a car with styling they consider to be attractive, but would reject a car that stands out or gets noticed.

Safety and comfort

Accessorized Americans have very definite views on the accessories and features their cars must have. After all, for those in this segment, driving isn't just a utilitarian experience of getting from one place to another. Of the four Car

Purchase segments, only Accessorized Americans are adamant about having front wheel drive. Comfort and a car's ease of handling are concerns for those in this segment, who believe that a car's suspension system should make it easy to turn corners.

Perhaps because their girth has increased with maturity, Accessorized Americans consider lots of head and leg room very important in a new car purchase. Accessorized Americans clearly prefer cars with an automatic transmission.

Besides an interior that looks and feels comfortable, Accessorized Americans are concerned about certain automobile features that have important safety implications. These features include airbags and disc brakes, which this segment considers to be safer than drum brakes. Concerned with safety, Accessorized Americans are profoundly disinterested in a car with lively acceleration. Owning a car that can zoom down the expressway entrance ramp isn't one of their needs.

Trust and reliability concern Accessorized Americans, not only in a car they might buy, but also in the dealership they work with. Accessorized Americans want to buy their car from a dealership they trust, preferably one near where they work or live. They, along with the Uninvolved segment, would appreciate it if dealerships would make the car buying experience a less stressful one. Even if a car has all of their desired features, they believe it should also come with a good warranty. And it should also be a dependable car.

STYLISH FUN

Those in this segment admit they spend more money than they should on their cars. Stylish Fun can't help it: they love cars and consider driving to be fun. They read car magazines, even when they're not in the market. Stylish Fun want to drive a car few people own, a stylish car with lively acceleration. Such a car will probably be imported, because Stylish Fun consider American cars to be inferior. Reliability isn't a top issue with this segment.

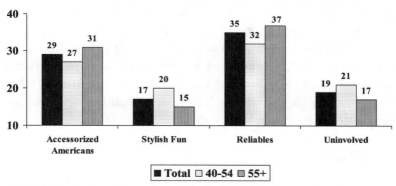

CAR PURCHASE SEGMENTS:
PERCENT OF TOTAL AND AGE GROUPS

Figure 10: *At a statistically significant level, lower percentages of Stylish Fun and Uninvolved exist among those 55 and older as compared to those 40 to 54. At the same time, higher percentages of Accessorized Americans and Reliables exist in the older population as compared to the younger.*

Relationship with car

Stylish Fun have a love affair with their cars, and they admit they usually spend more money on them than they should. For those in this segment driving is fun. They don't think of cars as transportation, but as objects that give them pleasure and joy. A utilitarian view of cars as a way to get to work or do grocery shopping is far removed from the Stylish Fun's perspective. Because for them driving is solely fun, they see no danger in it: no need for Stylish Fun to be defensive drivers.

Cars are so important to the Stylish Fun that they read car magazines and articles even if they aren't in the market to buy a car. When it comes to cars, they always want to be on top of the latest developments. Stylish Fun, who consider themselves to be experts on cars, reveal that they don't pay attention to reports from J.D. Powers & Associates when buying a new car.

The psychological importance of cars to the Stylish Fun is seen in their desire to drive a car few people own. Best-selling cars driven by hundreds of thousands of consumers have absolutely no appeal for this segment. They want to turn heads when they drive their fire red Audi TT down the street. Since they feel their car is an extension of their personality, they think they can tell what a person is like by knowing what kind of car he or she drives. They are the only Car Purchase segment that feels it has this gift.

Zip and drive

In appealing to this segment, car companies can keep their warranties, five-year road-service packages, and safety features. Energy efficiency is too mundane an issue to be of importance to the Stylish Fun. Neither is reliability a major factor for this segment, who would be bored with a less expensive, although dependable, car.

Stylish Fun want lively acceleration, which they believe can be found in a small, stylish car with a stick shift. In their view, such a car can also be a safe car. They want a comfortable interior, but they don't need a lot of head and leg room. While front wheel drive isn't important to them, a good suspension system is.

Open to imports

Stylish Fun don't consider it unpatriotic to buy a foreign car. They are convinced that American cars are inferior to imports, and small Japanese cars are much better than similar American cars. This segment has no concerns about the availability of parts for an imported car.

Just as Stylish Fun are open to a car from a foreign country, the dealership from which they would buy a car could be anywhere, not necessarily in the neighborhoods they frequent. There's no ill feeling in this segment against new car dealers. After all, these dealers sell a product Stylish Fun crave.

RELIABLES

Those in this segment have a profoundly utilitarian view of cars and driving. Reliables are totally focused on cars as providing nothing more than safe, reliable, and economical transportation. This segment pays little attention to a car's appearance when deciding whether or not to buy it. As the most research oriented of the Car Purchase segments, Reliables are prepared to encounter any car salesman: they are not intimidated.

A functional perspective

For those in this segment, a car is a car is a car. They have a profoundly utilitarian view of driving in which cars are simply machines providing transportation. For those in this segment, a car does not give them an emotional lift, nor is it viewed as an investment. For the Reliables a car is just a tool to help them get things done.

Reliables don't care if the car they buy is popular or unique, as long as it provides reliable transportation. Reliables wouldn't feel special if they drove a car that few people owned or one that gets noticed. It doesn't matter to them if their friends like their car or not. Since they have reduced cars to a purely functional role, Reliables can't detect someone's personality traits based on the car he or she drives.

Desired features

Reliables want a safe, reliable, and inexpensive car. Those in this segment would be happy with a generic, non-branded vehicle that meets their requirements. Reliables aren't going to be swept away, paying more for a car than their budget allows. The car they buy should have a good warranty. It should be extremely fuel efficient and, therefore, inexpensive to run. While the resale value of their car is unimportant, a five-year road service package is of interest.

Reliables don't need a great deal of leg room. While they prefer a stick shift, they aren't focused on acceleration. They concede, however, that they'd like to buy a car with the most performance they can afford.

Safety is a major concern for Reliables. Because of this perspective they don't consider wearing automatic seat belts to be a bother. Reliables recognize the hazards of driving and consider themselves to be defensive drivers. While they don't view small cars as safe, if they were to buy a small car, it would be from a Japanese manufacturer.

Looks not important

If a car meets their criteria of reliability, safety, and low cost, it doesn't matter to the Reliables that they don't like the car's looks. In fact, Reliables hardly pay attention to the appearance of a car when deciding whether or not to buy it. This mindset is another indication of how Reliables have reduced cars to the level of generic products.

Sales process

Reliables are not at all intimidated by the process of buying a new car. For this segment, car dealerships don't need to improve the sales process. After buying their cars, Reliables feel comfortable bringing them back to the new car dealership for service. The dealership itself doesn't have to be one with which they are familiar.

Reliables go to a dealership to buy a car having thoroughly researched the car or cars in which they are interested. It's almost as if they are pre-sold. One source Reliables rely on very heavily is *Consumer Reports*. Other sources of information and advice on cars include J.D. Powers & Associates and friends and family. They would only consider buying a car from a recognized manufacturer.

UNINVOLVED

Those in this segment know little about cars and intend to stay uninformed. Uninvolved view cars and driving as just a way of getting from one place to another. Instead of researching a car before buying, Uninvolved fall back on what is evident: a car's popularity and its looks. These cri-teria, along with reliability and low cost, are used by the Uninvolved in buying a car. Uninvolved loathe new car dealers and cringe at having to bring their car back for ser-vice.

Plan to stay ignorant

The Uninvolved know little about cars and don't want to know anything about them either. The entire subject of auto-mobile trends is of little interest to the Uninvolved. Even before they go to buy a new car, Uninvolved don't do any research. They are oblivious to whatever *Consumer Reports* or J.D. Powers & Associates may say about a specific model.

Cars as transportation

This segment, like the Reliables, views driving as a utilitar-ian event. Cars are just transportation, with, they hope, live-ly acceleration. While the Uninvolved prefer an automatic transmission, front wheel drive isn't important. Even safety features are of little interest to the Uninvolved. They regard an automatic shoulder belt as an uncomfortable nuisance and consider airbags to be unimportant. It isn't surprising that the Uninvolved don't see themselves as defensive drivers.

Lacking the information or knowledge to judge cars on technical details, Uninvolved can fall back on what is obvious and apparent: popularity and styling. If the Uninvolved don't like the way a car looks, they wouldn't buy it no matter what its features. Styling is one of the first things that someone in this segment notices about a car, and if the car generates a lot of attention, so much the better. The fact that a car is a best seller would make an Uninvolved feel more comfortable about buying it.

The Uninvolved would be happy, they tell us, with a car that is both inexpensive and reliable, with reliability being a major issue. Lacking any technical knowledge about cars, the Uninvolved would opt for free five-year road service, but are less interested in a car's warranty.

While Uninvolved would not view it as unpatriotic to buy a foreign car, they consider small American cars to be just as reliable as their Japanese counterparts. In general, they believe American cars are just as good as most imports.

Detested dealers

The process of buying a new car is troubling to the Uninvolved, and they would like car dealers to make this experience less stressful. As it is now, Uninvolved hate both doing business with new car dealers and bringing their car back to them to have it serviced. Distrustful of all dealers, the Uninvolved hope that those beyond their neighborhoods or near their work will be more trustworthy.

Chapter 21

THE CAR MAINTENANCE SEGMENTS

CAR REPAIR SAVVY

Those in this segment consider themselves to be good car mechanics. Besides saving money, fixing their car is something the Car Repair Savvy enjoy. Acknowledging that cars have become more difficult to repair themselves, this segment persists in wanting to do so. They are very willing to read and attend seminars in order to keep up to date. Car Repair Savvy are committed to maintaining their car, but don't consider a car dealership the best place to go for such service.

Experienced mechanics

Of the three Car Maintenance segments, only the Car Repair Savvy consider themselves to be good car mechanics, able to do more than just simple repairs and maintenance. If faced with a major job, however, they concede that they would have someone else do the repair. Compared to the other two Car Maintenance segments, Car Repair Savvy derive much pleasure from maintaining and repairing their own cars: it's something they really enjoy.

Commitment to repair

While car technology has changed radically over the past ten to fifteen years, Car Repair Savvy cling to the idea of repairing their own cars. Acknowledging that the need for sophisticated equipment is making it more difficult to do repairs, those in this segment deny that their ability to make such repairs is coming to an end. According to them, new cars aren't too complicated for them to work on and such work isn't reserved only for experienced mechanics with specialized tools.

The Car Repair Savvy plan to continue working on their cars, and this idea is entrenched in their minds. When they consider buying a car, for example, the ease of repairing it is one of their major considerations. Auto parts stores could ensure the Car Repair Savvy's loyalty if they would show them how to install the parts they buy from them. Those in this segment are interested in renting an auto bay providing tools and instruction if needed. Auto parts stores renting specialized tools and having more convenient hours would win the Car Repair Savvy's business.

Perhaps because of their knowledge about cars and their parts, the Car Repair Savvy, more than the other segments, will willingly accept rebuilt parts as being as good as new ones. They see salvage yards as good places to go for car parts. If these sources fail them, those in this segment feel extremely confident in buying parts at an auto parts store.

Saving money

The frugal and knowledgeable Car Repair Savvy would get several estimates on any major repair job. In their view, the main reason for repairing their car themselves is to save money.

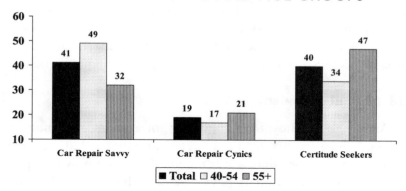

CAR MAINTENANCE SEGMENTS: PERCENT OF TOTAL AND AGE GROUPS

Figure 11: *At a statistically significant level, a lower percentage of Car Repair Savvy exists among those 55 and older as compared to those 40 to 54. At the same time, a higher percentage of Certitude Seekers exists in the older population as compared to the younger.*

Continue to seek information

Car Repair Savvy are sufficiently interested in their cars to want to maintain what they believe is their currently high level of expertise and would be willing to buy a comprehensive manual on auto maintenance and repairs. A retail store giving out brochures on cars provides a valuable service, according to the Car Repair Savvy. If new car or auto parts dealers provide seminars on maintenance and repairs, Car Repair Savvy would be most interested in attending. They'd like it if parts manufacturers provided more information on installation and maintenance. Those in this segment feel they would benefit from watching a mechanic repair their car: thus they would learn how to do it themselves.

Committed to maintenance

For the Car Repair Savvy, far more than for the other segments, car maintenance schedules are always top of mind. They have no trouble remembering when they last had their car's oil changed or if tires need to be rotated. More than the other segments, the Car Repair Savvy are concerned with automobile safety. Good maintenance, they feel, can help to ensure them of a safe ride. Even when they use their car on a vacation, those in this segment are always prepared and think it is a good idea to carry replacement parts, such as a belt.

Distrustful of dealers, service

As to where they take their car for repairs and maintenance, those in this segment aren't convinced that new car dealers know more than other mechanics about how to repair their vehicle. Car Repair Savvy believe that car dealers are good at selling cars, but not at repairing them. For those in this segment, getting a car repaired at a dealership means paying the highest prices for parts, something that irks the frugal Car Repair Savvy.

Those in this segment would feel more comfortable if they knew that the mechanic who worked on their car was licensed by the state: after all, he or she provides an important service. The pay mechanics receive is sufficiently high, according to this segment, to attract the very best people. Whatever their qualifications, however, Car Repair Savvy don't trust the service person to get them the best deal on parts.

This segment doesn't expect the mechanic to back up his or her work with a warranty, something the other two Car Maintenance segments seek. Perhaps Car Repair Savvy believe they know enough to catch shoddy repairs. This position is supported by the fact that they would like the mechanic to return all the parts taken out of the car and guarantee all replacement parts for the life of the car.

CAR REPAIR CYNICS

Car Repair Cynics resent any type of car-related regulation or restriction. Finding it impossible to deal with their increasingly complicated cars, those in this segment have largely given up on trying to repair them themselves.

Instead, Car Repair Cynics turn to the new car dealer as the best source for repairs. Wherever they take their car, however, they are convinced they will be cheated. To protect themselves, Car Repair Cynics want warranties on service.

Resenting control

Car Repair Cynics resent any type of car-related regulation or restriction, whether from the government or from car manufacturers. According to Car Repair Cynics, cars have gotten more expensive to run and more complicated to repair because the government has piled on a series of new laws. For this segment, such things as pollution controls are certainly not worth the extra cost. Car Repair Cynics feel that the government's regulation of the speed limit to 55-miles-per-hour was not a good idea. Mandatory auto inspections aren't something Car Repair Cynics would support, and they are the least supportive of state licensing of car mechanics.

Adding to the cost of maintaining cars are the manufacturers themselves. Car Repair Cynics see them as focused on creating production efficiencies, not on making cars easier to repair.

Can't work on cars

Given these extra regulations and the complexities they bring, Car Repair Cynics are only willing to attempt very minor car repairs. They believe that new cars are so complicated that only highly experienced mechanics with special tools can work on them. Lacking such tools, Car Repair Cynics have largely given up fixing their own cars. Those in this segment believe the days of being able to repair their car are coming to an end: new cars are just too complex. Not only are they unable to repair their car, they also no longer consider the neighborhood service station up to this task.

Not seeking more information

Car Repair Cynics don't have much interest in becoming better informed about how to deal with the maintenance needs of their high-tech cars. Those in this segment see themselves as sufficiently knowledgeable about cars already. Car Repair Cynics believe the owner's manual they received when they bought their car gives them enough information regarding necessary maintenance. If either new car or auto parts dealers offered seminars on maintenance and repairs, Car Repair Cynics wouldn't attend.

Concerned about cost

If their car needs repairs, Car Repair Cynics turn to their new car dealer, the shop they consider more knowledgeable about their particular car than any other. They do so while acknowledging that new car dealers are an expensive option: they charge more for auto parts than do retail auto parts stores. But taking their car to places like Sears for repairs isn't something Car Repair Cynics are interested in doing.

Distrustful about repairs

Wherever their car is being serviced, Car Repair Cynics believe they will be cheated, and service people certainly won't give them a break on the price of parts. They believe flat-rate manuals used by car repair shops are nothing more than thinly disguised price fixing and that giving mechanics a commission on the parts they install turns them into thieves. The only way to get a good deal is to wait for a sale to buy tires and batteries. Perhaps because of their interest in buying before they have a need, Car Repair Cynics like cars with gauges versus indicator lights. By buying ahead, they'll save money and exercise some measure of control over their car's repairs.

Warranties on service

The warranties that Car Repair Cynics seek appear to be on service, rather than on parts, and from the immediate vendor or provider of the service, rather than from the manufacturer. They place the least emphasis of any of the Car Maintenance segments on a part being guaranteed for the life of their car and would buy a car even if it didn't have an extended warranty. What they want is for the mechanic to back up his or her work with a good warranty.

Unconcerned about environment

Despite all the talk about global warming, Car Repair Cynics have no interest in buying a small, fuel-efficient car in the future. Of the Car Maintenance segments, Car Repair Cynics have the least amount of interest in an electric car run on batteries.

CERTITUDE SEEKERS

Those in this segment admit they don't know very much about cars, and they intend to stay that way. Certitude Seekers do not enjoy working on cars. Instead of knowledge, they rely on external guarantees, including governmental regulations, certificates, warranties, and paying the highest prices. With little actual knowledge, Certitude Seekers view both their mechanic and the manufacturer of their car in a favorable light.

Untutored buyers

Certitude Seekers admit that they don't know very much about cars or how they work. Those in this segment feel ashamed of their ignorance about making even basic repairs or doing simple maintenance on their cars. Certitude Seekers very strongly deny that they are knowledgeable car mechanics. Whether cause or effect, Certitude Seekers don't enjoy working on cars. And, say those in this segment, newer cars are too complicated to work on anyway.

Certitude Seekers, not inclined to handle a wrench, certainly don't want to find themselves in an auto bay they could rent by the hour in order to repair their car. Joining a car club made up of people who own the same make and model of car in order to share upkeep and repair tips isn't at all appealing to this segment. Certitude Seekers wouldn't give more of their business to auto parts stores even if these stores instructed them on how to install parts or made specialized tools available for rent.

Certitude Seekers don't know what the mechanic does to their car, and they intend to remain ignorant on this subject. They have absolutely no interest in watching a mechanic repair their car so that they can learn how to do the repair themselves the next time. Since selecting and purchasing car parts from an auto parts store is too much for them, Certitude Seekers have even less interest in buying the parts and taking them to a mechanic to install.

They know very little about how to repair cars and have no plans to increase their knowledge. The amount of information provided by their owner's manual regarding maintenance is enough for this segment. Although Certitude Seekers admit they have a hard time keeping track of their car's maintenance requirements, they see themselves as carefully following their manual's guidelines. Given the fact that their manuals are an adequate source of information and that they don't want to do car repairs or maintenance themselves, buying a comprehensive manual on auto maintenance is nothing Certitude Seekers would do.

Trusting a guarantee

Considering the fact that Certitude Seekers know next to nothing about repairing cars, they rely instead on external guarantees. By putting their faith in certificates, governmental regulations, and paying the highest prices for what they believe will be the best quality, Certitude Seekers are convinced they will lessen the chance that they will receive inferior service or bad parts.

To begin with, Certitude Seekers see repair persons in a favorable light: they trust them to give them the best deal on parts. Even giving mechanics commissions on parts won't turn them into crooks, say those in this segment. Certitude Seekers would get even more peace of mind if they knew that the same mechanic would be working on their car each time they bring it to the shop. With all their trust, however, Certitude Seekers would still like a mechanic to back up his work with a good warranty.

Specialization also gives Certitude Seekers confidence in their mechanics and their repairs. A mechanic would get extra points from Certitude Seekers if he or she has had specialized training. If their car's muffler needed work, they would take their car to a specialty repair shop, such as Midas.

Certitude Seekers wouldn't consider buying a car unless it had an extended warranty, and all parts that go into their cars have to be guaranteed for as long as the car lasts. A rebuilt part will never find its way into a car owned by a Certitude Seeker. Those in this segment won't be found prowling a salvage yard searching for parts. Certitude Seekers are convinced that a guarantee indicates that a car part has higher quality.

Seeking reassurance

In terms of car maintenance, Certitude Seekers see the government in a positive light. Certainly Certitude Seekers don't believe the government has added to the expense of having cars repaired by passing a variety of laws regarding them. To the contrary, such laws have actually given Certitude Seekers greater peace of mind. Those in this segment believe that every state should require car inspections, impose a 55-mile-per-hour speed limit, and mandate pollution controls.

Certitude Seekers don't feel that car manufacturers add to the difficulty or expense in getting their cars repaired. According to this segment, inefficiencies in repairing a car are not the result of how the car was manufactured. Certitude

Seekers deny that car manufacturers build their cars to break down after the warranty expires.

Price may bring protection

Besides the peace of mind that guarantees and warranties may bring them, Certitude Seekers also consider that paying the highest price may protect them from car-repair disasters. Certitude Seekers have no interest in waiting until a sale to buy a battery. They tell us that they will happily pay more to get the best-quality products for their cars and deny that the markup on car parts is too high. The prices at which new car dealers sell car parts is not, in their view, higher than those charged by auto parts stores. Flat-rate manuals are not equated in their minds with price fixing.

Environmental concern

If an energy crisis occurred, Certitude Seekers would become even more concerned about car maintenance. One reaction they would have to such a crisis would be to reduce the amount of driving they do. In the future, Certitude Seekers see themselves driving a small, fuel-efficient car.

Chapter 22

LUXURY CARS: WHO BUYS THEM?

Car sales center on mature market

The mature market's garages bulge with cars such as the Cadillac Escalade, Porsche Boxster, Audi A8, and Mercedes-Benz CL, as well as more common marques. While car makers continue to focus much of their attention on younger buyers, one fact is inescapable. Baby boomers and their elders account for the majority of new vehicle sales, and they will continue to dominate the market for the next several years.

The J.D. Powers & Associates' 2000 Vehicle Quality Study points out that baby boomers 35 to 54 are 39% of all new-vehicle buyers, while those 55 and older account for 33% of this group. Together baby boomers and their elders then make up almost three-quarters (72%) of all new car buyers.

Calculations based on the U.S. Department of Labor's 2000 Consumer Expenditure Survey show that households headed by those 35 and older accounted for 75% of U.S. consumer expenditures on new cars and trucks. Some of those in the automotive industry clearly understand the importance of this market. Nate Young, former group vice president of market planning at Johnson Controls, a large automotive components manufacturer, believes that "Aging baby boomers are the biggest and most significant buying group in the population."

Searching the haystack

While the mature market dominates sales, it's still incredibly difficult for car manufacturers to find anyone ready to buy a new car at any price. In 2000 only 5% of the U.S. population 18 and older purchased a new car. Identifying and reaching that 5% is extremely expensive. Finding and motivating those who buy luxury cars is even more difficult. In 2000, fewer than 3% purchased a new luxury car that cost $35,000 or more.

Securing the attention of potential buyers of new, luxury cars and influencing their purchase is a daunting task. Car manufacturers typically spend up to twice as much on measured media for each luxury car sold as compared to a non-luxury car. These marketing efforts can become more efficient and effective through the use of a psychographic segmentation. Targeting a specific psychographic segment of receptive consumers through their preferred activities and media makes it far easier to reach a small, but important, population. Focusing on receptive consumers includes creating messages relevant to them.

No "average" prospect

There is no "average" luxury car buyer. All markets are always made up of two or more segments with diverse views. When averaged, these views don't reflect anyone's true motivations or interests. Consumers exhibiting a specific behavior — such as buying a luxury car — aren't all motivated by the same factors. Motivations toward the purchase of a car are complex and differ by each psychographic segment. Sources of information and media also change radically for each of these psychographic segments.

Unfortunately, even attitudes and psychographics can be averaged, a process which renders them virtually useless.

Some marketers begin by segmenting a market before they conduct research, often on the basis of an arbitrary demographic variable. Having segmented their respondents based on age or gender or income, psychographics are then applied. An example of this process is drawn from J.D.Powers & Associates' APEAL study. This study concludes that "The major difference between the over-50 and under-50 buyers is psychographic—why they buy what they buy."

As presented by the study, these major psychographic differences are essentially seen from two age groupings: younger and older buyers. According to this viewpoint, older buyers want sensible vehicles with "quality, reliability, and durability," as well as "comfort and convenience." In contrast, younger buyers want "fun and emotion," as well as "sex appeal and flash." But such psychographic generalities are of little use to target marketers because they are not sufficiently specific.

Some baby boomers and their elders want flash and sex appeal, as do some of those under 50. At the same time, some of those under 50, as well as some older buyers, seek only to drive a highly reliable car, purchased, of course, at a great price, that will deliver an exceptional number of miles per gallon of gas.

Limited value in cohort approach

Segmentations such as this one created by J. D. Powers & Associates dividing a market into older and younger consumers appear to spring from a cohort approach. Using the generalities that make up a cohort's supposed profile can be useful in explaining some preferences, usually the ones based on experiences shared by virtually everyone in that generation. Such is the case, for example, with the popular music a cohort listened to when they were teenagers or young adults. But cohort analysis is far too general to explain motivations that are more complex, specific, and individual.

The impossibility of marketing to an "average" is illustrated by an article in *Brandweek* describing the representative or average attitudes of baby boomers toward buying a car. In a fashion similar to the story of the blind men attempting to describe an elephant by grasping its various parts, each marketing expert has a different, and sometimes contradictory, take on what baby boomers want. Such views provide no prioritization of needs, making it impossible to make marketing decisions based on what is most important.

The article tells us that "'With boomers, status and prestige comes from how you feel about yourself...'" One car brand has been marketing to the "holistic values of baby boomers." "Fun," we learn, "has also become the anchor of many a luxury car marketing strategy [targeting boomers]." In a corporate image campaign Mercedes stressed the values of "fun, passion, security and service..." One car marketer believes that "'Service is one of the things we need to talk about.'" Quick delivery of exactly the model desired is touted by one car maker trying to attract baby boomers. But "Despite such efforts," the article concludes, "the value-consciousness of baby boomers seems to be the strongest trump card for luxury car marketing."

Attitudes drive car choices

How can car marketers effectively target baby boomers when they see them as simultaneously valuing service, fun, security, and low price most highly? These contradictory motivators can be sorted out through a segmentation strategy based on psychographics or attitudes. We will see, for example, that safety is of little concern to one of our Car Purchase segments overwhelmingly focused on fun. In contrast, reliability and a car's exceptional value are of paramount importance to another segment.

Because of the mature market's importance to car manufacturers, as well as to those who sell and service them, we've developed two psychographic segmentation strategies, the Car Purchase segments and the Car Maintenance segments. These two segmentations are fully described in Chapters 20 and 21. The Car Purchase segments include the Accessorized

Americans, the Stylish Fun, the Reliables, and the Uninvolved. The Car Repair Savvy, the Car Repair Cynics, and the Certitude Seekers are our Car Maintenance segments.

Viewed solely from a demographic variable, such as having a pre-tax household income of $75,000 or more, the market for luxury cars would include all four Car Purchase segments. The conflicting views and interests of the four Car Purchase segments would then be merged into a murky mass. If a study based on averages finds a certain percent of respondents interested in a car's safety features, such a perspective does not enlighten us on the Uninvolved's obliviousness to them. Advertising messages about a car's advanced airbag system would not attract the attention of the Uninvolved.

Appeal by segment, not age

If one segments the car market, and particularly its luxury component, from a strictly demographic perspective, then it also appears difficult "to appeal to younger people and keep the older ones. How can you be both?," asks Dan Gorrell, an auto expert at a marketing research company. The answer to this dilemma is to begin with a segmentation defined by psychographics and motivations and then layer on demographics, behaviors, and media and Internet usage.

This approach is exemplified by Volkswagen. A spokesperson for the company reveals that Volkswagen does not "target any age group." Instead, Volkswagen targets "a psychographic that is active and performance-oriented..." Volkswagen's advertising campaign, "'Drivers wanted,' is an invitation to that experience." It is true that within various age groupings psychographic segments can increase or decrease in size. For example, Stylish Fun are 20% of baby boomers 40 to 54, but only 15% of those 55 to 64, as well as 15% of those 65 and older. At whatever age, a thorough understanding of the Stylish Fun's attitudes and motivations toward cars can be overlaid with additional data to further define the target.

Motivations remain stable

The Stylish Fun's motivations and attitudes toward cars do not change as they age, although the features they need and want may increase or decrease in importance. In selecting the top four features they look for in a new, unused car from the 25 features included in our studies, fewer Stylish Fun who are 65 and older selected a powerful engine (12%) as compared to those in this segment who are 55 to 64 (14%) and those 40 to 54 (17%). That a car has sleek, modern styling is more important to those Stylish Fun who are 40 to 54 (17%) as compared to those 65 and older (9%).

While these features decrease in importance as Stylish Fun age, they are still more important to the Stylish Fun than to the total 40 and older population. When it comes to sleek, modern styling or a powerful engine, only 9% of the 40 and older population would select either of these features as being among their top four. Viewed from another perspective, Stylish Fun, who are 17% of the 40 and older market, are 39% of those who would select a powerful engine as one of their top four features and 37% of those who seek a car with sleek, modern styling.

Focus on luxury cars

Even as the stock market pitches and dips, there is reason for car makers to focus on the luxury segment of the market. As Justin Hyde of Reuters notes, such vehicles "offer larger and more reliable profit margins than any other part of the business. And luxury sells well in fair or foul economic weather." According to Forbes.com, the "sales of luxury cars in the U.S. haven't contracted in more than 20 years." Susan Jacobs, a respected car industry analyst, believes "The luxury segment is the most promising segment for growth over the next 10 years."

The sale of such luxury vehicles is very much tied to the 40 and older market. In 2000, according to Auto Pacific, Inc., a marketing research and consulting firm, the majority of luxury vehicle buyers were 40 and older (76%). Jacobs sees this trend continuing as baby boomers move "into their 50s, becoming empty nesters" with "more discretionary income." As the article in *Brandweek* notes, "Baby boomers, and not an elite few representing landed wealth or nouveau riche, have made the lap of luxury more ample and are the principle target for cars priced in the $40,000 and up price range." At the same time, J. D. Powers & Associates finds that 50 and older car buyers "generally purchase more expensive vehicles, ranging from high end midsize cars to top-of-the-line luxury automobiles and premium sport-utility vehicles."

Using 2001 luxury car sales figures and conservatively factoring in 10% lower sales over the next five years resulting from a persistently soft economy, we project those 40 and older could account for $167 billion in sales of new luxury cars priced at $35,000 and above. This market is simply too big to ignore.

Because they have typically segmented this market solely by age, many car makers are unaware that the luxury car market is actually dominated by three very distinct attitudinal or psychographic segments. While Stylish Fun are 17% of the 40 and older market, they are 30% of those who own a luxury car and 31% of those planning to buy such a car. Stylish Fun are also 38% of those in the 40 and older population currently owning a Japanese or European luxury car.

Accessorized Americans are 29% of the 40 and older market, 29% of those who currently own a luxury car and 33% of those who plan to buy a car that costs $35,000 or more. Uninvolved are 19% of the total 40 and older market, 24% of those who currently own a luxury car, and 18% of those who intend to buy such a car. Which of these segments presents the best target for car manufacturers?

Segments differ dramatically

While they are described fully in Chapter 20, we can quickly see the dramatic differences among these three segments. Uninvolved view driving as just a way to get from one point to another. Their involvement with the car category is very low.

Those in this segment don't do research before making a new car purchase, and they are the only segment that admits knowing very little about cars. It is painful for the Uninvolved to relate to new car dealers, whether they are attempting to purchase a vehicle or having it serviced. Car safety is not a major concern for the Uninvolved, who admit that automatic shoulder belts are a hassle. Those in this segment believe that American cars are as good as most imports.

Accessorized Americans have their own unique viewpoint on what they want in a car. Compared to the other Car Purchase segments, Accessorized Americans believe it is unpatriotic to buy a foreign car. For Accessorized Americans a new car is an investment, and resale value is a major concern. Instead of a car that is unique or different, Accessorized Americans feel more comfortable buying a best-selling car. This segment is extremely loyal and will only buy a new car from a trusted dealership located close to where they work or live.

Stylish Fun view cars as much more than transportation: they are fun. Those in this segment are convinced that imported cars are far better than American ones. Stylish Fun look for a car with lively acceleration and style. They have a love affair with their cars, and, because of this, they spend more than they should when buying a new car. They're the only Car Purchase segment that keeps up with car trends, even if they're not contemplating a purchase.

The Uninvolved

Car makers will find the Uninvolved difficult to motivate. Having little interest in the product category, the Uninvolved are not receptive to car advertising. There is little a car manufacturer can do to appeal to them or even get their attention. Projected at the Uninvolved, messages of safety, power, and resale value will fall on deaf ears. Since they don't pay attention to car advertisements, those in this segment aren't motivated to move to the next step and seek information about a car, whether on the Internet or in a show room.

Because of their lack of involvement with the category, the cost of acquiring an Uninvolved customer will be far higher than that of attracting someone in a receptive segment, such as the Stylish Fun. Marketing to the Uninvolved will also require a great deal of time and patience. Having acquired Uninvolveds as customers, it will be difficult to engender brand loyalty in them. In our view, the Uninvolved are not good short- or long-term targets for makers of luxury cars.

Accessorized Americans, a declining target

Accessorized Americans are not over consumers of luxury cars: their incidence in the population equals the percentage of them who own such cars. They do, however, represent almost a third of the luxury car market among those 40 and older. The allegiance that Accessorized Americans have toward American cars is seen in their preference for Cadillacs and Lincolns.

The decline in sales in the U.S. of American cars compared to their foreign competitors parallels the decrease in the size of the Accessorized American segment as it ages. Beginning in 1975, U.S. car manufacturers steadily lost market share to foreign brands, with sales of foreign makes overtaking those of domestics in April 2001. Makers of American luxury cars should take note of the fact that the number of Accessorized Americans in the mature U.S. population declines to 27% among those 40 to 54 from 31% among those 55 and older.

Unless radical action is taken, a likely scenario is that American luxury cars will continue a slow decline in sales against foreign competitors. Lincoln, for example, has succeeded in attracting younger buyers "averaging in their mid-50s" to its LS sedan and Navigator sport utility vehicle. The Lincoln Town Car buyer, however, still has an average age of 66.

Stylish Fun best target

For the purpose of this analysis, we've defined affluent consumers as those with $75,000 or more in pre-tax household income. Our data shows that among these affluent consumers only 13% who intend to buy a car will buy a luxury car, defined as a car that costs $35,000 or more. The vast majority (87%) of those defined demographically as affluent will buy a Ford or Toyota, not a Volvo or BMW. It is clear that affluence alone does not define the luxury car buyer.

Findings similar to ours are related in *The Millionaire Next Door* by Stanley and Danko. In researching millionaires, the authors found that half of those they surveyed had "never spent more than $29,000 in their entire lives for a motor vehicle." More than a third (36%) of these millionaires drove cars with nameplates such as Chevrolet, Ford, Buick, and Toyota. Among the millionaires they interviewed, only 24% drove new cars, regardless of brand, and "25.2% have not purchased a motor vehicle in four or more years."

That the elusive affluent market cannot be captured solely by demographics serves to underscore the importance of a psychographic segmentation. This type of segmentation helps us to understand and identify the Stylish Fun. Among those who are affluent in this segment far more (22%) intend to purchase a luxury car than affluents as a whole (13%). Among affluent, mature U.S. consumers who plan to buy a car and intend to spend $35,000 or more on it, 58% are Stylish Fun, clearly the dominant segment.

Conversely, many of those who plan to buy a luxury car wouldn't even be targeted by car makers using the artificial demographic criterion of high income. Our data show that of those who plan to spend $35,000 or more on a car, 40% have a pre-tax household income of less than $75,000. And their plans aren't just wishful thinking. Of those who currently own a luxury car, 67% have pre-tax household incomes of less than $75,000.

Data from our ongoing studies show that luxury car buyers are defined by some level of discretionary income or access to credit, as well as by their motivations. Many of those who are strongly motivated to buy a luxury car will do so, even if it is beyond their means.

Stylish Fun own luxury cars

Of those 40 and older, 12% currently own a luxury car. Among the affluent, 20% own a luxury car. But twice as many affluent Stylish Fun (40%) own a luxury car. Luxury European car marques have the greatest appeal for the Stylish Fun. This segment is clearly the best target for luxury car manufacturers, whether BMW, Volvo, Saab, or Mercedes-Benz.

Stylish Fun more often in market

Luxury car manufacturers should also pursue Stylish Fun because they own newer cars. Although they represent 17% of the 40 and older market, Stylish Fun are 30% of those who own cars two years old or less. Besides currently owning newer cars, more Stylish Fun, whether affluent or not, also intend to purchase a new, unused car this year or next (26%) as compared to the 40 and older population (22%) as a whole.

Stylish Fun use Internet

Reaching Stylish Fun via the Internet should be regarded as an emerging strategy, but not currently a primary one. About one in four Stylish Fun (22%) have home Internet access. While that's higher than that of the overall 40 and older population (17%), the vast majority of Stylish Fun are still not accessible through the Internet. More Stylish Fun also have a computer in their homes (55%) as compared to the overall 40 and older population (45%). And 20% of the Stylish Fun use their home computers for 11 hours or more per week.

While the Stylish Fun are above average in their use of computers and the Internet, far more Reliables have a computer at home and Internet access. Viewed from the perspective of the 40 and older market as a whole, Stylish Fun make up 19% of those with a computer in the home, while information-seeking Reliables represent 33% of this population. Before buying a car, Reliables go to the Internet for the detailed information they need.

Mass media can target Stylish Fun

Using our Simulator media optimization software we analyzed the most efficient media to reach the Stylish Fun. Because it's based almost totally on demographics, current media research is extremely convenient to gather and use. But demographics, which only infrequently correlate with motivations, cannot effectively discern between receptive and non-receptive consumers. In order to increase the efficiency of their media buys, car makers will have to reach a receptive buyer defined first by his or her psychographic segment, and then by related behaviors, demographics, and media usage.

Our media optimization found that among those 40 and older, Stylish Fun are 25%, but Accessorized Americans are 47%, of those who subscribe to or regularly purchase *Forbes*. While Stylish Fun are 27% of those who subscribe to or regularly purchase *Condé Nast Traveler*, Accessorized Americans are 32%. Reliables are 33% of those who subscribe to or regularly purchase *Martha Stewart Living*, compared to only 16% of the Stylish Fun. While placing advertisements for Mercedes-Benz in *Martha Stewart Living* makes little sense, ads for Honda and Toyota are a perfect fit. Reaching the Stylish Fun is best done through car-oriented magazines.

Mass media buys can be farther targeted to those regions or states with exceptionally high populations of Stylish Fun. For example, 58% of all Stylish Fun who plan to buy a luxury car live in the West or Midwest.

While cable television has been touted as a great way to reach the mature affluent, it doesn't draw vast numbers of Stylish Fun. The majority of affluent Stylish Fun watch cable television for 10 hours or less a week (48%) or don't watch it at all (19%). Compared to affluent persons 40 and older (22%), Stylish Fun are only average (23%) in watching cable television for 11 or more hours per week.

Incorporating attitudes into databases

Models based on demographics and behaviors have improved the effectiveness of databases, such as those used for customer relationship management (CRM) and direct marketing. But even better results can be obtained by incorporating the insights obtained from a psychographic segmentation into a database. If databases are examined solely on the basis of behaviors, or a combination of behaviors and demographics, a predictive leap is necessary in order to find markets for entirely new products and services. Knowing the attitudinal configuration of one's database helps immensely in predicting the market for products and services that have never before existed, such as vehicles appealing to aging baby boomers.

Tying a strong attitudinal segmentation to the demographics and behaviors in a database provides us with a comprehensive understanding of the market. The composite profile developed in this way is far richer than one derived from assessing only behavioral and demographic data. There is little doubt that by identifying and appealing to the Stylish Fun, particularly at a younger age, a car maker can develop a very profitable long-term relationship.

In order to map attitudinal or psychographic segments onto a car maker's database, the process requires that sufficient common demographic and behavioral data exist in both the attitude research set and the car maker's database. If a common set of variables discriminating between the segments can be found in both the segmentation study and the car maker's customer files, it is possible to categorize the car maker's entire customer base.

Going beyond golf

Many luxury car makers focus on golf as the way to target luxury car buyers, but they actually only reach a small percentage of them. While about one in three (32%) affluent Stylish Fun plays golf once a month or more, a higher percentage of affluent Stylish Fun (43%) never play golf.

Sponsorship of a tennis event makes even less sense when examined by a targeted psychographic segment. Among male Stylish Fun only a small percentage play tennis once a month or more (4%), while 80% never play tennis. And Stylish Fun 40 to 54 are only average in watching sporting events on television (39%), something done by more Accessorized Americans in this age group (44%). In contrast, more Stylish Fun 40 to 54 attend professional sports events (35%) than do those in this age group overall (26%) or Accessorized Americans (25%).

But if tennis sponsors want to reach Stylish Fun, the few hundreds of them in the stands will not compensate for only average numbers of them in the television viewing audience. Given the Stylish Fun's above average loyalty to the brand of their existing cars, it makes more sense to spend marketing dollars on a CRM retention strategy than a loosely focused sports sponsorship.

Reach segments through entertainment

Makers of luxury cars need to consider additional lifestyle venues for promotions and relationship marketing efforts that reach Stylish Fun. Phil Guarascio, a former advertising executive for General Motors, sees marketing through entertainment as "the next big sector." This position makes sense in marketing to the affluent Stylish Fun because 67% of them go to a full-length movie in a theater once every three months or more. One in three Stylish Fun who intends to buy a luxury car goes to a museum (33%) or attends a play in a theater (35%) once every three months or more.

The current link between car marketing and fashion is supported by the Stylish Fun's interest in designer clothing.

While 41% of those in the 40 and older population who currently own a luxury car have purchased designer clothing over the last three years, it's something that 47% of the Stylish Fun have done. Even more Stylish Fun who plan on buying a new car have purchased designer clothing within that time span (57%). One problem, however, with linking fashion to car marketing is that Stylish Fun are a predominately male segment (62%). A second problem with the fashion-to-car linkage is that virtually every car marque from BMW to Toyota, Jaguar to Mercedes-Benz is sponsoring a fashion event. Today fashion sponsorship doesn't differentiate between marques.

The third problem is that a car maker's decision to sponsor a fashion event results from silo thinking facilitated by the use of averages. It is true, as Fern Mallis, director of the Council of Fashion Designers of America, points out that "Women are a huge target audience for buying cars right now—the car companies recognize this and capitalize on it." But the women Mallis refers to are nonexistent "average" women. The psychographic Car Purchase segments that skew female are Reliables (64%) and Uninvolved (62%). Reliables, as you may remember, will buy a car whose looks they dislike if it meets their criteria for reliability and economy. Their position is hardly a fashion-conscious one. Cars are not something the Uninvolved really care about, and the fact that Mercedes-Benz sponsors Fashion Week would be of little interest to them.

Cross promotions to the Stylish Fun

Car makers should consider targeting the Stylish Fun where they work. Many of those in this segment are frequent business travelers. For example, among consumers 40 and older, Stylish Fun are 24% of those with a membership in American Airlines' frequent flier program and 27% of those in Delta's.

Predicting future sales

Because the mature consumer is so important to car sales, and particularly sales of high-end vehicles, car makers are trying to figure out what will entice aging consumers to purchase a car. Lacking a crystal ball, a psychographic segmentation is highly useful in uncovering motivations and attitudes that haven't been previously articulated. Unmet needs can be discovered through such a segmentation. A psychographic segmentation can also be linked to the specific product attributes preferred by each segment.

In ten years, today's oldest boomers will be 65, while the youngest of them will have reached 46. Core motivations and attitudes toward cars will remain constant, unless the physical and emotional changes experienced by a segment are cataclysmic. We have noted that the percentage of those in some of our Car Purchase segments increases or decreases with age. Fewer Stylish Fun, for example, exist in the 65 and older population, as compared to those 40 to 54.

The market for the sporty, stylish European cars preferred by the Stylish Fun will shrink over the next ten years if the present trend continues. Car makers can modify their vehicles so that all consumers, even those with physical limitations, can drive them easily and safely. And they can also simultaneously increase their focus on the younger component of the Stylish Fun.

Designing a car for mature consumers

The efforts of car manufacturers to create a car, whether luxury or not, that is suitable for aging car buyers focus on physical changes, including limitations such as those caused by faltering eyesight, arthritis, and an increased girth. Ford Motor Co., for example, has developed a Third Age Suit which designers wear to "simulate the movements of an aging person." Mazda North American Operations had drivers 55 to 75 select the features they wanted in a car and design its interior. But not all mature persons age at the same rate or exhibit the same limitations. Car makers deciding what aging boomers want and need in a car must move beyond the average and focus on a multi-layered target.

It is true that the girth of mature Americans has increased over the past ten years. In 2000, for example, virtually one in four among those 40 to 49 and those 50 to 59 were obese (22.9% and 25.6%), up from 16% in 1991. Obesity has increased considerably among all age groups. But not all mature consumers are obese.

Having calculated each respondent's body mass index (BMI) from self-reported heights and weights, we found that at a statistically significant level more Stylish Fun are either normal or under weight (46%) and fewer of them are either obese or severely obese (13%) as compared to the other Car Purchase segments. For example, one in four Accessorized Americans (25%) is either obese or severely obese. Viewed from a different perspective, Stylish Fun are 12% of those who are obese or severely obese within the 40 and older population, while Accessorized Americans are more than a third (35%) of this population. The expanding girth of the mature population in the U.S. should be of greater concern to Cadillac and Lincoln, than to BMW.

Considering only arthritis, one of the 25 diseases we track, we find that among luxury car owners, fewer Stylish Fun (15%) report having arthritis as compared to Accessorized Americans (17%). While 9% of these Stylish Fun take a prescription drug for their arthritis, 15% of the Accessorized Americans do so. In fact, 45% of Stylish Fun who are luxury car owners take no prescription drugs, as compared to 28% of the Accessorized Americans.

As they conceive of cars for an aging population, car marketers must avoid generalities about the mature market and its projected disabilities. A more actionable view of the mature market and its needs will be created by starting with the psychographic segments most receptive to their cars. Adding insights on desired features and physical limitations to the segments will create a detailed road map to success.

Car repair revenues important

In 2000 households headed by baby boomers and their elders accounted for 79% of the $68 billion in consumer spending for car repairs and maintenance according to the Consumer Expenditure Survey. As the profit margins on new vehicles sold continue to erode, car repairs and maintenance become increasingly important to a dealership's survival. An article in *Business Week* points out that "Repair services and parts now make up 10% to 12% of revenues at the big dealer chains.... At Auto Nation, parts and services bring in just 12% of revenues but 35% of net profits." Dealers must succeed in capturing and retaining new vehicle repairs and maintenance.

From the perspective of the mature consumer, the dealer's ability to provide high-quality car repair and maintenance is an important factor in selecting a car marque. In buying a new car, excellent dealership service is one of the top four features selected by 22% of the 40 and older population and by even more Stylish Fun and Accessorized Americans (both 27%). In contrast, fewer Uninvolved selected such service as one of their top desired features (17%).

When we overlay our Car Purchase segments on to our Car Maintenance segments we find that the Accessorized Americans are split into two segments, the Car Repair Savvy and the Certitude Seekers. In contrast, large numbers of both the Stylish Fun and the Reliables (40% and 44%), the two segments most motivated to learn all they can about cars, are also Car Repair Savvy. Their knowledge about cars gives the Reliables and Stylish Fun a great deal of confidence in buying and repairing cars. It isn't surprising that half (51%) of the Uninvolved are also Certitude Seekers. Uninvolved know very little about cars and, because of this, can only go by warranties in judging the quality of a car or its repair.

We would expect males to dominate (80%) those Stylish Fun who are also Car Repair Savvy and females to make up the preponderance of Uninvolved who are also Certitude Seekers (78%). But it is surprising to see that there are more females (56%) among those Reliables who are also Car Repair Savvy than males (44%). This subsegment of mature female car buyers who know a great deal about car maintenance is the sort of insight that would be submerged and lost in an averaged perspective of the market place.

The next phase

Not all affluent people want to buy a luxury car, in fact, few do. Finding and attracting potential car buyers is, as we have seen, a daunting task. Facing continually escalating media costs and splintered audiences, car marketers will find that integrating all marketing efforts around a receptive psychographic segment or segments will create marketing efficiencies. From CRM programs to media selection, brand management to dealer training, public relations efforts to the creation of advertising with relevant messages and imagery, a psychographic segmentation will provide a reliable platform for focused marketing.

Understanding how baby boomers and their elders will react to the physical, economic, and psychological changes they will undergo as they age is of the greatest importance to car makers. For the next ten years this population, which accounts for 67% of all licensed drivers, will continue to be responsible for the vast majority of new car sales. The crest of the baby boom, after all, has not yet reached 50. Even while marketing to those in their 20s and early 30s, car makers must continue a profitable relationship with today's primary customers: baby boomers and their elders. Approaching this marketing problem armed with only demographics or a cohort analysis is insufficient. The generalities arrived at from these types of data will not lead car marketers to the strategies they will need to survive and grow. Focusing on one or two psychographic segments and overlaying other types of data will substantially increase car makers chances of marketing successfully to mature buyers.

REFERENCES

2001 Ward's Automotive Yearbook. "Demographics of new vehicle buyers and initial vehicle quality, 2000 model year."

Krebs, Michelle. "Shifting gears." *American Demographics* January 2000.

Gelsi, Steve. "Class for the masses." *Brandweek* 31 March, 1997.

Halliday, Jean. "Lexus spends $35 million to bag younger LS buyers." *Advertising Age* 18 September, 2000.

Wellner, Alison Stein. "Who is in the house?" *American Demographics* January 2000.

Hyde, Justin. "Automakers aim for luxury to improve profits." *Reuters* 11 April, 2001. 3 March, 2002 www.auto.com.

Kirkman, Alexandra. "Maserati's mystique." *Forbes Global* 14 May, 2001. 5 March, 2002 www.Forbes.com.

Hyde, Justin.

Gelsi, Steve.

Krebs, Michelle. "50-plus and king of the road." *Advertising Age* 17 April, 2000.

Flint, Jerry. "Backseat driver, America's car problem." *Forbes* 11 June, 2001.

Halliday, Jean. "Lincoln campaign aims to snag younger drivers." *Advertising Age* 4 December, 2000.

Stanley, Thomas J., and Danko, William D. *The Millionaire Next Door: The surprising secrets of America's wealthy*. Atlanta, Georgia: Longstreet Press, 1996.

Jackson, Kathy. "Big marketers get personal by going local." *Automotive News* 10 December, 2001.

Tsui, Bonnie and Halliday, Jean. "Keep cars fashionable." *Advertising Age* 9 April, 2001.

U.S. Department of Labor. *Consumer Expenditure Survey* 2000.

U.S. Department of Transportation, Federal Highway Administration. "Distribution of licensed drivers by sex and percentage in each age group and relation to population 2000."

Welch, David. "Can car dealers keep the profits rolling?" *Business Week* 14 January, 2002.

Chapter **23**

REACHING
BEST CUSTOMERS
WITH MASS MEDIA

Dissatisfaction with mass media

At the same time that marketers increased spending on mass media through the '90s, their frustration with it also grew. As audiences for mass media have withered, the problem of accountability has never been resolved. As Randall Rothenberg remarks, "No one understands how, or even if, advertising works." Dissatisfied with the results of their immense advertising expenditures, marketers have shifted their budgets from magazines to television to the Internet. While they've attempted to introduce accountability by reducing commissions to advertising agencies and paying for performance, the fundamental problem remains.

A downturn in the economy in 2001 could only have exacerbated many marketers' dissatisfaction with mass media, and many slashed their advertising spending. And the events of September 11th dramatically accelerated the decline in advertising expenditures. CMR, a marketing company specializing in advertising tracking, estimates that advertising spending reached $94.6 billion in 2001, a decline of 9.4% from 2000. While CMR predicts that advertising will increase by 1.5% in 2002, mass media's lack of accountability remains.

The goal: best customers

Admittedly, buying mass media based on a psychographic segmentation cannot remedy all of the unresolved issues inherent in such a purchase. It can, however, assure that the most *receptive* audience will be reached. According to the results of a poll for *Advertising Age* released in early 2002, "The ability to target the client's best customers was rated an important media attribute by 85% of respondents." Far more respondents, who were both ad agency executives and advertisers, rated reaching these "best customers" as an important media attribute as compared to others, such as negotiating lower costs (66%) and documenting a campaign's effectiveness (50%).

This interest in targeting "best customers" has no doubt contributed to the creation of some newer publications, such as *Real Simple* and *More*, which target a psychographically, rather than a demographically, defined group. *More*, for example, is designed to target "the mature woman who feels young, *is* [their italics] young and won't accept a different label." In contrast to these very general psychographic positions, our psychographic segmentation approach is based on a specific product or service and is, therefore, more targeted.

Using behaviors and demographics specific to the product, our psychographic segments can be further qualified, thereby assuring an even closer fit. If two magazines deliver a receptive and qualified audience as determined by our process, the final step is to compare the cost of one to the other. This is precisely what our Simulator media optimization program does using data from our studies on the mature market and media costs furnished to us by our clients.

Applied to three markets

We've used our Food segmentation strategy to illustrate the purchase of mass media by psychographic segments. Attitudinally each Food segment, as we've shown in Chapter 10, has very different motivations and attitudes toward food and its preparation. These motivations have been confirmed in the Food segments' food choices. Certain mass media are better places as compared to others in which to advertise the food products that each segment prefers.

Reaching the Food segments

Demographics takes us only to the point of telling us, for example, that mature males — on average — eat more salty snacks than mature females. We do not know *why* they continue to buy such snacks, nor do we know which messages would motivate them to buy a salty snack. Behaviors provide historical data, but do not help us if we are introducing a new product or trying to move light users into the heavy-user category. A magazine's general psychographic viewpoint, such as that of *O, The Oprah Magazine*, which "skate[s] over age boundaries" and presents "a soothing and stress-free aura" does not help us in advertising a specific product, such as salty snacks.

Rather than relying solely on demographics or even general psychographics, manufacturers of various types of food and beverage products can select media by our Food segments. Linked to demographics, behaviors, and specific mass media, our Food segments lead marketers to not only the most relevant message that can be developed, but also the specific media that should be used.

For example, baby boomers and their elders have been drinking beer all their lives, and many will continue to do so as they age. A brewer may decide to target Traditional Couponers, more of whom drink beer than the other Food segments. Within the mature population, the size of the Traditional Couponer segment remains stable, regardless of age. We see that among those 40 to 64, Traditional Couponers are

21% of the population versus 19% among those 65 and older. In our hypothetical scenario a beer maker has decided to target Traditional Couponers 40 to 64. Our beer marketer must decide which mass media to select to best target Traditional Couponers in this age group.

Cable TV good choice

If a marketer wants to use television to reach Traditional Couponers, it would be a reasonable choice. Slightly more than one in three Traditional Couponers (35%) watches network television 11 or more hours per week, which is just above average (33%) and the highest of all the Food groups. But it is cable television which attracts even more Traditional Couponers. Three-quarters of Traditional Couponers have cable television, about the same as the total market of those 40 to 64. Among those in this age group who have cable television, 35% watch cable television 11 or more hours per week as compared to 42% of the Traditional Couponers. In sharp contrast, only 32% of the Nutrition Concerned in this age group watch cable television for this many hours a week.

Of the cable television networks we track, Traditional Couponers 40 to 64 with cable television prefer certain cable networks as compared to others. Among the Food segments, they are the least apt to watch programming on the Arts & Entertainment (A&E) network or CNN. But slightly above average numbers of Traditional Couponers (38%) as compared to this age group as a whole (36%) watch the USA network several times a week or more.

Among the 14 types of television programming we study, Traditional Couponers prefer talk shows. These shows attract above average numbers of Traditional Couponers in this age group (28%) as compared to the total 40 to 64 age population (26%). The type of television programming that is best at reaching Traditional Couponers 40 to 64 is sports, something 46% report watching a few times a week or more compared to 41% of those in this population overall.

Traditional Couponers not readers

It will be difficult to reach younger Traditional Couponers through magazines and newspapers. While 8% of those 40 to 64 spend 11 or more hours per week reading magazines, only 5% of Traditional Couponers in this age group do so. Of the 60 magazines we include in our studies, measuring subscribers or regular purchasers, Traditional Couponers 40 to 64 are average or below average in the percentage who read them, as compared to those in this age group overall. Subscribership and regular purchase is only slightly above average among Traditional Couponers in this age group for three magazines: *National Geographic*, *The Smithsonian*, and *TV Guide*.

Just 15% of Traditional Couponers spend 11 or more hours a week reading a newspaper, only slightly higher than average (14%). Whether the newspaper in question is a local daily or a community paper, fewer Traditional Couponers 40 to 64 read it regularly.

Radio is not an outstanding choice for reaching Traditional Couponers 40 to 64. Among Traditional Couponers in this age group, 31% listen to radio 11 or more hours a week, as compared to 29% for this age group as a whole. Listening to radio declines severely among Traditional Couponers 65 and older, with only 21% listening 11 or more hours a week.

Nutrition Concerned exotic fruit target

As we've noted in our chapter on the Food segments, the Nutrition Concerned are most interested in consuming fresh fruits and vegetables, and their behaviors parallel these attitudes. If an importer wished to attract Nutrition Concerned to a line of exotic branded fruit, he or she should be targeting the Nutrition Concerned, a very large market. Nutrition Concerned are 43% of those 40 to 64 and 50% of those 65 and older. Our hypothetical marketer has decided to target Nutrition Concerned 40 and older, or 45% of the 40 and older market.

Should our marketer advertise his or her branded mangoes and star fruit on television in order to reach the Nutrition Concerned? Those in this segment are just average in watching network television 11 hours a week or more (35%). Among those who have cable television, the Nutrition Concerned are actually below average (36%) in terms of watching cable television 11 or more hours per week, something 39% of the total 40 and older population with cable television does.

Certain cable networks, however, do draw more Nutrition Concerned than others. Nutrition Concerned favor the Arts & Entertainment (A&E) network, with 47% of them reporting that they watch it several times a week or more. Nutrition Concerned are also above average in the percentage of them watching the Discovery Channel this frequently.

News and education preferred

When they do watch television, they focus on specific types of programming. For example, fewer of them watch situation comedies and soap operas as compared to the other two Food segments. In contrast, more Nutrition Concerned 40 and older watch educational shows (29%) several times a week or more as compared to the Fast & Health (24%) and Traditional Couponers (23%). More Nutrition Concerned also watch news and current affairs programming daily (61%) as compared to the Fast & Healthy (54%) and Traditional Couponers (53%).

Heavy readers

Nutrition Concerned 40 and older are above average in reading magazines 11 or more hours a week. In contrast, Traditional Couponers and Fast & Healthy are just average magazine readers at this level. As compared to the other Food segments, more Nutrition Concerned subscribe to or regularly purchase several magazines. These magazines include *Better Homes and Gardens*, *Family Circle*, and *Reader's Digest*. One in four Nutrition Concerned females subscribes to or regularly purchases *Better Homes and Gardens*, compared to one in five female Fast & Healthy and Traditional Couponers.

Other possible advertising venues that reach above average numbers of Nutrition Concerned include newspapers. Among the Nutrition Concerned who are 40 and older, 80% read their local daily newspaper regularly. More of them also read community newspapers (31%) as compared to the 40 and older population as a whole (28%). Advertising in *Parade* or another Sunday newspaper magazine, however, will reach equal percentages of Nutrition Concerned and Fast & Health (52% and 52%).

Nutrition bar seeks Fast & Healthy

Nutrition bars have proliferated on grocery and drug store food shelves. If a manufacturer of a nutrition bar, packed with protein, vitamins, and minerals, but offering the taste of a candy bar, decides to target consumers 40 to 64, his or her best prospects are the Fast & Healthy. This Food segment is too busy to cook meals and instead snacks through the day.

Fast & Healthy are 36% of the 40 to 64 age group. As we've seen, they are not motivated to cook complete meals, except for major family celebrations. Their lack of interest in cooking from scratch parallels the fact that, compared to the total 40 to 64 population, more Fast & Healthy are single. While 43% of those in the 40 to 64 age group are single, more than half (53%) of the Fast & Healthy are in this situation. In addition, Fast & Healthy are busy people with more of them working full time as compared to the other Food segments.

Our hypothetical nutrition bar marketer will not have an easy time reaching the Fast & Healthy through the mass media. Perhaps other marketing communications options, such as public relations, direct marketing, or special events, should be considered. Overall those in this segment are average to below average consumers of network television. For example, just an average one in three Fast & Healthy watches network television 11 or more hours a day.

Of those Fast & Healthy with cable television, 36% watch it 11 or more hours per week, just average for this age group (35%). In contrast, more Traditional Couponers (42%) watch cable television this frequently. And no cable network we measured appeals to the Fast & Healthy.

Sitcoms and soaps

When they do watch television, whether cable or network, Fast & Healthy are above average (43%) in watching situation comedies several times a week or more as compared to those 40 to 64 (40%). Fast & Healthy favor soap operas and are above average in watching them several times a week or more as compared to the total 40 to 64-year-old population. While 30% of the Nutritional Concerned in this age group watch educational shows several times a week or more, far fewer Fast & Healthy do so (22%). Game shows, sports, news and current affairs, and talk shows are all watched by below average numbers of Fast & Healthy.

Compared to the total 40 to 64 population, Fast & Healthy are below average in the time they spend reading newspapers and listening to radio. Magazines are also not a good way to reach the Fast & Healthy. More of those in this segment never read magazines (18%), the highest percentage of Food segments 40 to 64. In addition, below average numbers of them spend 11 or more hours a week reading magazines (7%). Of the magazines we track in our surveys, the Fast & Healthy reveal themselves to be only average or below average subscribers or regular buyers of them. As we've pointed out, marketers will have to work very hard to reach Fast & Healthy through the mass media.

A new approach

Marketers' frustration with mass media is escalating, and its efficacy is being called into question as never before. The selection of mass media vehicles is still heavily dependent on demographics, although some optimizer programs have introduced a behavioral perspective. Considering the millions they spend on mass media, marketers should consider a truly innovative way of selecting media. Rather than simply oil the rusting mechanisms that exist today, they would benefit from thinking in an entirely new way about media selection.

We've demonstrated that it is feasible and worthwhile to select media based on psychographic or attitudinal segments. Further defining segments *receptive* to the product or service using demographics, behaviors, and media preferences increases the probability that the best customers are reached most efficiently.

References

Rothenberg, Randall. "Bye-Bye: The Net's precision accountability will kill not only traditional advertising, but its parasite, Big Media. Sniff." *Wired* January 1998.

"CMR forecasts slight rise in overall ad spending for 2002." *CMR* 22 January, 2002. 22 February, 2002 www.cmr.com.

Cardona, Mercedes M. "Advertising under pressure." *Advertising Age* 18 February, 2002.

Wellner, Alison Steiner. "The female persuasion." *American Demographics* February 2002.

Wellner, Alison Steiner.

Chapter 24

WORDS AND
IMAGES KEYED
TO SEGMENT

We've all had the experience of watching or reading an advertisement and wondering to whom it was targeted. Certainly not ourselves. Having seen or heard the ad, we are now aware of the product or service, but are convinced that it must be for someone on another planet. We certainly aren't interested in checking it out.

An advertisement that fails to find *receptive* consumers and deliver a message they consider *relevant* will have great difficulty in generating sales. Conversely, when advertising hits someone's "hot buttons" it has succeeded in conveying a relevant message to someone open to receive and consider it. It has generated interest, not just awareness.

Advertisers are obviously targeting messages to the consumers of products and services in an attempt to generate sales. Unfortunately, consumers themselves are very frequently left out of the loop in determining which messages would motivate them to buy. Today much messaging springs from product specifications, rather than the consumers' interests or needs. Because some producers consider a certain product attribute or twist unique, they leap to the conclusion that what enthralls them will move the entire market.

A recent example of a company creating advertising out of sync with the needs of potential buyers are the ads which TiVo ran for its personal digital recorder (PVR) in 2000. According to *Advertising Age*, "TiVo intended to spend $50 million on the campaign." After all these expenditures, TiVo has a "subscriber base of 280,000, a blip against the 105 million American TV households." The company's humorous ads attempted to attract young consumers by stressing TiVo as a way in which they could liberate themselves from television's control. If the ads had provided basic information about this new type of product to consumers, perhaps more of them would have bought it.

At other times, marketers create messaging by observing the market place and developing their own assumptions of what is motivating buyers. Marketers see increasing sales of larger cars. They may then craft messaging around the comfort of driving their large cars, attributing their popularity to the consumers' expanding girth. The reality may be that those buying the cars are motivated by the safety offered by a large car.

A step up from intuiting which messages will motivate consumers is simply asking them directly. Traditionally, attitudes or psychographics have been used in the creation of messages and the selection of images. Conventionally, marketers use focus groups or a more traditional survey, asking a few attitudinal questions for this purpose.

Instead, we advocate using a psychographic segmentation in which attitudes are both quantified and thoroughly developed for this function. Such a segmentation serves as a platform on which a marketer can integrate every aspect of marketing, from messaging to product development, and from media selection to customer relationship management (CRM).

Applied to our segments

Once a marketer finds the psychographic segment that is the best fit for his or her product or service, the process of creating messages that motivate that segment is relatively straightforward. We've used a few of the segments from our nine segmentation strategies on the mature market to illustrate how a psychographic segmentation can be used to create messages and select imagery. This process, we believe, makes the creation of messaging and the selection of imagery reliable, forthright, and consistent with other marketing and sales activities.

Lifetime learning

Among the Lifestyle segments, the Upbeat Enjoyers are the natural market for programs such as Elderhostel. Messages that refer to their commitment to *exploring new intellectual horizons* are key in connecting with Upbeat Enjoyers. They want to *remain mentally active* and their memories, they believe, are just as good as ever. Such educational courses should be positioned as the next step in *a process of lifetime learning*. Learning in the *company of others* should also be played up for this sociable segment. And, of course, those pictured in the ads should look 10 to 20 years younger than the targeted demographic. Upbeat Enjoyers feel *young, energetic, and attractive*.

Safety prime motivator

A product finding its natural market with the Threatened Actives, another Lifestyle segment, is a device which senses motion and automatically turns on a light in a room as one enters. This device would give the Threatened Actives a measure of *control over their lives*, something that is very important to them. Threatened Actives believe their neighborhoods are unsafe. This product would increase the Threatened Actives' *sense of safety*, providing them with a *feeling of security*.

Another message should convey the idea that the device will allow them to *continue to live in their homes*. Threatened Actives are absolutely committed to never having to move out of their homes. An image showing a Threatened Active couple enjoying their brightly lit home would suggest that the device had brought them safety, security, and the satisfaction of living in their own home.

Videos for health

A marketer of a video on breast self-examination has decided to target the Internal Health Actives, one of the six Health Information segments. Those in this segment retain the locus of control over their own health, and they would be a receptive market for such a video. Key messages in targeting Internal Health Actives for this product would include that they *accept responsibility for their own health*. In addition, Internal Health Actives would respond to a message that the video would help them make the *everyday choices* that would help them to enjoy good health. The message that Internal Health Actives *make the time* to take care of their health is an important one. The pay-off for those in this segment is that breast self-examination will help them enjoy *a long and healthy life*.

Guaranteed repairs

Car dealers who market their repair services to the Certitude Seekers should not position themselves as low-cost providers. Certitude Seekers want guaranteed reliability, not low prices. Because they know so little about how cars work, they have to rely on externals. Seeking to attract Certitude Seekers, a dealership must *emphasize guarantees and warrantees* in its messaging.

Its mechanics must be touted as *highly skilled and specialized*, with their work backed up by a *good warranty*. Messages should inform Certitude Seekers about the *quality of parts*, which are also guaranteed. That the dealership provides *continuity of service* — or the semblance of continuity

— is a message that should also be conveyed in order to attract Certitude Seekers.

Easing frustration

At the other end of the spectrum, a car parts store should target the Car Repair Savvy. This segment enjoys repairing its cars, but is frustrated by not having access to the tools and information needed in order to continue to be able to repair its cars. A car parts store should emphasize that it *facilitates the repairs* that Car Repair Savvy wish to make. This facilitation includes training, manuals, brochures, seminars, tools, and auto bays that can be rented. The car parts store becomes *a partner* in helping the Car Repair Savvy *realize their dream*. The store will help this segment *recapture the days* when everyone could repair his or her car if they wanted to. An image showing a Car Repair Savvy, a grease smear across his or her cheek, working happily away on their car in a bay rented from a car repair store says it all.

A structured trip

A large packager of escorted tours to Europe has decided to structure tours specifically for the mature market and wants to attract Anxious Travelers. In terms of both their attitudes and behaviors, Anxious Travelers are currently the best target for such tours.

The escorted tour company knows that messages directed at Anxious Travelers must stress *personal safety*. The *familiarity* the tour company has with the language, foods, and customs of the country to be visited should also be conveyed. An image showing a traveler eating a meal the Anxious Traveler can recognize, in a setting that looks familiar, and chatting with others who look much like him- or herself would convey the safety and security that Anxious Travelers crave from a travel experience.

In addition, that the tour is *a great value*, both in terms of costs and experiences, must be promoted to appeal to this segment. The escorted tour company has to communicate that it will provide *detailed travel plans*, so that Anxious Travelers will know what they are doing every minute of every day. Planning and structure reduce the Anxious Travelers' misgivings and concerns about travel.

A pure experience

Independent Adventurers are the best target for those marketing destinations *undiscovered* by U.S. tourists, such as Chile's Lake District, an area it shares with Argentina. In promoting travel to its Lake District, Chile's tourism office should stress the fact that this region provides *a pristine experience* in a setting of *great natural beauty*. With breathtaking mountains and deep, blue lakes, the Lake District delivers Independent Adventurers with a *unique experience* providing solitude, where they *won't be besieged by hoards of tourists*.

Experiencing the area through *outdoor activities*, such as canoeing and hiking, should also be conveyed, as well as the fact that the trip is one *the entire family would enjoy*. The Independent Adventurers' image of their ideal trip is conveyed by a family of hikers, alone in the wilderness, making their way on a trail, a lovely lake and a ring of mountains in the background.

Computer banking

A financial institution wanting to move more of its customers to an online relationship has decided to target Self-reliant Savers. Attitudinally this segment is most receptive of all the Financial segments to using technology to complete financial transactions. The messages that those in this segment would find relevant include the ability to *manage their money on their own*. The use of online financial services through their institution will enable them to *monitor their spending*. Messages should emphasize the *great independence* they will enjoy and how they will be on the *forefront of technology* by using these online services.

In sharp contrast to the Self-reliant Savers, Credit Consumers avoid technology and don't recognize any of its benefits. A financial institution should focus on targeting loans to this segment, which admits that it spends too much and saves too little. Those in this segment have the second highest pre-tax household incomes and could perhaps be considered good credit risks.

Instead of emphasizing low interest rates, a financial institution targeting the Credit Consumers for a home equity loan should stress *the ease of getting the loan*. This messaging mirrors the Credit Consumers' motivations toward acquiring a loan, and images should focus on how quick it is to get a loan, with hardly any time having passed from completing the application to receiving the check.

The appeal of emotions

The importance of emotional versus rational appeals in messaging varies by product or service. Certainly, the more discretionary the purchase, the greater the importance of tapping into the consumer's emotions. But the thread of emotion runs through the purchase of every product, no matter how mundane. One strength of a psychographic segmentation is that it reveals both the rational and emotional motivations underlying the purchase of a specific product or service. Having identified what motivates his or her best prospect or customer, a marketer can focus on creating relevant messages.

REFERENCES

"4As speakers fault TiVo marketing campaign." *Advertising Age* 15 February, 2002.

Chapter 25

RELATING TO
YOUR PUBLICS

Just what is public relations?

Trying to define public relations is somewhat like trying to grasp and control a slippery eel. Some authorities label it as a type of promotion. Others stress that it is a management function, perhaps to distinguish it from mere press-agentry. In 1988 in order to clarify the role of public relations, the Public Relations Society of America (PRSA) developed a brief, one-sentence definition of it. Public relations, according to PRSA, "helps an organization and its publics adapt mutually to each other."

Public relations activities range from research to issues management, publicity to fund raising. In our complex and diverse society, public relations, according to a PRSA Foundation monograph, helps many various types of institutions "develop effective relationships with many different audiences or publics." Those who manage these institutions need the assistance of public relations so they can "understand the attitudes and values of their publics in order to achieve institutional goals." With the help of public relations, organizations can "plan, implement and measure activities to influence or change the attitudes and behavior" of their publics.

Since the type of segmentation research presented in this book focuses on attitudes and motivations, it is extremely well suited to define the attitudes held by various publics, as well as those of segments within each public. Our research also reveals the relative importance of these attitudes and motivations by segment.

Driving into the sunset

In a hypothetical case, a public relations firm has been hired by a state department of transportation. The number of accidents, some of them fatal, involving older drivers has been escalating. The department wants to create awareness of this situation. It also has to convince voters to support a plan requiring re-testing when someone 65 and older applies to renew a driver's license. Those 65 and older will also be required to present documents signed by a physician stating that they are physically able to drive safely.

The public relations firm has been hired to conduct research to isolate voters' attitudes regarding these proposals. If a series of focus groups are conducted with mature respondents, perhaps 50 or 60 persons will participate. Among those randomly selected persons we would find all four of our Lifestyle segments. During the course of these focus groups those in the public relations firm will hear and report a wide variety of views. After conducting focus groups, the firm will have no way of ranking the importance of these views, the intensity with which they are held, nor the percentage of mature voters in the state who hold these views.

In order to quantify the views they have heard, the public relations firm decides to conduct a telephone study of 500 persons 65 and older in the state. The questionnaire asks these voters to respond to a lengthy battery of attitude statements. Do they agree or disagree that mature drivers should be re-tested with an on-the-road test? Do they agree or disagree on a seven-point scale whether or not the eyesight of mature drivers should be examined by a medical doctor before a driver's license is reissued? This hypothetical survey reports that 35% of the respondents *on average* agree with re-testing, while 48% agree *on average* to have their eye sight tested. The very real differences between the Lifestyle segments on these issues have been submerged into averages. But communicating with an "average" is impossible, since an average person does not exist.

Pinpointing the problem

At the end of this research, the public relations firm has only averages. It will not know, for example, that the most vociferous objectors to the department of transportation's plan are Threatened Actives. In essence, the public relations firm will not be aware of the fact that it does not need to "influence or change the attitudes and behaviors" of all mature voters. It needs to focus its efforts on Threatened Actives, facilitating their understanding of the situation and obtaining their acceptance of re-testing. The public relations firm must communicate with Threatened Actives so that they can "mutually adapt" to each other. Unfortunately, it doesn't even know the Threatened Actives exist.

The reality, however, is that the Threatened Actives' attitudes on this particular point will be exceptionally difficult, if not impossible, to change. If the public relations firm had these insights into the Threatened Actives' intransigence, its client, the department of transportation, could realistically evaluate the Threatened Actives as a political constituency and the impact of their highly probable resistance.

A health event

A hospital's health fair publicizing its new Bone Health Clinic will draw more Proactives than Faithful Patients, two of our Health segments. Proactives are committed to taking care of themselves and concerned about doing all they can to preserve their health. Interested Proactives will be engaged by information on bone density screening, load-bearing exercises, and necessary vitamins. But fewer of the Faithful Patients, who avoid taking responsibility for their own health, will attend.

If the hospital knew that these Health segments exist and wanted to reduce osteoporosis among all mature women, not just Proactives, it would decide to make a special effort to attract Faithful Patients. It would use messages that Faithful Patients consider relevant, as well as the communication channels they prefer. Without such a targeted effort to the Faithful Patients, the hospital will find itself preaching to the converted—the Proactives.

In order to change the Faithful Patients' attitudes and behaviors the hospital will have to make a special effort to reach them through their physicians. Advertisements, news releases, and seminars on taking responsibility for one's own bone health won't motivate Faithful Patients to go to the health fair. What will work is their doctor giving them a brochure promoting the health fair and the new Bone Health Clinic as an important resource. The physician must clearly signal to the Faithful Patient that bone health is an important issue and that attending the health fair would be a positive move for them to take.

Getting geared up

In another hypothetical scenario, the Sunnyvale Garage, a small neighborhood car-repair shop, has invested in all the latest electronic equipment. Although it has highly skilled and trained mechanics it has not been able to compete successfully with car dealerships for business. The garage is owned by three brothers who are responsible for different parts of the business and also work as mechanics. Through a public relations program, including publicity and marketing communications, the Sunnyvale Garage hopes to inform those in its trading area of its expertise and high-quality service, as well as change any unfavorable opinions about it to positive ones.

The Sunnyvale Garage has decided that its garage should be positioned to reach Certitude Seekers. The management of this very professionally run garage is confident it can attract those in this segment. In addition, the garage is willing to offer the types of warranties and guarantees that Certitude Seekers want. And with long-time employees, the Sunnyvale Garage can also offer Certitude Seekers the promise that the same team of mechanics will always work on their cars.

In order to reposition itself in the eyes of its target segment, the garage issues news releases throughout the year highlighting car care. These releases offer tips on how to work with an auto mechanic and how to identify a well-run garage. These news releases are often printed in the two community newspapers which serve the garage's market area. In addition, a top mechanic from the garage regularly participates in a local call-in show at the local college's radio station, answering questions regarding car maintenance and repair. Another Sunnyvale mechanic teaches seminars through community education on basic car care.

Over a period of three years these publicity efforts have increased business at the Sunnyvale Garage from 12% to 16% each year. By understanding the motivations of the Certitude Seekers, this small business has focused all of its miniscule public relations budget on the messages considered relevant by Certitude Seekers, the psychographic segment it wants to attract.

Opening a farmers' market

Public relations includes community relations activities which seek to improve the community as a place to live. A neighborhood organizing council has decided to open a farmers' market in the local grammar school's parking lot. The parking lot is not being used for cars and a farmers' market would be a positive addition to the neighborhood.

While they hope to attract the entire neighborhood to visit the farmers' market, the organizers realize that not everyone will shop there. Those responsible for the market know that since they will not be offering convenience foods, such as bagged salads or pre-cut broccoli, they will not attract many Fast & Healthy. They are also convinced that few Traditional Couponers will visit, and if they do, it will only be to buy a sack of potatoes. By selling locally produced fruits and vegetables, the organizers of the new farmers' market know that most of their customers will be Nutrition Concerned, who will be most involved with the farmers' market, making the most visits to it.

With this insight the organizers can begin planning for the market and focusing its public relations campaign on this segment. News releases issued about the farmers' market will stress the fact that the produce will be free of pesticides and certified as grown organically. They reveal that the produce will be exceptionally fresh, having traveled from a nearby field to the market within five hours. The names of the farms where the produce was grown will be displayed prominently. The organizers have invited the local extension agent to visit the market and share recipes on cooking some lesser-known, but highly nutritious, vegetables, such as kale and collard greens.

In a crisis

A company offering cruises to the Caribbean is the long-time client of a public relations firm. During the second day of one of its cruises an unfortunate incident occurs: a water pipe bursts and some of the rooms are flooded. While those affected were moved to other rooms and their clothes were cleaned, the cruise line recognizes it must do more to compensate these customers.

The public relations firm realizes that most of those on the cruise are either Pampered Relaxers or Global Explorers, two of our Travel segments. In order to deal with the crisis and make it right, the firm must quickly develop one or more compensation strategies that will appease these two very different types of cruisers.

The firm develops two offers based on the attitudes and motivations of Pampered Relaxers and Global Explorers. Those affected by the burst pipe are told they can select one offer. The first package includes an hour-long massage, a free shampoo and styling at the ship's beauty shop, a superb fruit basket and a bottle of very good champagne. The second package includes a day-long shore trip with all expenses covered by the cruise line. The cruisers selecting this package will enjoy encountering a culture very different than their own.

The first package was designed for Pampered Relaxers, the second for Global Explorers. It is obvious that dealing with the crisis by offering just one compensation package would have left one segment or the other still disgruntled because of its experience. Pampered Relaxers have little interest in encountering a new culture. Conversely, Global Explorers value new cultural experiences far more than a shampoo and blow dry.

Measuring attitudes for public relations

As defined by PRSA, the measurement of attitudes in order "to influence or change... attitudes" is at the heart of public relations activities. Those in public relations must "understand attitudes." Rather than rely on their own intuition, feedback from non-quantifiable focus groups, or attitudinal measures reported on a mythical average, public relations practitioners would find it of value to use the type of psychographic segmentation research we have described in this book.

The quantifiable psychographic segments we develop would give public relations practitioners a thorough understanding of the attitudes they are attempting to reinforce or change — and how these attitudes relate to one another. Whatever the public relations activity, the use of a robust, precise, and highly targeted psychographic or attitudinal segmentation strategy would shape more actionable and accountable programs. Basing its strategies and tactics on such segments would increase the legitimacy of public relations and further integrate its activities into other marketing efforts.

REFERENCES

"Public Relations: An Overview." *Public Relations Society of America Foundation*. 5 March, 2002 www.tampa.prsa.org/pr101.

Chapter 26

IMPROVING INTERNET CONNECTIONS

Reality versus buzz

According to the IAB Internet Advertising Revenue Report compiled by PriceWaterhouseCoopers, revenues from Internet advertising sales tripled from 1996 to 1997. Over the next three years, expenditures on advertising via the Internet doubled each year to reach $8.2 billion in 2000. Then, for a variety of reasons, Internet ad revenues plummeted in 2001 to their 1999 levels.

That the industry was ill-prepared for this dramatic downturn is evidenced by the tsunami of buzz that hit in 1999 and early 2000. At that time, market researchers forecast that banner ad sales would reach astronomical highs. AdZone Research Inc., for example, predicted that "online ad sales would hit $16 billion" in 2001. Instead, in that year ad revenue hit only $7.3 billion, "10% lighter than in 2000."

Admittedly, advertising sales in all channels declined in 2001. But the fact that Internet banner advertising sales did not increase was especially painful in the light of immense expectations. Born in the years of go-go growth, the nascent Internet advertising industry had never before experienced a recession. The dot com implosion of 2001 took the air out of Internet advertising's hot air balloon and advertisers began to question their assumptions regarding this channel. The events of September 11, 2001 dealt yet another blow to Internet advertising, as well as to the entire advertising industry.

Disillusionment sets in

And, finally, Internet advertising, which had been introduced as a panacea for the ills of mass media, was being examined by marketers in the cold light of reality. For many, yet another cure for advertising's malaise had proven unequal to the task. Commenting on expectations of the Internet, Fred Rubin, director of iDeutsch, says that "It's a myth that this medium should respond like a mature medium. It's an unbelievably immature medium . . . A new medium is not made overnight."

Click-through was, until recently, the ultimate measure of a banner ad's success. And many marketers were stunned to learn that "just 0.3% of Web surfers" click-through. The evolving industry responded to criticism with new formats and different types of advertising. The result is that banners, which accounted for 50% of revenues for the first nine months of 2000, fell to only 36% of revenues during the same period in 2001. Emerging sources of revenues, such as slotting fees, took up the slack, as did the growth in classified advertising.

In late 2001 and early 2002 online revenues held steady, a fact Greg Stuart, president of the Interactive Advertising Bureau (IAB), viewed "as a positive sign . . . the Internet is holding it's [sic] own against what we have been hearing about other advertising sectors, confirming that advertisers are not deserting the medium and in fact are committed to the Internet long term." Today the highest prediction for online advertising revenue in 2002 comes from eMarketer Inc., which forecasts $9 billion in sales.

Studies by Morgan Stanley Dean Witter, Marketing Intelligence, Nielsen Media Research, and others show that online advertising works. Dynamic Logic reports that "online ads produce a 4 percent lift in brand awareness, a 15 percent lift in message association, a 1 percent lift in purchase intent, and a 30 percent lift in ad recall." A demonstration project conducted by multiple sponsors, including the Advertising Research Foundation (ARF), on Unilever Home & Personal Care's Dove Nutrium Bar further validates the value of online advertising, finding that its "share in the media mix can have a significant increase in the effectiveness of an overall advertising campaign."

Mature market spurs Internet sales

In 2001 the allure of the Internet as the hottest medium around melted into the reality that it had become just another mundane communication channel, one used by persons of all ages. That year the Gartner Group found that two-thirds of American adults use the Internet once a month or more. In terms of which demographic group uses the Internet most heavily, a survey from Media Metrix showed that in a month Americans 45 to 64 "went online an average of 6.3 days more than the 18-to-24-year-old 'Internet Generation,' stayed on more than two hours more, and visited an average of 150 more unique pages a month."

But the myths surrounding the Internet are pervasive and extend to those who are on it. Those marketing on the Internet are far more interested in Generation Y, as opposed to baby boomers and their elders. The reality is that marketers advertising on the Internet should be targeting a far older demographic.

In terms of present sales, the Gartner Group study found that teenage Internet users are far less likely to purchase online as compared to online adults. And purchases made by online teenagers are typically funded by a credit card belonging to mom or dad. This study revealed that those who are 55 and older are "better customers than the youngest." For example, Americans 55 and older spent $92 on average online over the first quarter of 2001. In contrast, those 18 to 24 didn't even spend half as much ($40). The Gartner study points out that baby boomers "were responsible for more than half of all online sales in the first quarter of 2001."

Great potential in mature market

And older shoppers are increasing their reliance on online shopping according to a study conducted in 2002 for eMarketer. The study reports that more than half (54%) of Internet shoppers 35 to 54 buy online more now than they did a year ago, while shopping among those 55 to 70 has increased by 50%. In contrast, only about one in three (37%) of online shoppers 18 to 34 reported that they are shopping more online now as compared to last year. Regarding future sales, demographically those 55 and older represent a far larger potential market as compared to those under 35. Among those 18 to 24, nine million are online buyers as compared to 33 million baby boomers 35 to 54 in this category.

Besides the fact that baby boomers and their elders represent an immense, lucrative, and growing market, the Gartner study also demonstrates that online buying has "nearly peaked." This study supports the view that "there is a limit to the total proportion of users who are willing to use the Internet for commerce...now almost all browsers are also buyers."

If this argument is accepted, knowing the psychographics of current buyers, as well as those of browsers, becomes even more critical. And an understanding of the psychographic segments within the mature market, the Internet's best customers, is especially important. In-depth insights into the motivations of these groups would help Internet merchants present *relevant* messages to *receptive* psychographic segments.

Boomers fuel e-travel sales

A study released by IDC in 2001 projects that the online travel sector will enjoy a boom fueled by the increase in baby boomers. IDC concludes "that aging baby boomers are poised to become a significant purchasing force." IDC describes baby boomers as a group having both the "time and funds to travel." But, as we've noted, significant attitudinal and behavioral differences exist among our Travel segments.

Among these segments, the Global Explorers and Independent Adventurers are attitudinally most open to the idea of making travel arrangements through the Internet. From a behavioral perspective, when asked about activities in which they regularly participate, one in five of both Global Explorers and Independent Adventurers give the Internet as an interest, signaling the highest level of Internet participation among the Travel segments.

In terms of the hours they spend on the Internet, their access at home to the Internet, and their ownership of a computer in their homes, Independent Adventurers are the best targets for Internet travel sites. While Global Explorers aged 40 to 64 are average as compared to this age group as a whole in the number of them who spend 11 hours or more on the Internet a week, Independent Adventurers in this age group are 50% higher.

Global Explorers are just average in terms of Internet access and having a computer in the home, whereas far more Independent Adventurers exceed the average for the total 40 to 64 age population. For example, 50% more Independent Adventurers than the total 40 to 64 age population have Internet access in their homes. The Internet appears to be a very good medium for travel companies to use in reaching Independent Adventurers.

Independent Adventurers key

The success that airlines will have in moving ticketing and other travel functions online will be heavily dependent on Independent Adventurers. Fortunately for the airlines, a key motivator for those in this segment is the use of airline frequent flyer miles when traveling. This Travel segment's attitude is dramatically reflected in its behaviors. From 11 airline frequent flyer clubs in our surveys in which our respondents could note their participation, only two have double-digit membership levels within the 40 to 64 age population. In sharp contrast, six frequent flyer clubs have double-digit membership levels among Independent Adventurers in this age group.

That the Independent Adventurers are worth pursuing online is reinforced by the fact that they also enjoy the highest median pre-tax household income among Travel segments in the 40 to 64 age group. While the median income for this age group is $43,397, that of Independent Adventurers is $55,876. One in five Independent Adventurers enjoys a pre-tax household income of $100,000 and above.

But marketing to the Independent Adventurers requires an acute knowledge of their motivations to travel, which we explored in Chapter 6. Overlaying our Travel segments onto our Lifestyle segments reveals that disproportionate numbers of Independent Adventurers are also Financial Positives. This Super Segment shows many Independent Adventurers seeking not only a pristine, natural experience when they travel, but also demanding high quality and great value. To succeed with this segment, marketers will have to apply these kinds of insights to their marketing programs, including those on the Internet.

Health through the Internet

Examining our Health Information segments leads us to conclude that in the 40 to 64 age population more than half (53%) are not motivated to access health information. In Chapter 15 we discussed the motivations and attitudes of the Uninvolved Fatalists, Self-directed Positives, and Fearful Listeners. Pharmaceutical companies, health-related associations, medical device manufacturers, distributors of wellness products, and others must concede the massive impediments that exist in reaching half of those in this age group who are not at all receptive to what they have to sell or say. In various ways, the remaining 47% of those 40 to 64 are interested in health information and fall into the Internal Health Actives, Confused Compliants, and External Health Actives segments. The deep attitudinal chasm that exists between these two groups of Health Information segments must be factored in when planning a health information site.

Among the three Health Information segments interested in health-related information, Internal Health Actives are most involved with the Internet. More Internal Health Actives access the Internet each week and are above average in the hours they spend on it. More Internal Health Actives 40 to 64 report that the Internet is an activity in which they regularly participate (30%) as compared to this population as a whole (24%). In terms of having accessed the Internet for health information in the past 12 months, Internal Health Actives are 33% higher than average on this point. In contrast, the other Health Information segments are below average or average in accessing the Internet for health-related advice.

Prefer lifestyle changes

As we have noted in other chapters, Internal Health Actives are far more committed to lifestyle changes than taking pharmaceutical drugs. These attitudes translate into the fact that fewer Internal Health Actives 40 to 64 take a prescription drug (53%), compared to the 40 to 64 population as a whole (57%). While 19% of those 40 to 64 take three or more prescription drugs daily, only 15% of the Internal Health Actives do so.

Internal Health Actives are committed to exercise and taking care of their health. For example, more Internal Health Actives 40 to 64 exercise to an aerobic level four or more times a week (44%) as compared to the 40 to 64 population as a whole (33%) and to each of the other Health Information segments.

Optimizing health

While Internal Health Actives are an excellent target for companies selling products and services to increase or optimize health, they are less attractive to pharmaceutical companies. As we've noted, fewer Internal Health Actives 40 to 64 take a prescription drug. While pharmaceutical companies are pouring increasing dollars into Internet websites and DTC advertising in this channel, those 40 to 64 who are using the Internet are most apt to be Internal Health Actives, who are not an optimal Health Information segment for pharmaceutical sales.

A preference for using the Internet itself to sell pharmaceutical drugs can also be questioned. There is nothing inherent in Internet access that promotes pharmaceutical sales. Our studies show that in the 40 to 64 population, those with Internet access are not more prone to ask a doctor about an advertised drug (28%) as compared to those without Internet access (29%).

Viewed from another perspective, having seen a direct-to-consumer (DTC) advertisement, below average numbers of Internal Health Actives check out a prescription drug on the pharmaceutical company's web site. They are far more apt to ask a doctor or pharmacist about it. In contrast, in this situation above average numbers of External Health Actives access the pharmaceutical company's web site.

An evolving medium

Now that Internet hype has been replaced by a more realistic perspective, the medium must now work harder and smarter to prove its effectiveness to marketers. Certainly the mosaic of information on online shoppers and browsers should be continually added to and refined. To measurements of what is being viewed and the length of someone's visit, the Internet must also provide more information on who is visiting and why.

One way of doing so is to use psychographic insights to tailor website visits to the attitudinal segments of those who browse and shop online. The psychographics of online shoppers or visitors can be obtained in a number of ways: by asking visitors to register and provide information, appending data to an existing database, and extrapolating from mouse clicks. By focusing on the psychographics of those who browse and buy online, the Internet can position itself as effective in reaching best customers, regardless of age group.

Collaborative filtering, suggesting alternative products to shoppers based on related selections made on other visits or by other shoppers, is useful in establishing a relationship with shoppers, but only at the most minimal level. This methodology offers only general suggestions and lacks any ability to identify a shopper's motivations. Rather than merely suggesting yet another swimsuit at the Land's End website, the classification of a shopper into a psychographic segment would allow for products and messages that would forge deeper bonds. If Land's End knew a shopper was committed to value; or was only interested in handmade, unique items, or craved luxury, products with these attributes could be suggested and described in relevant language.

Instead of sliding into the morass of a mass medium, the Internet should strive to be increasingly relevant to those who go online. By using psychographics, Internet marketers can enrich online relationships.

REFERENCES

PriceWaterhouseCoopers, *IAB Internet Advertising Revenue Report.* Third quarter 2001.

Crockett, Roger O. "Beware of optimists." *BusinessWeek* 18 February, 2002.

Rosner, Hillary. "Reality check." *Brandweek* 4 February, 2002.

Crockett, Roger O.

PriceWaterhouseCoopers.

PriceWaterhouseCoopers.

Crockett, Roger O.

Rosner, Hillary.

"Internet is powerful complement to traditional advertising media" *IAB* 6 February, 2002. 16 March, 2002 www.IAB.net/news.

Schehr, David. "The Internet market you're overlooking: Go for the gray." *Gartner/G2* 22 August, 2001. March 15, 2002 www.bethetweezer.com.

Cook, Rick. "One year ago: Internet not just for kids anymore." *E-commerce Times* 4 April, 2001. 5 March, 2002 www.ecommerce-times.com.

Schehr, David.

"eMarketer: Older shoppers buying online more" *NUA* 7 March, 2002. 12 March, 2002 www.nua.ie/surveys.

Schehr, David.

Saliba, Clare. "Study: Baby boomers to drive e-travel sales." *E-commerce Times* 18 May, 2001. 5 March, 2002 www.ecommerce-times.com.

27

DIRECT MARKETING'S NEXT STEP

It *is* the market

Those 40 and older are clearly the dominant demographic in direct marketing, however one measures it. The vast majority of direct marketing purchases (73%) are made by those 40 and older. Catalogs ranging from L.L. Bean to Land's End, from J. Jill to Lillian Vernon all depend on the mature market for the bulk of their sales.

Miniscule results

It's true that direct marketing holds out the promise of accountability so lacking in mass media. But with all its modeling and tracking, profiling and emphasis on qualifying prospects based on RFM — that is, recency, frequency, and monetary value—a response rate of 2 or 3% is a goal to which direct marketers aspire. What can be added to the direct marketing proposition to improve response rates and make certain that the tons of offers and catalogs mailed each year reach receptive and qualified prospects? To date the industry has relied overwhelmingly on demographics and behaviors. We support its emerging interest in adding attitudes and psychographics to databases in order to improve response rates.

Rejuvenation by mail

As a hypothetical example of the direct marketing approach we can consider a large packaged goods company that has recently acquired a line of intensive treatment products specifically targeting mature skin. The company knows that whether measured by the numbers of buyers, the volume they purchase, or the dollars they spend, women 55 and older are clearly over consumers of facial treatment products. For example, at mid year 2001 Information Resources, Inc. reported that female heads of households 55 and older indexed at 133, that is, 33% higher than the national average, in the category of facial moisturizers by dollars spent. By every measure, females 34 and younger are vast under consumers of facial moisturizers.

Our hypothetical company wishes to introduce these products to mature women, enticing them to purchase them by direct mail. The company has decided to target the Lifestyle segments, specifically females 40 and older in the Financial Positive segment, 29% of this population.

Targeting Lifestyle segments

In examining the attitudes of those in the Financial Positive segment, we know that they, along with the Insecure, are the most concerned with looking younger. Of all the Lifestyle segments, Financial Positives are by far the most motivated to use cosmetics, hair dyes, and treatment products for the skin. They don't think they look as good as they did when they were younger and are committed to preserving at least the allusion of youth, whether through creams or plastic surgery.

Unlike the Insecure, Financial Positives have high household incomes with which they can purchase expensive creams. Female Financial Positives have a pre-tax household income of $42,563, the highest of all the Lifestyle segments and far higher than the median income for females 40 and older ($30,808). Female Financial Positives are then both highly receptive to treatment products and able to pay for them.

Over consumers of treatment products

Financial Positives are massive over consumers of such products as sunscreens, eye creams, moisturizers, and treatment products. Those in this segment are clearly the best customers for companies such as Lancôme, Estee Lauder, and Elizabeth Arden. Financial Positives repeatedly demonstrate that compared to the other Lifestyle segments, more of them regularly use skin-care and wrinkle-reducing products. Among female Financial Positives, 34% report regularly using a wrinkle-reducing cream as compared to 23% of females in the total 40 and older market. While 29% of female Financial Positives use an eye cream, 18% of females 40 and older do so.

Not only are Financial Positives over consumers of treatment products, they are also the best consumers of color cosmetics in the 40 and older market. From lipstick to foundation, mascara to eye shadow, Financial Positives are clearly on a mission to look as young and as attractive as possible. More female Financial Positives regularly dye their hair (40%) as compared to all women 40 and older (31%). More female Financial Positives (61%) wear mascara as compared to females 40 and older (49%).

Reaction to merchandise catalogs

But our hypothetical direct marketer of treatment products through direct mail should also know that when they receive a merchandise catalog via direct mail, female Financial Positives are just average in their reactions to it. Similar percentages of female Financial Positives and the 40 and older female population as a whole are apt to toss away a merchandise catalog they've received through direct mail unopened (8% and 9%). Female Financial Positives 40 and older are also only average (71%) in opening a direct mail catalog selling merchandise and reading it, as compared to the total female 40 and older population (70%).

More female Insecure open and read merchandise catalogs (74%) compared to all the Lifestyle segments and the total 40 and older female population (70%). Unfortunately, because of their lower incomes, they are the least able to purchase from a catalog. We see that female Insecure spend less on personal grooming items wherever they are purchased. While female Financial Positives spent the most on personal grooming over the past four weeks, a median of $26.15, the Insecure spent the least, a median of only $17.63.

In considering purchases made through a catalog in the last three months, female Financial Positives spent a median of $151.58, far more than any other Lifestyle segment and more than females 40 and older ($128.00). While more female Insecure are reading catalogs, their expenditures in this channel over the past three months is the lowest of the Lifestyle segments, a median of just $110.92.

The best customers

Selling cosmetics and treatment products to female Financial Positives makes sense. They are by far the segment that is attitudinally most *receptive* to the use of such products. Financial Positives also demonstrate their motivation to use such products through their behaviors. In addition, they also have the financial resources to purchase expensive products. Our data shows that the challenge for someone selling cosmetics and treatment products by direct mail and targeting the Financial Positives is to woo them away from other channels of distribution.

In offering these products to the Financial Positives through direct mail, we must understand not only their motivations in purchasing them, but also their current sources of such products. Over the past three months, 17% of female Financial Positives have purchased wrinkle-reducing products in a drug or discount store as compared to 11% of the total 40 and older population. Another 8% had purchased such products in a department store as compared to 5% of females 40 and older. But only 3% had purchased wrinkle-reducing products from a catalog through direct mail as compared to 2% of females 40 and older.

We know then that more female Financial Positives are making purchases of wrinkle-reducing products at a drug or discount store, while fewer of them are buying such products from a department store or catalog. That the female Financial Positive's preferred source for cosmetics and treatment products is a drug or discount store underscores their value orientation.

Predictive capability

The strong predictive capability of the type of psychographic segmentation strategies we create suggests that Financial Positives could be lured away by a trusted brand name offering them a great value through direct mail. A Caswell-Massey offer of a 32 ounce bottle of high-quality almond-scented hand cream at a 33% savings is the type of value proposition Financial Positives would find appealing. L'Occitane, a French manufacturer of cosmetic, aromatherapy, and treatment products, rewards frequent catalog buyers with a 10% discount card. And both of these brands offer the high-quality products Financial Positives are motivated to buy.

Overlaying a custom-designed psychographic segmentation on the purchase of cosmetics and treatment products through direct mail onto the Lifestyle segments, and specifically the Financial Positives, would further develop our understanding of *why* an attitudinally based segment would switch from its current channels and purchase more treatment products from a catalog. Wrapping demographics and behaviors around a motivational segmentation strategy, a marketer would be able to reach his or her best customers with products they want and messages they consider relevant.

Credit card mania

As credit card offers continue to overwhelm mail boxes, direct marketers at VISA and American Express should consider targeting the Financial segments. The Savvy Investors, 24% of the 40 and older market, enjoy the highest median income of $54,757 as compared to $35,752 for this population overall. Among Savvy Investors, 42% have a pre-tax household income of $75,000.

Unfortunately for credit card marketers, when Savvy Investors receive a credit card offer in the mail, their overwhelming reaction (72%) is to throw it away unopened. In contrast, the Strapped Spenders are least apt to take this action (53%). Savvy Investors are also less apt (4%) than the Strapped Spenders (14%) to put the piece aside for later reading. Perhaps Strapped Spenders are searching for a credit card offering a lower interest rate.

The Financial segment with the highest income, Savvy Investors clearly believe they have enough credit cards. While Savvy Investors are not afraid to incur credit card debt, they are attitudinally committed to paying off such debt each month. Savvy Investors will not generate late fees and interest payments on balances for credit card companies.

Ability to pay

Strapped Spenders, who feel they spend too much and save too little, are far more apt to incur such fees and charges as compared to Savvy Investors. With a median income of $29,100, lower than the median income of those 40 and older ($35,752), will Strapped Spenders be able to make even minimum payments on their unpaid balances? In marketing to Strapped Spenders, credit card companies walk a tightrope between this segment's motivation to charge and incur debt and its ability to keep current on its debt payments.

Current methods lacking

Direct marketing offers the accountability that mass media lacks. Marketers can determine which appeals, products, and mailings yield the highest response rates. The problem remains, however, that response rates in the direct marketing industry are typically in the low single digits. It is apparent that current conventional approaches are not yielding cost-effective results. As the cost of paper and postage escalates, alternative methods of reaching best prospects and customers become increasingly appealing. Complementing a catalog with an online presence is one such improvement.

Current methods of identifying the best prospect or customer, such as demographics, behaviors, life stage, and lifestyle, have not succeeded in vaulting the direct marketing response rate into the double digits. Identifying those prospects or customers receptive to buying through a catalog, favorable to specific catalog brands, and open to certain offerings by their psychographic segments will give direct marketers increased refinement in their targeting.

Identification of their key psychographic segment(s) will also allow direct marketers to integrate all of their efforts, from layout to product offerings, messaging to customer service, based on a segment's motivations and needs. It is true that adding a known — not intuited — psychographic tag will take additional time and entail an increased expense. But the overall results will make such an effort worthwhile.

REFERENCES

Abacus news release. "Abacus trend report details catalog buying habits" 14 November, 2000.

Chapter 28

Attitudes Improve CRM Efforts

Lots of data, fewer insights

Computers with massive storage capabilities whirl away, data is collected at a ferocious pace, and analysts build complex models to identify best customers. But customer relationship management (CRM), once touted as the newest marketing panacea, has recently suffered from increasing dissatisfaction. According to one commentator, marketers who pursued CRM now feel "more like the Seven Dwarfs than Prince Charming, overwhelmed by a mountain of data and chastised by a consumer base that refuses to be interpreted in binary terms."

While currently practiced imperfectly, many marketers remain committed to CRM. Virtually everyone agrees that identifying and retaining customers is less expensive than acquiring them. This belief and the need to inject accountability into marketing spending are certainly still evident. Commitment to CRM is also demonstrated by the millions of dollars devoted to it. Over the next two years, expenditures on CRM are forecast to exceed those on any other major information technology projects. According to a Jupiter Media Metrix survey, 26% of U.S. businesses will spend $500,000 or more on CRM tools in the next 24 months.

CRM objective often forgotten

Perhaps many have lost their way in the CRM forest because they have forgotten its fundamental objective. That CRM is "learning to *understand the values* that are important to individual customers and using that knowledge to *deliver benefits the customer really wants* [italics ours] and making it easier to do business with the company" is not posted on any mainframe computer. To date, the focus of CRM has been primarily on information technology (IT) expenditures and the collection of data, not on the consumer.

It must be admitted that the definition of CRM varies from guru to guru and company to company. Jean-Yves Hepp, general manager of McCann Relationship Marketing (MRM) in Paris, notes that "lots of companies now claim to do customer relationship marketing but information technology companies sell an IT-led approach, direct marketing agencies are direct marketing-led, and so on."

The reality is that companies are failing every day to understand their customers and this situation hobbles CRM efforts. An examination of only one industry, financial services, suggests the extent of the problem. A recent study conducted by the Peppers & Rogers Group, the one-to-one marketing gurus, in conjunction with LOMA, an international association of insurance and financial services companies, shows that in the United States "the failure to build meaningful relationships costs banks and financial institutions about $700 million per year." Such losses will continue as long as companies focus solely on behaviors and demographics in their attempts to develop an in-depth knowledge of their most profitable customers.

Many obstacles in the way

But fulfillment of CRM's promise is too often blocked by a multitude of obstacles, ranging from an organization's structure to its culture. A successful CRM program necessitates a massive investment in training, as well as computers. And it can only be realized by a commitment at a company's highest levels. Our approach to segmentation research cannot address all of these issues directly, but it can influence many of them. It does, however, have direct application to understanding the motivations of a company's best customers. As Jean-Yves Hepp notes of his agency's CRM efforts, "We want to understand why people call and focus on providing content and quality—a different way of managing customer contacts."

The type of segmentation strategy described in this book can help marketers more easily reach the objective of all CRM efforts: being relevant to the most receptive and profitable customers. Our approach to psychographic segmentation covers both the rational, and sometimes irrational, reasons why customers buy. By understanding customers' motivations, as well as their demographics and behaviors, organizations can plan their most effective campaigns for retention, up-sell, cross-sell, and win-back. By appending segment identifiers on customers in a CRM data mart, *relevant* products and appeals will be targeted to the most *receptive* audience.

Mapping attitudes on a database

How can this strategy be accomplished? Attitudinal data are not found in today's customer databases. And collecting such attitudinal data on all of a company's customers would be an impossible task. The method we propose involves correlating psychographic segments with demographic or behavioral patterns and mapping the results on to customer databases statistically. The graphic below shows third-party demographic and behavioral data merged into a company's database. Motivational segments such as those described in

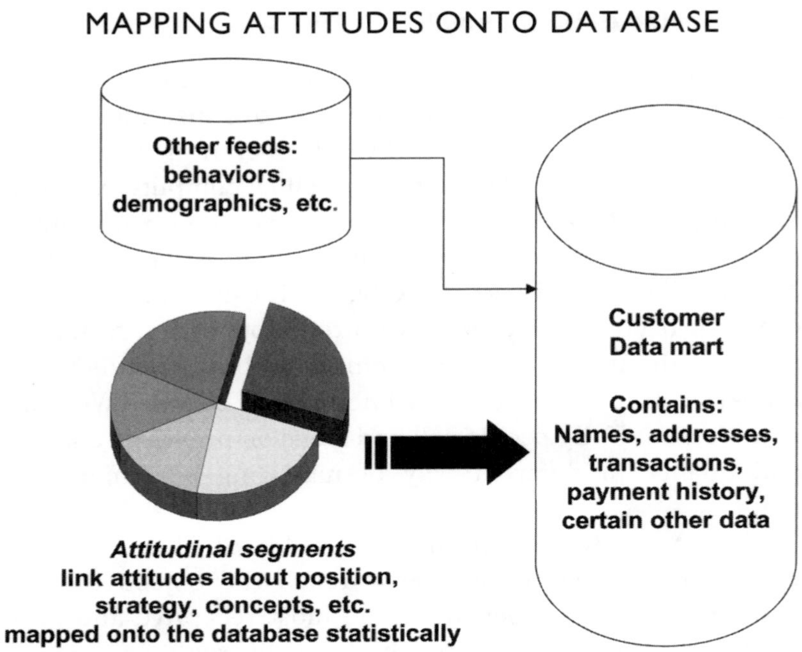

MAPPING ATTITUDES ONTO DATABASE

Figure 12: *Customer databases are enhanced dramatically with the addition of third-party demographics and behaviors. Using these data as inputs to statistical models, each customer's attitude segment can be predicted.*

this book can then be mapped analytically onto a CRM database.

An application to car sales

Exactly how a marketer can apply the approach we've outlined above is seen in the following hypothetical example. An American car manufacturer is introducing a sporty new luxury car specifically designed for baby boomers. The company decides that the primary market for the car is among affluent 40 to 60-year-old customers with pre-tax household incomes of $100,000 and above. Among this demographic group, the Stylish Fun, one of our Car Purchase segments, is selected as the optimal psychographic target.

The car manufacturer will begin its CRM program with a direct-marketing effort. Third-party demographics and lifestyle data have been appended to the company's database and the car manufacturer's IT department has used this data, as well as existing behaviors, to create a model identifying each of the Car Purchase segments, and specifically the Stylish Fun. As a next step, the IT department extracts Stylish Fun who meet the demographic criteria from the database. This sub-sample of Stylish Fun is also limited to those customers who have not purchased a car from the manufacturer for three years or more. Stylish Fun typically buy a new car far more frequently than our other Car Purchase segments.

Those in this sample receive a total of three mailings, two of which invite them to go to their local dealer to test drive the new luxury vehicle. Before that, however, they receive an initial invitation to a gala cocktail party at a local art gallery where the new luxury car will be introduced as "a work of art." A variety of celebrities will attend the event, including an internationally famous artist, a world-class race car driver, and a fashion designer who works exclusively in leather. He has created the leather interior of the new luxury car. Those who have been invited to attend have been asked to RSVP.

Tailoring responses to segment

When the call center operator pulls up a customer's record, a flag identifies him or her as a being in one of the Car Purchase segments. In the case of a Stylish Fun who has received an invitation, the operator can confirm a reservation to the cocktail party and answer any questions, always tailoring responses to this segment's interests. At the dealership level, if the direct mail recipient calls to arrange a test drive, the salesperson will see the same record flagged with the Stylish Fun label.

Customers or prospects going to the manufacturer's web site to request information or arrange for a test drive, will give their names and addresses. They will also be asked to answer the four or five classification questions placing them into a classification in a Car Purchase segment, including the Stylish Fun. Although this will be a duplicative effort in the case of existing customers, it will also be a way to check the accuracy of the classification model.

Surfers who visit the site but don't make a request for additional information or contact can also be given the opportunity to answer the classification questions. This classification adds an additional dimension to real-time personalization. While the car manufacturer will not know who has visited the site, he or she will know which psychographic segment(s) accounts for most visitors. In addition, the car manufacturer will be able to examine the information each psychographic segment accessed. This perspective will reinforce the system and provide valuable marketing insights.

Upping compliance for prescription drugs

While billions of dollars are made through the sale of pharmaceutical drugs, an immense black cloud overhangs these transactions. Whether the drug is for high cholesterol, such as Lipitor; or for osteoporosis, such as Evista; or hormone replacement therapy, such as Premarin, virtually every drug shares the same problem of non-compliance. Studies show that "about 50 percent of people fail to take medications for chronic conditions as ordered by doctors." Dr. Jerome Avorn, an associate professor of medicine at Harvard Medical School and an expert on the subject, calls non-compliance "a dirty little secret in health care."

"It is extremely difficult to get people to do anything on a routine basis," said Dr. Dennis Sprecher, the lead investigator in a study on whether cholesterol-lowering drugs work as well in "day-to-day-practice as they do in…formal experiments." The study found that 66% of those monitored "benefited less than would be predicted." The decrease in the drugs' benefit, the study concluded, resulted from non-compliance, not from the drug's lack of efficacy. The problem of non-compliance is widespread with large percentages of those who are prescribed a drug taking it only intermittently or not taking it at all. Increasing compliance by even one or two percent would generate immense revenues for pharmaceutical companies.

A CRM program for patients

According to Diana Long, principal of DML Consulting, a good CRM program "will find ways to educate and encourage patients to complete the treatment regimen." To increase compliance through a CRM program for patients currently on a drug, for example, a statin, they must be enrolled in a pharmaceutical company's database.

Because of privacy issues, enrollment can be facilitated through a physician's office, community center, health club, direct-to-consumer (DTC) advertising, a managed care organization (MCO), or through the Internet. In the case of a statin, the type of drug most typically used to treat high cholesterol, the pharmaceutical company would set up programs reinforcing lifestyle changes that will complement taking it.

While programs encouraging healthful behaviors may appear to contradict the pharmaceutical company's own best interests, this view is short sighted. Consumers in many of our psychographic segments want practical programs to help them improve their health. The reality is that they also take prescription medications to help them accomplish these goals. The opportunity exists for pharmaceutical companies to partner with the patient, MCO, and doctor in facilitating these efforts.

Specific programs may allow patients to plan menus, record what they have eaten, monitor their exercise, and keep track of stress levels for each day. Patients enrolled in a smoking cessation program could be sent helpful tips to best ensure a successful outcome as they monitor their efforts.

Classifying the patient

In order to participate in these lifestyle programs, a patient must currently be on a statin. The call center operator records which statin is being taken as well as other pertinent information. A handful of classification questions are also asked, placing the caller into one of our Health Compliance segments.

Knowing the patient's psychographic segment, the pharmaceutical company can also obtain insights on segment differences among the various statins. Perhaps Zocor is attracting more Informed Avoiders, while Lipitor is more successful in getting Trusting Believers to take its medication. While many things influence a patient's being given a certain pharmaceutical drug, this insight provides valuable feedback. It also suggests a host of new questions that must be answered on the DTC advertising of statins and the psychographics of the physicians writing these prescriptions.

Programs shaped by total profile

Of course, each patient's goals for lifestyle changes will be based on the behaviors and demographics furnished. Knowing into which Health Compliance segment a patient falls enables the pharmaceutical company to tailor all contacts and communication specifically to that segment.

For example, in the case of the Informed Avoiders the pharmaceutical company will know that those in this segment are typically on the statin only as a last resort. Taking the drug should be strongly positioned as complementing lifestyle changes. The programs offered by the pharmaceutical company will help Informed Avoiders do a better job staying in control of their health.

In contrast, most Trusting Believers will be offered a version of the lifestyle programs that are less demanding than those for Informed Avoiders. They aren't as motivated to participate in such programs as compared to the Informed Avoiders. Programs for Trusting Believers will stress the doctor's involvement in the patient's efforts, with the two of them working closely together to accomplish somewhat modest goals.

In each case e-mail messages and newsletters will be sent to participants on a weekly basis that are relevant to his or her Health Compliance segment. Participants will also be sent information on health-related events, such as walks and health fairs in their area, as well as supportive local and national resources, including yoga centers, health clubs, and health-related associations.

Knowing why they buy

Focused on IT processes, too many businesses to date have implemented CRM by spending huge sums of money on technology to collect, update and manage enormous customer databases containing information on transactions, behaviors and personal data. Today we know *who* buys *what* products, but that's not enough. Companies have to know *why* customers buy specific products and services. Effective CRM requires moving beyond behaviors to understand our customers' motivations.

The mapping of attitudes onto a company's database will bring the promise of CRM closer to reality. A company that can identify its customers by their psychographic segment will be able to design more suitable offerings, craft more relevant messages, utilize better channels of communication, and better satisfy its most profitable customers. Such a company has the keys to how and what to offer when up-selling and cross-selling. The integration of CRM with other marketing efforts will also be facilitated by a shared view of the customer extending beyond behaviors and demographics to include attitudes.

REFERENCES

Fuller, Peter. "A Two-Way Conversation." *Brandweek* 25 February, 2002.

DiPasquale, Cara B. "Study: CRM Spending to Increase." *Advertising Age* 25 February, 2002. 6 March, 2002 www.AdAge.com.

Newell, Frederick. *Loyalty.com.* New York: McGraw-Hill, 2000.

"Towards a closer relationship with customers." *Financial Times* 6 March, 2002.

"Financial services institutions lose millions annually in profit opportunities, reports LOMA and Peppers and Rogers Group." *Peppers and Rogers Group* 11 January, 2002. 2 March, 2002 www.Peppers & Rogers Group.

"Noncompliance appears endemic." *StarTribune* 10 March, 2002.

"Study: Heart patients not taking drugs." *StarTribune* 12 November, 2001.

Millar, Bill. "Writing its own prescription." *1to1 magazine* September 2001.

Chapter 29

MAKING THE
SALE

Searching for hot buttons

The salesperson looks for cues in dress, eye contact, voice —gleaning insights about the prospect in front of him or her. Sales persons analyze body language, the manner in which the prospect communicates, and involvement with the product or service. What is the prospect's underlying and basic emotional motivator, wonders the salesperson. Unfortunately, all these approaches are limited, yielding generalities, not precise information.

Some salespersons are less skilled than others in intuiting a prospect's motivations, and they remain so, regardless of experience. Training someone in these skills is a long and expensive process, something not likely to happen with today's reduced training budgets. Yet the problem remains: a salesperson is driven to discover the prospect's hot buttons in order to make the sale.

Without a defined view of the prospect's motivations, salespersons find it difficult to cross-sell and up-sell. For example, we have found consumer segments who are attitudinally unwilling to place all of their financial accounts with one institution. Trying to sell consolidation to someone in such a segment is likely to be futile because it is extremely difficult to change attitudes and motivations. Conversely, other segments are highly favorable to consolidation. The objective is to quickly and accurately discern one from the other.

Answers to the why question

While access to demographics and behaviors on prospects or current customers is useful in qualifying them, these do not yield insights into motivations. A marketer or salesperson at a financial institution may know a customer's pre-tax household income, but does not know whether he or she is motivated to save or invest and *why*. And the behaviors we know are limited to our portion of a customer's purchase history. We can't access his or her accounts or purchases with other institutions or companies. In addition, behaviors report past history and aren't necessarily applicable to the sale of new types of products or services.

With the process we propose, every salesperson, regardless of skill or experience, would be able to quickly and easily place a prospect into a psychographic segment *directly linked to the product or service at hand*. Rather than spend the bulk of an interview in directionless probing, a salesperson, with a very clear idea of a prospect's motivations, would be able to focus on refining his or her questions and actually closing the sale.

Being able to quickly categorize a prospect or existing customer into a motivational or psychographic segment also helps a salesperson decide whether the prospect is worth pursuing or not and how much time and energy to invest in this pursuit. If the prospect's motivations and attitudes show that he or she would be highly resistant to the sales message, however tailored, it may be best to move on to a more likely prospect. On the other hand, if a prospect's attitudes indicate receptivity to what is being sold, the salesperson knows which sales messages to use.

Our experience in creating segmentation strategies shows that persons in some segments are motivated by the lowest cost, while others are relatively unconcerned about what they pay. Some demand a high level of attention or service, while others prefer to be left alone. For some segments, attention must be provided in person, while others are very happy with contact through e-mail. Some segments will be excellent conduits for sales to their many friends and contacts, while others don't produce one lead. Some clients are sophisticated in their knowledge of a product or service, while others are ignorant and intend to remain so.

Setting up a system

In the process we advocate, the prospect's motivations would be identified and understood with a high degree of reliability and uniformity. For the sales process, this methodical and quantifiable approach provides immediate insights into a prospect's motivations. If the prospect becomes a customer, the categorization process is formalized, captured, and then integrated into all sales and marketing activities.

These goals can be accomplished in two steps. In the first step the salesperson informally and conversationally asks certain key questions which indicate into which psychographic segment a prospect belongs. With this guidance the salesperson can tailor his or her sales messages and strategies to the needs, interests, and motivations of this prospect. The salesperson knows the hot buttons.

If the prospect does indeed become a customer, the enrollment process would include five to eight questions categorizing him or her into a psychographic segment with a high degree of accuracy. If some of the attitudes are sensitive, less touchy parallel or surrogate questions can be used in the model. At that point, the customer's responses are fed into a computer and analyzed. The customer, now classified into a psychographic segment, is labeled as such in the database. This information then helps to shape and inform all marketing efforts, from customer-relationship management (CRM) to strategic planning, media selection to product development. All contacts and messages are keyed to the psychographic insights that are known.

This approach can be used in any sales situation where there is one-on-one contact with the prospect. The following examples illustrate this approach.

Focusing on financial sale

The bank representative, insurance agent, and stockbroker all have personal contact with existing clients and prospective ones. The opening of a new account, for example, is a good time to ask the questions necessary to place the prospect into a psychographic segmentation and thus gain the knowledge of what motivates him or her. And yet in most financial institutions this opportunity is lost.

Categorizing prospects into psychographic segments could show that two prospects opening checking accounts on the same day have very similar asset levels and incomes, but very different needs and motivations in reference to financial products. The offerings, services, and messages, the way of relating to a customer who is a Worried Frugal, as compared to one who is a Self-reliant Saver, will be very different—and yet they could have virtually identical demographics.

Boosting timeshare sales

Global Explorers are the Travel segment most motivated to buy a timeshare. Unfortunately, when timeshare companies hold sales presentations they attract Pampered Relaxers and Highway Wanderers, who have no interest in timeshares, as well as Global Explorers. Getting prospects to a timeshare presentation is expensive, often entailing free meals and entertainment and subsidized stays at the timeshare.

Sales would be increased and related costs reduced if audiences were composed of more receptive Global Explorers and fewer Highway Wanderers. Timeshare companies hire waitpersons and others in contact with the public to extend invitations to presentations. These persons can help winnow out non-receptive Travel segments. Answers to a question or two would help such intermediaries decide whether or not an invitation to a timeshare presentation should even be extended.

Once the timeshare sale is made, the buyer would answer a handful of questions placing him or her in a psychographic segment. This tag or label would then reside on the timeshare company's database, useful for further sales activities. Existing timeshare owners have demonstrated that they are the very best prospects for additional sales. And knowing that a buyer is a Global Explorer gives a timeshare company the ability to craft *relevant messages* for future sales.

Selling a hybrid product

In the sale of a complex product that touches on motivations related to different areas, it is beneficial to overlay segments. Doing so develops the profile for the best prospect and the sales approach that should be used. Although long-term care insurance is a product that has been offered for several years, until recently it has had only minimal sales. Some mature consumers weren't ready to sign up for a type of insurance they weren't sure they needed.

Demographics, particularly assets, can make the first cut in determining good candidates for long-term care insurance. But salespersons need to go to the next step and determine which prospects are *receptive* to such insurance.

The decision to purchase long-term care insurance is motivated by attitudes toward finances, retirement, and health. In order to understand how these motivations and attitudes relate to one another, it's useful to create a Super Segment, one made up of segments from multiple segmentation strategies. One such Super Segment that is a prime candidate for long-term care includes persons who are simultaneously Proactives, a Health segment, Financial Positives, a Lifestyle segment, and Savvy Investors, a Financial segment.

These segments are bound together by their ability to project themselves into the future, their commitment to taking care of themselves both physically and fiscally, and an interest in preserving their assets. Initially categorizing prospects and then customers as part of the two-step process we've outlined would result in increasing sales of long-term care insurance.

Conversely, a Super Segment composed of those who are simultaneously Optimists, a Health segment, Upbeat Enjoyers, a Lifestyle segment, and Credit Consumers, a Financial segment, would be poor prospects for long-term care insurance. Optimists believe that they are now in excellent health and will remain so. Upbeat Enjoyers have a *carpe diem* viewpoint toward life. They live for today and spend little time thinking about their financial futures.

The third segment in the Super Segment averse to long-term care insurance is the Credit Consumers, financial neophytes with little interest in becoming informed consumers. Long-term care insurance is a gamble, and Credit Consumers seek to avoid risk in their financial dealings. Another type of avoidance is seen in their dream of buying a new house in a warm climate when they retire, while not factoring in the impact of aging on their finances.

Let's make a deal

Based on our data, we predict that in the years ahead Reliables, one of our Car Purchase segments, will dominate car buyers among those 40 and older. Those in this segment are knowledgeable about cars and focused on what they want. Because Reliables walk into a dealership having researched a great deal of concrete information, they are not apt to be swayed by a salesperson. Unless a dealership wishes to alienate those in this large and growing segment, it must have a strategy for selling to them and a way of identifying them as they enter the door.

Since both Reliables and Stylish Fun are knowledgeable about cars, a car salesperson must quickly differentiate between the two. Again, we suggest a two-step process. Initially questions are asked conversationally as part of the probing process to quickly categorize the prospect. Knowing that the prospect is a Reliable, the salesperson can move ahead with a sales pitch that relates to this segment's concerns and motivations.

If the sale is made, such questions can be asked as part of the closing process and captured for a database. Future contacts with this customer, now identified as a Reliable, can center on topics of concern to him or her. For example, Reliables are committed to getting the most miles per gallon out of their car. Instead of a car dealership merely reminding a Reliable that their car needs a tune up, a direct mail flyer to this segment could stress its benefits: increased gas mileage.

A new perspective

In order to make a sale, a salesperson has to know which messages motivate the prospect to buy—the prospect's hot buttons. But current sales approaches attempting to discern a prospect's motivations are imprecise and too general. If they are known, a prospect's demographics and past behavior do not reveal his or her critical motivators.

Sales are lost and the cost of making a sale remains high because salespersons know so little about the motivations of the persons to whom they are attempting to sell. Inexperienced salespersons have the greatest difficulty in reading a prospect's motivations. Their lack of effectiveness and efficiency in making sales frustrates them and those for whom they work.

Our approach quickly and easily provides insights into what motivates a prospect in a psychographic segment to buy or not buy a product or service. All salespersons, regardless of experience or skill, benefit from the same insights. The prospect's psychographic segment reveals areas of resistance or receptivity and guides the salesperson in shaping sales messages.

Besides increased sales, there are other benefits to the company itself in using our approach. When prospects and customers are categorized into a psychographic segment, the company achieves an objective and uniform way of codifying them. This process enables a company to analyze its database by psychographic segment, an important new dimension. A company may realize that its prospects are overwhelmingly in one segment or another, thereby gaining a strategically important insight. Learning a new customer's psychographic segment and entering it into a database becomes an important piece in the integration of all aspects of sales and marketing.

INDEX

About the authors

Carol M. Morgan and Doran J. Levy, Ph.D. are the founding principals of Strategic Directions Group, Inc., a marketing consulting firm specializing in creating motivational segmentation strategies and identifying receptive customers, the messages they consider relevant, as well as the channels of communication and distribution they favor. The company's unique Marketer® methodology determines robust segmentations from which advertising, marketing, product development, and customer relationship management (CRM) programs can be developed. The firm creates models and software applications based on its segmentations for use in media selection, database marketing and CRM.

Carol M. Morgan

Carol M. Morgan, president of Strategic Directions Group, has 20 years experience in marketing consulting for Fortune 500 companies. Ms. Morgan is a frequent speaker on motivational segmentation at national and international conferences, including the Conference Board of Canada's Tourism Research Institute, the International Symposium on Presbyopia, the Direct Marketing Association, the EPM Entertainment Marketing Conference, and National Association of Chain Drug Stores (NACDS). Her articles have appeared in numerous publications, including *Advertising Age*, *Brandweek*, *American Demographics*, and *The Wall Street Journal*. She has taught at several universities and holds a master's degree from Kansas State University.

Doran J. Levy, Ph.D.

Doran J. Levy, Ph.D., executive vice president, has been a leading proponent of market segmentation for 30 years. He has held positions of manager of consumer research at The Pillsbury Company; senior vice president, director of strategic planning at Young & Rubicam/Wunderman, Detroit and vice president, manager of marketing analytics, of Interelate, a customer relationship management outsourcing firm. He received his doctorate from the University of Missouri, Columbia, focusing on attitude research and the adoption of new products. He currently addresses segmentation as a columnist for *DM Review*.

Strategic Directions Group, Inc.

Quantifying attitudes

Strategic Directions Group, Inc. is an international marketing consulting firm specializing in the measurement of attitudes and motivations, often called psychographics.

Extensive experience

For 25 years we have used proprietary methodologies to identify our clients' most *receptive* targets and the messages these targets consider *relevant*. The robust segmentation strategies that we develop are far more comprehensive and actionable than those created by traditional techniques. The studies described in this book were conducted and analyzed using our proprietary methods.

Total perspective

Based on methods from psychometrics, our Marketer® system creates a *quantitative* view of attitudes and motivations *by segment*. We couple this information with demographics, behaviors, sources of information, media and Internet usage, and other data.

The segments we develop and related data provide a total perspective of a market. Marketer provides significant and actionable insights on a wide range of marketing, customer satisfaction, product development, and sales issues for both business-to-business and consumer applications.

Applications that work

Our software-based applications enable clients to apply the psychographic segmentation strategies we develop to media optimization, customer satisfaction, future research, one-on-one sales training, and building targeted databases. From being "nice to know," these applications move our psychographic segmentation strategies to being *actionable in the real world.*

Linking psychographics to databases

Strategic Directions Group links the psychographic segmentations it develops to databases for highly effective direct marketing and customer relationship management (CRM). Moving beyond demographics and behaviors, Strategic Directions Group defines *why* a prospect or customer is receptive to a product or service. Applied to databases, these insights vastly increase marketing efficiencies.